Advance praise for **Sweetwater**

"Robin M. Boylorn takes you intimately and viscerally into her life growing up and into the lives of the southern black rural women in her hometown. You hear women whispering and talking women-talk, see them worshipping and getting the spirit, smell the ham hocks cooking, sense the passion and pain of their daily romantic and family lives, feel their hearts beating and bleeding, share their resentment and love for the men who don't always do them right, and finally understand deeply the resilience it takes to get by no matter what challenges are thrown at you. Dr. Boylorn joins the creative genius of a Toni Morrison to the scholarship of black women's lives, exemplifying the ethnographic eye/I and ethical consciousness of the best of qualitative research. This is a stunning autoethnographic and narrative tour de force that will captivate students and scholars alike."

–Carolyn Ellis, Professor of Communication Studies and Sociology,
University of South Florida, and Author of Revision:
Autoethnographic Reflections on Life and Work

"Zora Neale Hurston is kicking dirt up out her grave! With Robin M. Boylorn's brave work, dust tracks become lineage and lines of text become clotheslines again. All that we are is hung out here to dry, wave surrender, or see morning. In content and form Dr. Boylorn's *Sweetwater* actualizes the black feminist imperative to lift up our stories, in this case the stories of rural black women, as catalysts towards a world better understood, more deeply held, and more transformatively loved."

—Alexis Pauline Gumbs, Founder of the Eternal Summer of the Black Feminist Mind,
Co-Creator of the Queer Black Mobile Homecoming Project,
and Author of Spill: Scenes of Black Feminist Fugitivity

"The stories in *Sweetwater* are like oxygen after held breath—exhilarating, satisfying, and sustaining. Twiggy, Bread, and Bird love and scold, teach and hold each other, the women in their community, and the reader through their stories, lives, and worlds. Robin M. Boylorn is a writer who breathes air and life into her inheritance and shares the stories of her mothers with honesty, care, hope, and strength."

—Stacy Holman Jones, Professor in the Centre for Theatre and Performance,
Monash University, and Co-editor of The Handbook of Autoethnography

Sweetwater

Rochelle Brock and Cynthia Dillard
Executive Editors

Vol. 100

The Black Studies and Critical Thinking series
is part of the Peter Lang Education list.
Every volume is peer reviewed and meets
the highest quality standards for content and production.

PETER LANG
New York • Bern • Frankfurt • Berlin
Brussels • Vienna • Oxford • Warsaw

Robin M. Boylorn

Sweetwater

Black Women and Narratives of Resilience

REVISED EDITION

PETER LANG
New York • Bern • Frankfurt • Berlin
Brussels • Vienna • Oxford • Warsaw

Library of Congress Cataloging-in-Publication Data

Names: Boylorn, Robin M., author.
Title: Sweetwater: Black women and narratives of resilience / Robin Boylorn.
Description: Revised edition. | New York: Peter Lang, 2017.
Series: Black studies and critical thinking; vol. 100 | ISSN 1947-5985
Includes bibliographical references.
Identifiers: LCCN 2017005924 | ISBN 978-1-4331-3493-7 (paperback: alk. paper)
ISBN 978-1-4331-4222-2 (ebook pdf) | ISBN 978-1-4331-4223-9 (epub)
ISBN 978-1-4331-4224-6 (mobi)
Subjects: LCSH: African American women—Southern States—Social conditions.
Rural women—Southern States. | Boylorn, Robin M., 1978-—Childhood and youth.
African American girls—North Carolina—Biography.
Rural girls—North Carolina—Biography. | Southern States—Rural conditions.
North Carolina—Rural conditions. | Ethnology—North Carolina.
African Americans—Poetry. | Storytelling—Social aspects—North Carolina.
Classification: LCC E185.86 .B6496 2017 | DDC 305.48/896073075—dc23
LC record available at https://lccn.loc.gov/2017005924
DOI 10.3726/b11027

Bibliographic information published by **Die Deutsche Nationalbibliothek.**
Die Deutsche Nationalbibliothek lists this publication in the "Deutsche
Nationalbibliografie"; detailed bibliographic data are available
on the Internet at http://dnb.d-nb.de/.

The paper in this book meets the guidelines for permanence and durability
of the Committee on Production Guidelines for Book Longevity
of the Council of Library Resources.

In loving memory of my mentor
Dr. H. L. (Bud) Goodall, Jr.
Who once said:
*"I want to write stories that people will read and that will change
their lives,"*
and then taught me.

September 8, 1952–August 24, 2012
Big Love!

This book is dedicated to the women who raised me
To Grandma Gert, who told me once that she was like my father
and has always made sure her children never wanted for nothin'
To my mother, Bettina, for her beauty and faith
whose prayers prepared a platform for my words
To my aunt who taught me to respect her
by making me call her Mama Frances
years before she birthed her own children
To my Aunt Regenna, whose memories of my mother as a child
bore witness to my own stubbornness
And for being the first storyteller in my life
You taught me how to act
How to love
How to cuss
How to pray
How to fight
How to mend
How to breathe
You taught me
How to be myself without apology
And love what I see

Thank you!

Contents

*Window Poems by Mary E. Weems

Author's Preface to the Revised Edition

(Re)Telling

I was initially reluctant at the thought of doing a revised edition of *Sweetwater*. The first time I held the book in my hands, I inspected each page, fingering the edges and finding minor aesthetic errors that made me feel sick to my stomach. I had wanted it to be perfect. It wasn't perfect. But it was mine, and its imperfections were my imperfections. Pieces and fragments of my story held together by memory, pages, and time.

Sweetwater is what happened after years of collecting stories, writing, witnessing, remembering, and telling. Many people have said to me after reading *Sweetwater* that they wished there was more, and of course there is more. There is always more. Telling a story is always telling a partial and partisan account (Goodall, 2000). Stories are fragments of larger narratives, snapshots of lives that keep going long after the telling.

When I was writing *Sweetwater* I was intentional about the stories I told, and while editing sometimes leaves things out, things you intended be left in, I felt *Sweetwater* was the story I needed to tell at the time. The story is timeless and resonant, representative and generalizable (and not only to black women). *Sweetwater* is about living with and through complicated circumstances that center race and gender without being limited to race and gender. It is a living witness and history, archived evidence that the black women I wrote about exist(ed) and their lives are worth talking about. The interior lives of southern black women, and the intimacy of their knowing, offers an opportunity to analyze the context of their lives and the influence of factors including race, rurality, regionality, socioeconomics, and gender. I worried that retelling *Sweetwater* would disrupt or alter the importance of the first telling.

Talking with friends and colleagues led me to imagine the possibilities for a revision. While keeping the existing narratives intact, I could reconsider and reimagine how I framed them, adjust the introduction, expand the conclusion to make additional claims about the relevance of black women's stories, revise and focus the analysis, include feedback and reviews, offering my response, fill in some of the blanks, correct some of the aesthetic errors, make it more *imperfect*. I became excited about how a re/vision and re/telling could reconceptualize the story and make it available to an even wider audience.

The success of *Sweetwater* exceeded my expectations. I am humbled that it has been taken up in the ways that it has, and in the additional work and research it has inspired. *Sweetwater* has been taught in multiple disciplines (including English, Communication, Education, Sociology, Women's Studies, African-American Studies) and in multiple ways (to teach qualitative method, creative writing, interpersonal and family communication, the rhetoric of oral history, etc.). It received prominent awards including the inaugural H. L. "Bud" Goodall, Jr. and Nicholas Lee Trujillo "It's A Way of Life" Award in Narrative Ethnography in 2013, the 2013 Best Monograph Book Award from the National Communication Association Ethnography Division, and the 2014 Outstanding Qualitative Book Award by the International Congress of Qualitative Inquiry. In 2016, *Sweetwater* was included in the #LemonadeSyllabus, a digital collection of works celebrating black womanhood curated by Candice Benbow as an accompaniment to Beyoncé's Lemonade album, and shared widely across the interwebs. I have had the opportunity to teach *Sweetwater* in my classes, do readings and book signings at community venues (including Charis Books and More, in Atlanta, GA, the oldest feminist bookstore in the south) and promote the book on a late night TV Web Series (*Ladies Night*). I have visited and skyped with students who were assigned the book for their classes, given invited talks and lectures about *Sweetwater*, and published excerpts from *Sweetwater* in an academic journal. Panels dedicated to reflecting on and responding to *Sweetwater* took place at the National Communication Association Convention in 2013 ("Sweetwater along the Potomac"), and the International Congress of Qualitative Inquiry in 2014 ("Celebrating Sweetwater"). In response to those panels, a Forum on Sweetwater was published in the spring 2015 issue of *Departures in Critical Qualitative Research*, featuring eleven reviews and responses to the book (excerpts of which are included in this revised edition), many of which were first presented at one of those conferences.

While much has happened since *Sweetwater* was initially published, what remains is my commitment to privileging the lives and storied experiences of black women, and my investment in the ways we narrate and theorize the scripts and situations black women live in/with.

As a communication studies scholar, I am interested in the ways language creates reality and identity, and how black women's unique communication practices factor into the ways we understand and express ourselves. As a black woman, I am committed to contributing to scholarship that makes black women visible and viable. I am also curious about what stories tell us, teach us, and show us about ourselves and others. If meaningful communication is storied (Fisher, 1987), and stories are theoretical (Bochner, 1994), then how can we use stories to make meaning and make sense of our lives?

(Re)telling *Sweetwater* gives me an opportunity to make sense of the lives of Sweetwater women, myself included, in new and different ways. I intentionally did not disrupt the narrative of Sweetwater in this revision. I did not insert any new stories to the pre-existing chapters (though a significant revision was made to the Porch Premonitions/Interlude). Instead, I reconsider and revisit the framing of the book to respond to absences and fill in gaps, to clarify and expand, to think through and explain, and to reflect new theoretical considerations, new research, and new thinking. The revision is not about making *Sweetwater* perfect, it is about making *Sweetwater* even more discernable and accessible to black women who may never sit in a college classroom, but who will find remnants of their lives hidden in the pages of this book. I don't attempt to retell the stories of Sweetwater, only to reimagine what the stories suggest about how black women live meaningful lives despite oppressive circumstances. A student once said to me, in response to reading *Sweetwater*, that she saw it as a story that urges the reader to marvel, not at my resilience for leaving, but at the resilience of the women who stay(ed). I could not agree more.

—R. Boylorn
November 1, 2016

Series Editor's Preface

Sweetwater:
Country Stories With Ties to the City

"If ignorance is bliss then my life has been tragic, marked by the realization that despite my attempts to define myself, I'm often reduced to what the world says I am." When I read these words by Black woman–scholar Robin Boylorn, I was spun back through my own life, like a Black girl fast dancing with time. Although I was born and raised in the inner city, my ancestors on both my mother's and father's sides moved here from the south in the early 1900s, and the Sweetwater stories helped me revisit the connection between my southern ancestry and northern self.

I remembered all of the times we were out of Koolaide, soda, juice, and milk in one roach-infested apartment or another and the only thing I could fix my sisters and brother to drink was sugar water, something sweet seasoned with the taste of being poor—a fact I didn't realize until I started attending school. I remembered all of the times I watched programming in black and white that reinforced blatant stereotypes about Black people—and Black women in particular—and laughed.

Most important, this quote reminded me of the fact that even today, twelve years into the twenty-first century, media stereotypes about Black women are alive and well thanks to TV commercials that feature Black women cleaning houses and kitchens and cooking fried chicken; thanks to television programs with Black matriarchs running the household and their husbands too; thanks to reality shows where Black women act a fool for the camera and get paid; and films like *The Help* where the southern Black maid is stereotyped while her experiences in the mid-twentieth century are mythologized in ways that mock the brave women who endured racism, hard work, low wages, rape, and disrespect in order to help support their families.

Where is the programming featuring Black women business owners, doctors, lawyers, astronauts, and PhDs? Where are the stories featuring everyday black women as sheroes rather than caricatures?

Sweetwater: Black Women and Narratives of Resilience is first and foremost a journey through life in a country town through the experiences of its women. In it, Robin returns home, a trained scholar seeking to reconnect with her hometown family and the other people she grew up with in order to gather their stories one at a time and to tell her own. To the extent stereotypes are present in this work, it is not by design but rather part of telling what needs to be told as openly and honestly as possible, keeping the importance of the participants' feelings about the way they are written about as well as her goal of honoring both the past and present of their lives in mind. *Sweetwater* portrays Black women as we are: powerful, loving, intelligent, confused, challenged, *resilient*, and, in the end, hopeful for a better day for ourselves and our families. It is a southern book with a heart strong enough to reach Black women raised in the city.

After working on this project with Robin for two years, I received a creative surprise after the manuscript was completed and I was asked to help her increase the length of the book—Boylorn's words reached out to me and poems started to come. I was inspired to actively engage Robin's work as a city-born and -bred Black woman, interacting with rural cultural symbols (Blumer, 1969; Joas, 1987; Plummer, 1987, 1991; Denzin, 1992), making meanings that moved between the experiences of these women and my own, between city lights and pitch black country roads.

The resulting poems act as windows, which lead the reader out of one story and into the next, adding an additional, complex cultural layer while honoring the spirits of my paternal and maternal ancestors who migrated north more than five generations ago.

Like ancient and contemporary African griots, Robin is a storyteller, a keeper of the keys to part of our history, a scholar who has taken up the journey of making certain, like Zora Neale Hurston before her, that our stories are not only *not* forgotten but are recorded, published, and accessible to anyone interested in knowing more about the complexities of the experiences of Black women in the United States.

I am honored as a series editor in Black Studies and Critical Thinking to present *Sweetwater* as the second book in my "What's Going On?" Series. This may be the reader's first taste of Robin Boylorn's work, but it won't be the last. Enjoy the journey.

—Mary E. Weems, Series Editor
August 31, 2012

Foreword

H. L. (Bud) Goodall, Jr.

If you are a white middle-class suburban person, as I am, and you've spent time in the rural south, as I have, Sweetwater is one of many small African-American communities that you've driven through—usually by mistake—windows up, doors locked, eyes closed to everyone and everything in it, your only thought focused on how to find the quickest way back to the Interstate, to what is familiar and to what is understood.

To be fair about it, as a white middle-class suburban person you might also feel much the same general unease if you find yourself in a poor "white trash" neighborhood in the rural south (or rural anywhere), but chances are good that rednecks (I use the term in a strictly phenomenological sense)—even those toting loaded guns and driving pumped-up trucks with Confederate flags proudly displayed on them—don't make you feel quite as vulnerable or nervous. If you are white, you can always look away. Go on about your business. Ask for directions back to the Interstate.

This is an America, imperfect. This is America as a big beautiful idea about equality that has yet to be fully realized. This is America, just as it is, imperfect yet dreaming, and the images of its imperfection—of *our* imperfection—are everywhere apparent.

This is a *me* imperfect as well. No matter how I position myself in relation to Sweetwater—me as the educated liberal ethnographer in blue jeans, fresh out of the suburbs and with a flush bank account, for example—there is no way even in the Monopoly of advanced capitalism that I can buy myself a "get out of my suburban upper-middle-class white skin free" card.

I am as "Other" to the residents of Sweetwater as they are to me. And maybe I'm a good bit scarier, too.

What I need, what we need, is a translator.

*

What I want is someone I can trust to mediate the cultural distance between Sweetwater and me. Someone who knows the terrain, both the surfaces and what lies beneath them. Someone who is a native, but a native who left town long ago and has since returned with a more mature, perhaps even a more sympathetic perspective. Someone trained as a professional observer who speaks my language.

All of which is to say that what I want when I turn off the Interstate and find myself in this story about Sweetwater is someone who can help me make sense out of what I don't understand. To be that translator means to be aware of the profound cultural distance between a rural and relatively poor African-American southern community that has no clear or compelling voice and the storied world that I am already part of, a collective narrative made out of our predominantly white male, middle-class suburban ethnographic scholarship.

What I want from a translator, then, is what the philosopher Sarah Worth (2008) calls a kind of knowledge that can only be acquired through personal narrative—not a knowing *what* or a knowing *that*, but instead a knowing "what it is like to" live this way.

That "third way of knowing" is the core contribution that all ethnographies make in general and that personal ethnographies (e.g., autoethnographies, narrative ethnographies, etc.) have a special obligation to achieve. What I need, then, is a translator who not only meets the native cultural knowledge criteria but also can tell a credible, memorable *story*.

But I am ahead of myself.

*

This book is not a book about race or class, although what it shows us about race, class, and gender is part of its contribution. It is a book about people. Remarkable people, really. Resilient. It is a book about remarkable, resilient people with homegrown names like Cake and Black Charles and Bread, people who are born into impoverished lives they most often want to escape in skins that never will. So no, this book isn't about race or class in any traditional social science sense; it's not a hypothesis to be tested because residents of Sweetwater already know what being black and (relatively) poor means in their lives. Race and class are nothing special in Sweetwater, no more worth noticing or complaining about than the weather.

What about *gender*? Where does gender fit into the rural southern social-political-cultural mix? What do we know, really, about rural southern women? What do we know about rural southern women who are also black?

Which is to say, what do we know about the lives, the lived experiences, of women in a close-by but yet so far away place as Sweetwater? What goes on there?

How do the women of Sweetwater make sense of their circumstances, their families and friends and God and children, their hopes and dreams and jobs, and men and cars and sex, and all the rest of it, which is to say, what do we know about how they make sense out of their Sweetwater lives?

The succinct answer is, simply put, "Not a lot." Not a lot, that is, until Professor Robin Boylorn, native of Sweetwater and adept cultural translator, wrote this book.

*

There are many ways to write a book. For a communication scholar trained, as Robin was trained, in narrative inquiry, and beckoned by an interpretive ethnographic muse, the "choice" of how to *evoke* a sense of place (and, in the case of Sweetwater, the place she still calls "home") and how to *represent* the always complex, nuanced, and deeply historical lives found there (lives of people she has known and in some cases loved and/or feared) is less a choice strictly driven by the dictates of method and more one that is informed, and complicated, by "relational ethics" (Ellis, Adams, & Bochner, 2011).

The idea behind "relational ethics" is that how we write about others—about real people living real lives—ought to be guided by the realization that our ethical obligation is not only limited to revealing the truth of our experiences with them in the past but, moreover, it extends to the present and future. How might those lives be affected today by what we choose to say? How might our relationship to those we write about be altered in the future? Would members of our community—or of any Sweetwater you care to name—welcome us back if they had the opportunity to read what we said about them and their lives?

The "golden rule" of relational ethics is an ethnographic version of the Hippocratic oath to "do no harm." Yet, as Joan Didion (1976) explains it, telling a story is an "aggressive" act that destabilizes readers. She reminds us:

> In many ways writing is the act of saying I, of imposing oneself upon other people, of saying *listen to me, see it my way, change your mind.* It's an aggressive, even hostile act. You can disguise its aggressiveness all you want with veils of subordinate clauses and qualifiers and tentative subjunctives, with ellipses and evasions—with the whole manner of intimating rather than claiming, of alluding

rather than stating—but there's no getting around the fact that setting words on paper is the tactic of a secret bully, an invasion, an imposition of the writer's sensibility on the reader's most private space (pp. 17–18).

So, please, be forewarned: There isn't any pure ethical stance or one preferred style of narrating a story that guarantees good relational ethics outcomes. For no matter how we choose to tell the story of "these people in this place and time," when we do so we forever alter our relationship to those we write about and to their community. That process and consequence, too, is worth writing about.

This book is a *narrative* inquiry. Unlike traditional forms of scholarly reporting, it is not a process that "writes up" the results of a study after the research is conducted. Instead it teaches us how the writer came to understand her subject as part of that research process. What this style of writing aims for then—reading Didion's caution into the ethnographic heart of Sweetwater's darkness—is a kind of justifiable violence of the narrative kind. It is violence of language deployed in a local context, and of the realities created in and by it, a style of "showing" and "telling about" that attacks both the reader's naivety and the writer's taken for granted assumptions about the past, about people and relationships, and about the community. As the narrator learns, so must we. As the narrator changes and matures, so can we. Label it what you will, we are co-authors of what happens to us when we are called out about our Interstate ignorance. Bitch-slapped by one woman's truth. Blown away by what we should do now, what we teach now, because of what we now know.

This justifiable violence to our point of view is the why and how and "what it is like" when the most memorable ethnographies speak directly to us: Our narrative comfort zones are *called out* for what they are; our preconceived and naïve ways of knowing are *challenged*; and the experience of reading a scholarship infused and compelling story *moves us* emotionally and intellectually, so much so that we are transported to a new level of consciousness.

In other words, we want to be *changed* by what we read. If there is a little blood on the page, so be it.

*

Writing through the epistemic lens encouraged by relational ethics is very much an ethnographer's Heisenberg Uncertainty Principle: our very presence in the process of making sense out of a community alters it. Because there is no "purely objective" place to stand in relation to our work, to the stories we are sharing and the people we are studying, the best we can do while we are writing is make that uncertainty, that ambiguity, that conflict part of the ongoing narrative. This ability to write about how we question what we know lights the path for readers and encourages them to do the same self-reflexive work.

There are, of course, other ethnographic best practices to guide our writing about relational ethics, all of which Robin accomplishes in this fine book. These best practices include maintaining a critical, *self-reflexive* awareness of our place in a community as well as of the implicit power imbalance that grants to the writer a narrative authority to define persons, places, and things that, even if "true" in an empirical sense, may be interpreted differently by those whom we write about. This particular "best practice" does not mean that we avoid writing about "the hard stuff," but it does mean we must *own the story* as well as the *relational result*. For this reason you will find that Robin provides the details of sharing her stories with some of those persons depicted in them (sometimes with laugh-aloud results, some with necessary tears) in a strong singular voice that is vulnerable, tough, feminine, and empathetic.

Yes, there are many ways to write a book. But there are precious few books written this way—through a relational ethic of care—or this well. And I'll leave it to you to name another book that in showing us and telling us about the lives of rural southern women teaches us so much about race, class, and gender.

But aside from high-minded academic standards for evaluating the ethics of the research process and uniqueness of the narrative, this book—and the voice driving it—is the kind of accomplished writing we expect from creative nonfictionists of the first order. In part this is true because Robin thinks of herself as a writer and has taken the time and effort to become trained as one. And in part it is because as a writer schooled in a writer's craft she allows the messy organic stuff—the rhizome—of human relationships developing over time—the roots of hopes moving around broken shards of old shared memories, conversations, epiphanies, dreams, abandonments, betrayals, and at least one murder—to organize the beautifully entangled form these interconnected stories and poems acquire and through which their evolving meanings may be understood. The result—one part intense autobiography and two parts character-driven narrative ethnography—creates a new high standard for ethnographic scholarship.

*

You are going to love reading *Sweetwater*. It succeeds as a compelling, page-turning, OMG! kind of narrative that will have you turning off your cell phone and closing down Facebook to finish it. It also succeeds as scholarship, which is to say that it makes a new and unique contribution to the literature. I imagine that it will be required reading for any number of courses, both as an exemplary study of women in a rural southern community and as a fine piece of writing.

Now let me tell you a thing or two about Robin.

When I first met Robin she was working on an undergraduate degree in English and had dreams of becoming a writer. She had already left the real Sweetwater, but I didn't know anything about that. Not then. Sweetwater was her secret. Little did either of us suspect or even imagine that opening up that secret would also open up a new life for her, not only as a writer but as also as an academic.

The Robin I met back then was living in the long echo of Bird's childhood you will read about here. She was tall and shy. She was polite and smart. She had secrets. She also had that rare ineffable thing we call "potential" that even a lucky teacher like me gets to see only a few times during a long career.

I did the only thing I knew how to do. I encouraged her. I read her stories. I offered some criticism and some advice; I gave her a million books and articles to read. Eventually I talked her into graduate school with us at the University of North Carolina at Greensboro, where, two years later, I was fortunate enough to direct her thesis. Along with my other UNCG colleagues who had by then also become fans of hers and Bettina (Robin's mom and biggest fan), we finally convinced her to apply to the doctoral program at the University of South Florida. As they say in the south, this "took some doing." Her reluctance had nothing to do with USF and everything to do with Sweetwater. Which is to say no one from Sweetwater ever did anything so bold as to pursue a doctorate, much less move on her own (meaning without a man or because of one) to another state.

Think about that for a minute. Reminds me of the old line from William Faulkner about the long-term effects of the Civil War on the southern state of mind: "The past isn't over. Hell, it's not even the past." After you read *Sweetwater* you'll better understand that quote in relation to Robin's growth as a person and as a writer-scholar, as a woman from Sweetwater—from the stories that make Sweetwater what it is—but no longer bound by those stories.

*

The rest of the story is, and continues to be, a happy one. Under the wonderful mentoring of Carolyn Ellis and Art Bochner, Robin completed her doctorate at USF. She accepted a tenure-earning assistant professor position at the University of Alabama in Tuscaloosa, where today you will find her living the writer-scholar's life she once dreamed of when she was that shy little girl back in Sweetwater.

You are now holding in your hands the story that brought us here—you, me, and Robin—a story hard-won with her life and powerful enough to change our lives in the reading.

Go ahead. Turn the page. I dare you…

Acknowledgments

This book is the result of lived realities, good conversations, reminiscent reads, sleepless nights, provocative classes, disturbing memories, and realized dreams. I remember saying in prayer once, "God, if I can leave my mark in the world, let it be my voice." This offering is my voice.

I am deeply grateful for the people in my life who have made me a better writer and person and, thus, made this project possible. I thank my mentor, H. L. (Bud) Goodall, Jr., for telling me my words should be in books and inspiring me to get them there. I am thankful for the possibilities he made possible by believing in, challenging, and affirming me—and most especially for urging me to write my *blackgirl* stories. His faith and love have proven immeasurable in my journey to becoming a writer. I dedicate this book, and everything I (will) write and accomplish to him, as an extension of his legacy. I will miss him forever!

I also thank my academic parents, Carolyn Ellis and Arthur Bochner, for walking me through my ambitions and for making room for me in their lives. I am grateful for the time spent sharing stories, listening, mentoring, drying tears, calming emotions, reassuring, handholding, holiday meals, walking the dogs, climbing mountains, winning (and losing) sports bets, editing, co-writing, thinking through, working through, writing through, and mostly for just believing in me. Thank you for loving me through my insecurities. I love you both beyond words.

Tony Adams, thank you for your unfailing friendship, for co-writing and collaborating with me, and for helping me vision my dreams. This revision would not be possible had you not insisted I see the opportunities inherent in revisiting and re-visioning this work. Thank you for celebrating me, celebrating *Sweetwater*, and for being your wonderful self. You are my favorite!

I thank Mary Weems and Rochelle Brock for lending their ears and giving me a hearing—and a chance—and for embracing, supporting, and encouraging this project. Their careful feedback, constructive edits, and encouragement was immeasurable. Mary, your soulful wisdom has inspired me, your own work has haunted me, and you have informed my words, making them feel important, urgent, and necessary. Thank you!

I am grateful for mentors and colleagues who have continually inspired and supported me and my work over the years: Mark Orbe, Navita Cummings James, Cheryl Rodriguez, Christopher Poulos, Pete Kellett, Michael Parker, Eric Eisenberg, Rex Crawley, Eric Watts, Ron Jackson, Mark Hopson, Tim Terrentine, Stacy Holman Jones, Elizabeth Bell, Michael LeVan, Marcy Chvasta, Ken Cissna, and Norman Denzin (who published my first academic article).

To my praying mama, Bettina Boylorn, and my sister and first best friend Nicole Boylorn, thank you for teaching me unfailing love and fearless faith. We will always be each other's "person(s)."

I also want to acknowledge my proofreaders, prayer partners, friends, and colleagues whose patient listening and brilliant insight was immeasurable as I stumbled through the process of making this book (in its various iterations): Brittney Cooper, Susana Morris, Derek Bolen, Rachel Raimist, Aisha Durham, Anita Mixon, Antoine Hardy, Ally Rhodes Steinweg, Cara Mackie, Wren Levitt, Jeanine Mingé, Sheri Davis-Faulkner, Eesha Pandit, Ruth Nicole Brown, Patrick Santoro, Jillian Tullis, Tunisia Riley, Liz Edgecomb, Sara Dykins Callahan, Chris McRae, Nigel Malcolm, Rachel Gerakaris Tomko, Andrew Herrmann, Rachel Binns Terrill, Christine Davis, Chris Patti, Keith Berry, Cynthia Dillard, Alexis Pauline Gumbs, Elizabeth Straight-Wilt, Robert and Brenda Fruster, Natalie Sims, LaShay Stokes, Keysha Williams, Sheri Broner, Anne Copeland, Shawn Brass, Tremaine Brittian, Roshunda Terry, Sherica Bailey, Johnie Scott, and the Crunk Feminist Collective (CFC).

I would like to thank my colleagues who have engaged *Sweetwater* since it was first published in 2013, taught it in their classes, used it in their own research, and invited me to discuss it with their students. I especially want to express gratitude to everyone who participated, responded, and/or attended the "*Sweetwater* along the Potomac" panel at NCA in 2013, and the "Celebrating *Sweetwater*," panel for ICQI in 2014. I am also grateful to Stacy Holman Jones, Editor of Departures in Critical Qualitative Research for hosting the *Sweetwater* Forum in the Spring 2015 issue, and to everyone who generously contributed to the special issue, and/ or the book reviews and responses included in this revised edition.

I also thank Ravin Lawson for designing the book art, and Jazz Franklin and Lucas Porter for collaborating on the book trailer, available at www.robin boylorn.com.

I appreciate, additionally, the collegiality and support of my colleagues in the Department of Communication Studies and College of Communication and Information Sciences at the University of Alabama for creating a safe environment for my creative work. I also thank my beautiful students, former and future, both at the University of South Florida and the University of Alabama, for listening to my stories and for telling me theirs.

And finally, I thank my maternal family who I can't call by name without direct implication. I wrote this as a commemoration of where we come from and how far we have come. In particular, I thank the nine women who opened up their lives, their homes, and their hearts to me, and gave me their stories to tell alongside mine. Thank you for everything you have gifted me with through the benefit of (y)our experience and the patience of (y)our love.

Prologue

Telling

Overhearing the gossip of strangers in my mama's living room, I learned that you don't want your business in the street. It was the mantra of grown folk/who met at fences/and stood across ditches/and sat on porches and waved/and spoke into phone receivers/and exchanged knowing glances/and used their children to spy/ and whispered possibilities into the air/and made up endings to dry stories/and made judgments and justifications/and talked shit while shooting the breeze/and knew the comings and goings/beatings and leavings/badass kids and abortions/ and arrests/and grades/and girl did you know so and so was pregnant by such and such/and the bad credit and the repossessions/and the court dates and the bad checks/and the illegitimate children and the unfaithful wives/and the layoffs and the drop outs/and the fights and the fists and the tears and the spit/and the *lovehatelove*/and the husbands who left/and the incest/and the crimes and the schemes and scandals/and the drug money hidden in vents with more money than the neighbor left to her family when she died/and the donation the church made to help pay for the funeral cause they didn't have enough money to bury her right/to the deaths in the threes/and the births from fish dreams.

To know everybody's business while holding your tongue takes everything you got—
it robs you of the story you long to tell

the story that makes you feel *something*
The story comes when I am ready to release the pain and the past
that is attached to it.
The stories spill out, liberating me from the chains of shame,
hopelessness,
and disguise.
my business
balled up
like a fist
contained
between my lips
locked in my throat
because my story
is hers
and hers is mine
and what does it mean for me to tell our story?
my secrets are someone else's secrets
my pain unlocks someone else's pain
my memory is not the same as someone else's memory
I leave room for discrepancy
honesty

it is
my sorrow
my family's embarrassment
my father's abandonment
my business
it is
my sadness
my mother's scorn
my reflections song
of dried switches
cutting across
brown legs
& grown legs
wrapping around
the butterscotch skin
of a man who offered me

ten minutes of
affection
& lies

my business
of secret suicide tries
pill overdoses
funeral fantasies
and the barrel of gun in my mouth

walking
barefoot on broken glass in backyard
falling
on rusted nails
sitting
in broken down cars
waiting
for a change
that won't come
recalling
my business

Because telling all my business was, in fact, telling most of theirs. But to be a writer, and a good one, I had to learn to use all of the pain that was embedded beneath my skin to unlock the words—and through the words, the power—and the will—to tell.

Telling was murder and I anxiously became a coconspirator, killing the silence with the story. Killing the absence with my presence.

My stories are embedded with the ethics and politics of sharing,

ooooooooooh I'm gone tell it,
like lyrics leaving my tongue.

It comes with the consequences of reminding myself of some significant loss I can't immediately let go, and deep-seated secrets I promised to never tell.

*

This book, which began as a dissertation, is a result of me telling my story, and other rural black women telling theirs.

Telling is not without controversy.
There are multiple versions and multiple truths.

There are gaps and lapses I didn't fill in.

There are parts of the story missing.

All of our stories are a combination of secrets and salvation. *Sweetwater* is no different.

A common characteristic of Sweetwater stories is resilience. In the face of adversity, tragedy, violence, racism, and oppression, Sweetwater women exhibit, not just strength, but restraint. I examine our lives, over generations, to determine how black women use and pass down narratives to cope and communicate about their experiences as acts of social resistance. I use our lived experiences to theorize about how justice is negotiated and reconciled in the lives of black women, challenging presuppositions and offering alternatives to what it means to be a black woman in the rural south. Accordingly, this book is an interdisciplinary effort. I draw on the work and legacy of a wide range of black women writers, thinkers, and theorists who inform my understanding of myself as a black woman and the implications of that identity. I use *Sweetwater* to speculate about how stories help black women know themselves most authentically and unapologetically.

Introduction

The Call(ing) of A Rural Black Woman's Story

"The impulse, simply put, is to tell the story [...] to tell one's own story [...] as one has known it, and lived it, and even died it."

—*Maya Angelou*

Historically, "biases of racism and sexism as well as class elitism lead the American public to feel that black women's voices are the least compelling when serious issues are at stake" (hooks, 1999, p. 27). This critique has often caused black women to protect and maintain face by remaining silent about their stories; stories that Michele Wallace refers to as struggles (hooks, 1999). If black women's stories are struggles, they are also strategies, songs, testimonies, prayers, promises, warnings, offerings, poems, prophesies, co-constructions, and callings. *Sweetwater* calls forth untold and unearthed narratives of rural black women that celebrate and reflect their resilience, without being limited to their resilience. *Sweetwater* stories are also stories of resistance, stories of survival, and stories of silence(s).

Sweetwater is my effort to say something about the lived realities of rural black women and to talk through testimonies of being poor, black, and female. This project offered me a unique opportunity and responsibility to look at the language that is used about black women's lives, and the language black women use to tell about their lives (Smitherman, 2000), and make sense of them. The stories I share are exceptional and not necessarily representative of all rural black women's experiences, but they are resonant and palpable narratives that speak to generational lived realities in small towns.

As a former member of the community I studied, I, similar to other black women scholars before me, had to leave the environment in order to value it. Comparing her viewpoint to wearing a tight-fitting shirt, Zora Neale Hurston (1990/1935) stated, "I couldn't see it for wearing it. It was only when I was off in college, away from my native surroundings, that I could see myself like somebody else and stand off and look at my garment" (p. 1). Hurston realized that as a member of her community she was immersed in the culture and unable to "see" it from a perspective of appreciation or critique.

Alice Walker had a similar revelatory experience of the merits of southern, rural life. After growing up in the rural south and leaving, Walker later recognized the wisdom and beauty that was available to her there. Walker (1983) writes that the black southern writer inherits what she calls "double vision," the ability to "see [your] own world and its close community while intimately knowing and understanding the people who make up the larger world that surrounds and suppresses [your] own" (p. 19).

The intimacy and accuracy of Walker's dual knowledge and Hurston's homecoming experience allowed them to tell stories from a place of embodied understanding without diminishing the story of the "other." It is this double and external vision, my positionality as an insider/outsider, and my consciousness of the taken for granted gifts embedded in everyday life and language that inspired me to write about the people I grew up with as I see them, as they see themselves, and as they are seen by others, in all of their idiosyncrasies (Houston, 2000).

(Re)Defining Rural Black Womanhood

The stories black women tell about their lives are different from the stories other people tell about them (Bobo, 1991). Black women focus on strength and survival, not fairy-tale happily ever afters, and while they recognize the tragedies in their lives, they do not identify their lives as tragedies. As Audre Lorde (2007/1984) points out, "It is axiomatic that if we do not define ourselves for ourselves, we will be defined by others—for their use and to our detriment" (p. 45). This call for black women's self-definition, a hallmark of black feminism, has inspired black women to write themselves into visibility and out of pathology.

For generations black women overlooked themselves, accepting, sometimes without critique, the versions of their lives offered to them from the lens of white supremacy (Harris-Perry, 2011). Many of the available representations were negative, resting at their feet the blame of everything from the emasculation of black men (Wallace, 1999/1978) to the destruction of black families (Moynihan, 1965; Franklin, 2000). For some women, however, including the women in my home community, the publicized demonization of black women and black families was no different from the assaults of racism and sexism they endured every day.

In *The Black Woman: An Anthology*, Toni Cade Bambara (1970) offers a definition that proves black women do not have a homogenous identity and there is no "authentic" black womanhood (Ladner, 1971). She describes the black woman as:

> A college graduate. A drop-out. A student. A wife. A divorcee. A mother. A lover. A child of the ghetto. A product of the bourgeoisie. A professional writer. A person who never dreamed of publication. A solitary individual. A member of the Movement. A gentle humanist. A violent revolutionary. She is angry and tender, loving and hating. She is all these things—and more. (p. xviii)

Bambara's contradictory descriptions insist that black women are multifaceted, multilayered, and multioppressed. Black women are surrounded by myths claiming that they are inferior, physically and emotionally impervious, unfeminine, criminal minded, and sexually promiscuous (Jones & Shorter-Gooden, 2003). As a castrating matriarchate, Black women are presented as superhuman (Ladner, 1971), strong (Danquah, 1998; Morgan, 1999), and grossly independent (Wallace, 1978/1999). In addition, for women in the rural south the stereotypes deepen with layers that include ignorance, laziness, lack of opportunity, and backward thinking. Labeled unsophisticated, unstable, and stuck, rural black women are presented as unable to leave or better their situations.

Early studies of rural communities (Woodson, 1930) concluded that rural black folk suffer discriminations and racial restrictions at a greater degree than those in nonrural areas because of racism, white supremacy, classism, and a lack of education and resources. These limitations, however, do not necessarily impact how they see themselves and their communities.

A redefinition of (rural) black womanhood challenges stereotypes while celebrating and recalibrating what most matters. Rural black women value themselves and each other, concentrating on intergenerational relationships, old time religion, and family. Black women writers have long resisted traditional and canonical expectations of a well-lived life, expressing ambivalence if not disdain at respectability politics that never reflect their circumstances (Christian, 1997;

Morris, 2014), situating them simultaneously within and without their storied representations.

Outsiders-Within: Black Women Writing about Black Women

Patricia Hill Collins (1998) defines outsider-within spaces as locations that offer us new perspectives of oppression and are, therefore, "riddled with contradictions" (p. 5). Collins (2009) also likens the outsider-within to an "invisible Other" (p. 110). Similarly, Joni L. Jones (1996) adopts insider/outsider language to describe the shifting identity that ethnographers experience upon entering and leaving the field. She describes the benefits of self-othering, saying, "constructing the self as other. [...] lets one see one's self from an outsider's view, as tangential, as reference rather than referent. The self becomes the object in the process of otherizing" (p. 133). These multiple and shifting positions give black women a unique vantage point from which to write and analyze, which is why black women should be among the primary investigators of black women's lives.

Black women researchers can offer information about black women that others can't. Robert Blauner and David Wellman (1973), two white social scientists, admitted that "there are certain aspects of racial difference that are difficult—if not impossible—for nonminorities to grasp empirically and formulate conceptually. These barriers are existential and methodological as well as political and ethical" (p. 329). No one is more qualified to interpret what it means to be a black woman than a black woman. Black women's studies by black women allow black scholars to respond to earlier interpretations of their lives with their own perspective (hooks, 1989). Instead of adopting a nonauthentic voice to respond, black women can personally engage topics of discourse and communicate their lives in a shared language through everyday talk or sisterspeak (Houston, 2004; Houston Stanback, 1988a; Scott, 1995, 2000, 2002). Black women document their lives and experiences through stories, superstitions, sayings, metaphors, poems, parables, and thick descriptions. Whether studying black women as a subculture or the communities in which they live, black women researchers can offer a privileged standpoint for collecting and evaluating the raw data of black women's lives—but there are some potential challenges for black women primarily studying their own lives.

First, black women have an inevitable bias that may influence their interpretations. While black women spend a good part of their lives taking outsider views into account, a black woman's situated knowledge is intentionally subjective. Second, black women may dismiss or ignore significant information or findings they consider taken for granted or common knowledge. Because of the shared experiences and histories many black women have, they may not always pay attention to details that offer important context for nonblack women. Third, there may be professional conflicts or consequences for black women scholars studying themselves or their communities. Black women researchers who are committed to what Marsha Houston (2000) calls "community-cognizant scholarship," which is intended to be "liberatory for the masses of African American women" (p. 675), must negotiate the competing goals of representing our communities while advancing our professional careers. Black women researchers studying black women must defy the traditional, white-washed standards of the academy that would only accept scholarship that is inaccessible and illegible to the black women at the center of our analysis. Houston (2000) believes that black women researchers, as "insiders" (black women), must grapple equally with those considered outsiders (nonblack women scholars), to guarantee everyday black women's definitions and understandings are recognized, understood, and respected.

Focusing on Black Women's Communicative Lives

Spoken, written, and nonverbal communication accounts for how we use messages to make meaning. African-American communication concentrates on the identity-specific and culturally influenced communication practices unique to the black diaspora (Jackson, 2004). Studies of black women's communication urges an interpretation of communication that centers black women's knowledge (Houston & Davis, 2002) and privileges personal narrative (Bochner, 2014; Ellis & Bochner, 2000; Etter-Lewis, 1991; Houston, 2002), performance, (Davis, 2007, 2008; Johnson, 2013; Jones, 1996; Madison, 1993), orality, and storytelling, utterances that have always been central components of black women's communication practices (Etter-Lewis, 1991; Houston, 2002; Madison, 1993; Vaz, 1997). Marsha Houston (2004), a trailblazer of African-American women's communication research, insists that "any explanation of African American women's communication must, in some way, account for the heterogeneity of black women's lived experiences" (p. 157). In A Black Women's Angle of Vision on Communication Studies, Houston and Davis (2002) call for more scholarship "that explores the lived communicative experiences of African American women," and is found in "ordinary women's everyday conversations" (p. 3). While examining everyday talk and historical legacies are important, studying stories and narratives of black women, as communicative artifacts, offers a layered and nuanced perspective by focusing on the events and experiences they choose to tell, and considering the implications of the stories they silence.

Black women use communication and language as a way of making themselves visible and relevant (Houston & Davis, 2002) and to connect to those who share common experiences (Moraga and Anzaldúa, 1983). The dialectic of identity that emerges from black women's (often contradictory) affiliations and allegiances to their gender and race complicates their communication practices (Hecht, Collier, & Ribeau, 1993) and requires focused and intentional research to "uncover untold stories of Black women whose lives had been ignored and made invisible by hegemonic society" (Davis, 2008).

In Goals for Emancipatory Communication Research on Black Women, Brenda J. Allen (2002) suggests that research grounded in the communicative lives of black women should (1) be committed to improving black women's lives, (2) challenge homogenous assumptions about black women, (3) focus on the variegated experiences of black women in different contexts, (4) include a critique of the oppressive forces black women face, (5) uncover the benefits of black women's communication, (6) help black women get free, and (7) include a commitment to emancipatory research. These goals guide the methodological possibilities of interpreting Sweetwater as a communication text, and inform how Sweetwater stories can be understood independently.

Black women's studies is not, however, limited to one field of study. An interdisciplinary approach to studying the lives of black women can help identify how stories, silence, and deeds in ordinary everyday conversations (Houston & Kramarae, 1991), alongside critical and contextual analysis and self-definition, can be used strategically to confront and resist oppression. Further, because meaningful communication is storied (Fisher, 1987), stories are useful tools for understanding black women's communication and black women's lived experiences.

Theoretical Approaches to Understanding Black Women

By definition, theories describe, explain, predict, increase awareness, foster understanding, and critique. Theories are embedded in our experiences and the questions that emerge from our curiosities about the world. Theories are connected to praxis which allows a theory to be translated, carried out, rehearsed, and compared to the lived experiences of others. Theories are also stories (Bochner, 1994, 2002; Coles, 1989), and stories are theoretical, which means theorists and practitioners are story-tellers. Therefore, in some sense we are all, knowingly and unknowingly, intentionally and by accident, naïve theorists (Wood, 2005) and narrators.

In the collection of feminist writings, *This Bridge Called My Back*, Cherríe Moraga and Gloria Anzaldúa (1983) name theory, saying, "A theory in the flesh means one where the physical realities of our lives—our skin color, the land or concrete we grew up on, our sexual longings—all fuse to create a politic born out of necessity" and contradictions (p. 23). Theories that center black women are "fleshed out" theories that wrestle with identity politics and grapple with how race and gender representation inform our experiences. Three principal theories that can be applied to the study of black women's lives are black feminist thought/womanism, intersectionality theory, and muted group theory.

Black Feminist Thought and/or (Alice Walker's) Womanism

Often used interchangeably, black feminism (or black feminist thought) and womanism refers to a standpoint theory whose common objective is black women's self-definition (Banks-Wallace, 2000; Brown, 1997; Collins, 1998, 2009; Taylor, 1998; Walker, 1983). Some scholars conflate womanism and black feminism while others insist they are incompatible (Alexander-Floyd & Simien, 2006). For the purposes of my study, I use both approaches and terms synonymously.

Black feminist thought offers black women a view of themselves through interpretive frameworks, epistemological approaches, and empowerment (Collins, 2009). Black feminist thought is characterized by six related components or distinctions related to black women's experiences: (1) black women constitute an oppressed group; (2) black women have diverse responses to common challenges within a racist society; (3) black women's experiences represent a heterogeneous collectivity, therefore black women share a group standpoint; (4) black women intellectuals need to examine and investigate black women's viewpoints and experiences; (5) black feminist thought and black feminism must remain dynamic and changing to meet changing social conditions and needs; and (6) black feminist thought is linked to other social justice projects, linking the lives of black women to issues of human dignity, empowerment, and social justice (Collins, 2009).

Black women's epistemologies, or ways of knowing, are rooted in lived experience. The four dimensions of black feminist epistemology, which include lived experience as a criterion of meaning, the use of dialogue, the ethic of personal accountability, and the ethic of caring, are available to everyday black women and provide a blueprint for ordinary black women to craft knowledge outside of the academy (Collins, 2009; Phillips & McCaskill, 1995).

Alice Walker (1983) offered womanism as a substitute ideological approach to white feminist thought. In her collection of nonfiction prose, *In Search of Our Mothers' Gardens*, she defined a womanist as:

> A black feminist or feminist of color. From the black folk expression of mothers to female children, "You acting womanish," i.e., like a woman. Usually referring to outrageous, audacious, courageous or willful behavior. Wanting to know more and in greater depth than is considered "good" for one. Interested in grown-up doings. Acting grown up. Being grown up. Interchangeable with another black folk expression: "You trying to be grown." Responsible. In charge. Serious.

The definition continues to include,

> a woman who loves other women, sexually and/or nonsexually. Appreciates and prefers women's culture, women's emotional flexibility, and women's strength. Sometimes loves individual men, sexually and/or nonsexually. Committed to survival and wholeness of entire people, male and female. Not a separatist, except periodically, for health. Loves music. Loves dance. Loves the moon. Loves the Spirit. Loves love and food and roundness. Loves struggle. Loves the Folk. Loves herself. Regardless. (xi–xii)

Womanism, according to Walker, is a tradition of black womanhood and, therefore, a central part of black women's experiences. Her definition attempts to give agency to black women historically by privileging folk traditions and black women's ways of knowing. She presents the black woman as someone who seeks knowledge (even to her own detriment) and relies on her experiences and emergence into adulthood or "grown-up doings" to learn. Through her definition, Walker encourages self-love and a love of black people ("the Folk"), spirituality, and customs (music and dance). She also recognizes and celebrates the dialectics of black women's lives including her ability to be vulnerable and also courageous; outrageous and also serious; independent and also reliant on relationships (sexually and/or nonsexually with men and/or women).

Walker was not suggesting a feminist hierarchy but rather an alternative to white feminism. In an interview with David Bradley (1984), Walker explained that she did not feel black feminism described things correctly. She said,

> I don't choose womanism because it is "better" than feminism [...] I choose it
> because I prefer the sound, the feel, the fit of it, because I cherish the spirit of
> the women the word calls to mind, and because I share the old ethnic-American
> habit of offering society a new word when the old word it is using fails to describe
> behavior and change that only a new word can help it more fully see.I need a
> word that is organic, that really comes out of the culture, that really expresses the
> spirit that we see in black women. And it's just [...] womanish. (p. 94)

Walker's definitions and descriptions of womanism make it available and accessible to rural black women who may feel isolated from black feminism because
of its attachment to white feminism and academe. Layli Phillips (2006), who
distinguishes womanism from feminism, praises the verisimilitude of Walker's
womanism, and defines it as,

> a social change perspective rooted in Black women's and other women of col-
> or's everyday experiences and everyday methods of problem solving in everyday
> spaces, extended to the problem of ending all forms of oppression for all people,
> restoring the balance between people and the environment/nature, and reconcil-
> ing human life with the spiritual dimension (p. xx).

Phillips' connection between womanism and social justice is consistent with the
ways everyday black women engage in activism often in unintentional and unconscious ways.

Womanism, like intersectionality theory, has been criticized for its seeming
malleability and ubiquity. Both theories were created by black women to explain
and represent the unique experiences of black women, but are commonly used to
represent other marginalized positionalities as well.

Intersectionality Theory

Intersectionality is a term credited to legal scholar Kimberlé Crenshaw (1989;
1991) to explain the unique injustice black women faced in the criminal justice system. Intersectionality offers a way of investigating how gender joins other
identity factors to influence how black women experience oppression and gendered violence. Intersectionality theory is grounded in the idea that people live
layered lives and often experience overlap and "intersections" in their identities.
This means when multiple identity factors are considered, it is both possible to be
multiply oppressed, and to feel oppression in one area and privilege in others. For

example, black women are marginalized by race and gender but may be privileged in society as heterosexual or middle class.

Intersectionality is an interdisciplinary, multigenerational, social-justice focused theory that originated in the early work of black feminists who recognized how the particulars of their identity often informed how they experienced discrimination as black women. The Combahee River Collective's Black Feminist Statement (1982) argued that race, class, sex, and sexuality oppression often are experienced simultaneously by black women and, therefore, cannot be separated (p. 16). Setting the foundation of identity politics that Crenshaw (1989, 1991) would later build on, these feminist women recognized the interlocking nature of oppression in black women's lives.

In *Women, Race and Class*, Angela Y. Davis (1983) discussed the concerns of black women by emphasizing the relevance and significance of the intersection of class, race, and gender in the lives of black women. Davis found that these categories of oppression are not discrete and, therefore, must be explored where they have similarities. Her perspective does not overlook the oppressions individually or their distinct causes and consequences but rather acknowledges how a concerted recognition of interlocking oppressions creates a greater opportunity for resistance.

In her collection of essays and speeches, *Sister Outsider*, Audre Lorde (2007/1984) furthered the concept by encouraging an acknowledgment, rather than a dismissal, of differences among women, including but not limited to age, race, class, ability, and sexuality. Lorde used her work to challenge white feminists who ignored the inevitable differences in the lives of American women. By arguing for an acknowledgment of difference, Lorde urged feminists to consider the implications of who they are. By writing from the peculiarities of her own life as a black warrior woman, lesbian, feminist, mother, lover, and activist, Lorde teaches us that difference is significant and important.

Brittney Cooper (2016) cites a genealogy of intersectionality to the late 19th century. She attributes early iterations of the concept to public intellectual race women Anna Julia Cooper, Mary Church Terrell, and Pauli Murray, who all wrote about the joint implications of race and gender discrimination (Cooper, 2017). She also credits Frances Beale's double jeopardy (1970/1995), and Deborah King's "multiple jeopardy" (1988) with establishing foundational knowledge for intersectional theorization. Cooper (2016) states,

> Taken together, this body of proto-intersectionality theorizing advanced
> the idea that systems of oppression—namely, racism, classism, sexism, and

heterosexism—worked together to create a set of social conditions under which black women and other women of color lived and labored, always in a kind of invisible but ever-present social jeopardy (p. 386).

Cooper goes on to argue that intersectionality offers an account of power (-isms), not personal identity, to thwart the impulse to move toward post-intersectionality due to intersectionality's failures as a prescriptive theory of identity (Cooper, 2016).

While there are multiple and sometimes contradictory understandings of intersectionality, Collins and Bilge (2016) argue that intersectionality has six agreed upon tenets and themes when used as an analytic tool: inequality, relationality, power, social context, complexity, and social justice (pp. 25–30). Concentrating on the everydayness of intersectionality, they suggest it is useful both inside and outside of the academy as a way of theorizing injustice.

Muted Group Theory

Muted group theory attempts to represent nondominant or marginalized groups whose voices and experiences are often overlooked or silenced. Initially rooted in anthropological investigations of women (Ardener, 1978) and later applied to the discipline of communication (Kramarae, 1981; Orbe, 1998a, 1998b), muted group theory reflects the suppression of thought and can be applied to the ways black women's voices and experiences are silenced. Muted group theory states that dominant groups determine how (or if) the experiences of nondominant groups are communicated. In a summary of the theory, Cris Kramarae (2005) says,

> Muted group theory suggests that people attached or assigned to subordinate groups may have a lot to say, but they tend to have relatively little power to say it. Their speech is disrespected by those in the dominant positions; their knowledge is not considered sufficient for public decision-making or policy making processes of that culture; their experiences are interpreted for them by others; and they are encouraged to see themselves as represented in the dominant discourse. (p. 55)

Ardener (2005) distinguishes muted group theory from the act of muting. She states that while muting includes the suppression or repression of speech, alongside silencing, muted theory is also, or just as concerned with "what people say, and when they speak, and in what mode." This acknowledges that muted group theory engages recognition, representation, and removal.

Intercultural communication scholar Mark Orbe's co-cultural theory (Orbe 1998a, 1998b), which emerged from oral histories of marginalized groups, is informed by muted group theory and calls for underrepresented voices to be heard and understood, alongside as well as in reaction to dominant voices. Orbe states, "theorizing from a marginalized experience simultaneously unites and differentiates experiences without essentializing them" (p. 1).

As a muted group, black women's fight for acknowledgment and visibility includes an insistence on authenticity. In A Race for Theory, Barbara Christian (1987) reinforces black women writers' resistance to translate their work to fit the standards of white, "dominant" discourse, and expectations. Her suspicion of formal theorizing is based on the absence and dismissal of black women's voices and perspectives. While rejecting hegemonic ways of thinking, she forwards an acknowledgment of the everyday theorization of black women's lives by black women. She states,

> For people of color have always theorized—but in forms quite different from the Western form of abstract logic. And I am inclined to say that our theorizing (and I intentionally use the verb rather than the noun) is often in narrative forms, in the stories we create, in riddles and proverbs, in the play with language, since dynamic rather than fixed ideas seem more to our liking. How else have we managed to survive with such spiritedness the assault on our bodies, social institutions, countries, our very humanity. And women, at least the women I grew up around, continuously speculated about the nature of life through pithy language that unmasked the power relations of their world (p. 52).

While Christian's critique is based on literary criticism, it corresponds with the scholarship on muted group theory, not only by identifying black women as a muted group, vulnerable to erasure without a reimagination and renegotiation of academic priorities, but she expresses a commitment to use the language and stories of black women to ensure their self-defined semantic survival.

Any discussion of black women should include a discussion of difference within the lives of women (Lorde, 2007) and the "simultaneity of oppressions" (Combahee River Collective, 1982; Smith, 1983) they encounter. Their unnamed theories and often unheard voices not only legitimate their experiences as sites of knowledge but privileges their sense-making capabilities for strategizing and analyzing their lives.

"Seeing Myself Like Somebody Else": Mis-education and Research

Like Hurston (1990/1935), college education gave me an academic perspective to analyze my rural cultural upbringing. This project offered me the opportunity to interrogate the mis-education black women often receive about the veracity and importance of their lives as lived and the contributions their interior experiences offer to the academy (Collins, 2009; hooks, 1989; Phillips & McCaskill, 1995).

I had the opportunity to interrogate the ways my book and nonbook education affected my return to Sweetwater in terms of the changed lens, which caused me to see myself, my hometown, and community members differently. The comprehensive educated gaze allowed me to amalgamate my formalized education with the epistemic education I received at home. As a trained (auto)ethnographer, I suddenly "saw myself like somebody else" and used that lens simultaneously as both a subject and object of research (Jones, 1996).

There are clear distinctions between my college education and the education I received at home. My grandmother refers to this as the difference between book sense and good sense (or common sense). She would often say, "Common sense ain't all that common." My grandmother, and most members of my home community, appreciate the former but highly value the latter. She has told me on multiple occasions that "all of the learning I do" would make her head hurt.

Sweetwaterans realize that there are ways that education makes things accessible in the larger world, but can limit or distort the knowledge that is necessary for everyday existence (Dews & Law, 1995). Through gathering stories and using theoretical approaches to understand them, I use Sweetwater stories tolink my formal training to my community intelligence.

Sweet Home Sweetwater

I initially returned to Sweetwater—after having been away for ten years—for the purpose of participant observation research during the summer of 2006 as part of dissertation requirements. I became a character during my research, readopting, relearning, and re-remembering what it meant to live in the community full-time. I had to immerse myself in the experience while at the same time observing and recording and negotiating my inevitable exit. To protect the privacy and anonymity of participants, I used pseudonyms for all persons and places, and collapsed details to create composite characters and narratives to represent the experiences and stories of multiple participants. Unimportant details were fictionalized.

It is not possible to be fully detached as a scholar, participant, or observer because all of those roles require some attachment. My relationship with the community, prior to my research and return as an involved participant, clouded my judgment and perspective. I had been sent to school so that I could have a better life but no one had calculated what my ambition would mean and how it would translate to my nonacademic life.

Autoethnography

Autoethnographies are cultural, situational, political, self-conscious, and inherently critical (Boylorn & Orbe, 2014; Ellis, Adams, & Bochner, 2011; Madison, 2012). They are also autobiographical, multilayered, and introspective (Bochner & Ellis, 2016; Ellis, 2004a, 2004b; Ellis & Bochner, 2000). Autoethnographies allow researchers to use the materials of their personal lives and lived experiences to explain how and why they interpret things the way they do (Goodall, 2004), and to make informed connections between individual and collective experiences. By inverting the ethnographic eye on the self, autoethnographers are able to translate and story social and cultural experiences.

Because of its equal engagement of traditional ethnographic techniques and autoethnographic reflexivity, communication professor Chris Poulos describes Sweetwater as an "ethnographic autoethnography" or "autoethnographic ethnography." This distinction recognizes the dual purposes of my role(s) as a researcher and community member alongside my ethnographic I (Ellis, 2004a, 2004b). The content of Sweetwater stories are based on ethnographic research (Clifford & Marcus, 1986; Madison, 2012), but my mirroring of those stories in the second half of the book are autoethnographic.

Autoethnography requires me to not just tell my story but also to situate it among others and frame it theoretically and analytically (Adams, 2011). For example, what does my autoethnographic story do? What does it accomplish? What makes my story unique or representative, and how can it be useful for understanding the lives of rural black women? I am invested not only in telling my story but also in making my story useful and meaningful for others. It is important that other people find relevance in the stories I tell.

We can learn about our lives by reading about the lives of others (Ellis, Revision, p. 16). In that sense, autoethnography contributes to others' stories and involves other participants. The slash that is often added to auto/ethnography by many woman of color scholars notes the collective embedded in the individual (Mary Weems, personal communication, May 9, 2012). My story is our story.

Revisiting Sweetwater (Meta-Autoethnography)

In *Revision: Autoethnographic Reflections on Life and Work,* Carolyn Ellis (2009) returns to some of her earlier autoethnographies in an effort to "re-present, re-examine, and re-vision" stories previously published about her life. She revisits her original work, considers how people have responded to it, and writes autoethnographic accounts about the autoethnographies. She defines these accounts as meta-autoethnography, which include "current reflections, narrative vignettes, and analyses" (p. 12) as a way of bridging the past with the present. Meta-autoethnographies are autoethnograpic accounts about autoethnography, or autoethnographies about autoethnography. In Ellis' work, each revisited narrative chapter is anchored with a meta-autoethnography that explains, reconceptualizes, and reflects on its preceding story, in its original context and in its new iteration.

Ellis (2009) explains that academic writers are rarely given the opportunity to return to and reevaluate their work, because that is generally the work of critics and reviewers. She argues that revisiting autoethnographies can make them more meaningful. Ellis states, "re-examining the events we have lived through and the stories we have told about them previously allows us to expand and deepen our understandings of the lives we have led, the culture in which we have lived, and the work we have done" (p. 13). In this revised edition, the original narratives of Sweetwater are held in place, while the framing and analysis around them are reimagined and retold. Reviews of Sweetwater are included in order to put Sweetwater stories in conversation with its readers, and the revised framework that comes before and after the narratives offered me an opportunity to rewrite Sweetwater without restorying it.

Ellis' (2009) restorying impulse, however, is at the heart of the revised edition of Sweetwater. While I do not wrap the individual old narratives in larger "stories of the stories," like she does, retelling them with new insight, I reflect on the stories in the Prologue, and rewrite the introduction and analysis to better explain and theorize their meanings. I also include the feedback of scholars who have written or presented reactions to Sweetwater and consider how their questions, challenges, and affirmation influence the original work. In the new Sweetwater Re/Visions section, I reply to reviews and responses and explain the choices and changes I made. In the new Epilogue, I write a brief meta-autoethnography about revisiting Sweetwater and what has changed since the book was first published.

Relational Ethics: Taking Sweetwater Home

In order to conduct an ethical project I followed Ellis' (1995, 2007) advice who has reflected on emotional and ethical ways of carrying out research on intimate others. In addition to investing myself in the research and telling stories of my personal experiences in the field, I read the stories through the eyes of participants in order to consider how they might react to them. I also shared early versions of the stories with participants to get their feedback and permission to move forward. In the passages that follow, I consider how my mother and grandmother responded to an early draft of Sweetwater, followed by my personal convictions of writing and then publishing these stories.

"It Makes Us Look So Bad"

I read the first lines of the story about Twiggy and Cake fighting (Chapter 4) to my mother over the phone and she listened, quietly. When an extended pause marked the end, I asked for her reaction.

"Well [...] that's how it was."

That was all she said. I didn't know if that was a positive or negative reaction. I asked for more detail. She hesitated and then said, finally, in a voice that sounded suddenly sad,

"It just makes us look so bad."

I had not intended to make anyone look bad. The weight of her words paralyzed me to speechlessness. We sat on the phone in silence for several minutes.

The realization that the project was exposing secrets and dredging up painful memories made me feel guilty. I was unable to continue writing for several months. Every word felt like a betrayal. Despite the fact that I was fictionalizing the stories I felt responsible for the way my mother reacted. I was suddenly aware that regardless of my intentions I could neither predict nor control how people responded to the stories, including participants. I wanted to give them a reflection of their lives, as lived, in an academic context, but was that something they wanted or needed, or was it my own selfish need for rural black women's scholarship? What if my well-meaning project failed and did more harm than good?

My intention was to use the stories and experiences of rural black women to not only understand and construct a place for us in academe but also to establish my career. I was being influenced by academic pursuits and my allegiance to my black womanhood (see Ladner, 1971). Perhaps it was the reality of knowing that my livelihood and future were dependent on telling my truth that left me feeling implicated by the possible hurt the stories would cause to the women I interviewed. Suddenly my ambition felt selfish. I had to justify my study to myself.

My mother's initial response to the research eventually subsided and she became more comfortable with our private and family stories becoming public. Her original discomfort challenged me to think deeply about the ethical implications this research would have on people who could be readily identified, especially those, who by association with me, would be recognized. Autoethnography is an ethical practice (Ellis, 2007) and I needed to be prepared for the potential consequences of my stories. Regardless of the ramifications I knew I needed to provide my family with the courtesy of hearing the stories from me and the opportunity to respond.

"It Sounded Like a Real Story"

I decided to read the story out loud to my grandmother. I felt it was important to give her the opportunity to ask questions if she had them. Our interviews had been somewhat disappointing because, though I know my grandmother as a storyteller, she has always been stingy with words. She is more of an observer, taking people in with her eyes and ears.

Most of the stories I collected about her life came from her children. After interviewing them I would go to her to request details and ask about her version of the events. She seemed the least interested in my project but was willing to participate, even introducing me to other participants and recommending women who might be able to help me.

I sat with her at noon and I had thirty minutes before her stories (soap operas) came on. She sat in her black pleather recliner rocking chair, arms folded, wearing a beige sweater jacket over her blue and yellow family reunion t-shirt and men's Lee jeans with a crease down the middle. Her white slouch socks peeked above her black Reebok tennis shoes that she puts on as soon as she wakes up to walk around in the house. She is only barefooted when she sleeps. She has "sugar" (diabetes) which causes her to have cold chills regardless of the temperature. I waited for her to get comfortable in her favorite chair, which doesn't match the other furniture in the room, but that she insisted on keeping when the set it came with was thrown away. I turned the volume on the television all the way down without permission, knowing that she insists the TV stay on all day long, regardless if she is in the room or paying attention to it. It is one of her many daily rituals.

Butterflies danced in my stomach as I began reading the same story I read to my mother eight months earlier. I had chosen that story on purpose, think-ing that it was the "worst" of them. I was nervous about how my grandmother would respond, but realized that documenting and analyzing her response was a necessary part of the research process. I wondered if she would be angry with me. When I was a child, her anger was manifested in a raised voice, a good cussing out, and a butt whipping. What would she do to me now? I know that other family members who make her mad are immediately put on her "shit list," of which it is nearly impossible to get off. I wondered if she would ask me to change the story. And if she wanted the story changed, what would she want me to put in its place? Would she require me to start over by refusing to be a character? I won-dered if she would tell me I had it all wrong.

I read the story out loud. I was careful to change my intonation, ever so slightly, when I read the dialogue and to slow down when I got to the parts that I suspected she would have concerns about. When I finished reading, I glanced up at the burgundy antique clock on the wall. Ten minutes had passed. There would be time for us to talk about my story before her stories came on.

"Well," I said half to myself and half to my grandmother, "what did you think?"

When she did not respond immediately, I feared she was staring at me the way she looks at people when she's angry. She would generally wait for you to make eye contact so she could roll her eyes and then look away, refusing to reen-gage. I looked up and realized that she had dozed off.

"Mama!" I called, waking her up.

"What?" She sat up in her chair and rubbed her hands over her face.

"Were you listening? I was reading you the story."

"I heard it," she said.

I look at her suspiciously, not believing her.

"I heard it. It was good, it put me to sleep. It sounded like a real story." Looking at her innocence, I shook my head and laughed out loud, because I had been worried that the story would upset her.

When I asked my grandmother's permission to leave the story as it was she nodded her head, still trying to reassure me that she had indeed been listening, and hoping she had not hurt my feelings. "I like it," she promised.

I realized in that moment that my grandmother was not concerned about the story—I was. Having lived nearly eight decades, she was not concerned about people's opinions of her life. She was not apologetic or ashamed of her past. She was not worried about her reputation or legacy. She had lived a colorful life and made the best of it under the circumstances. She taught me a tremendous lesson in that exchange and told me she didn't need to hear any more of "my stories," a nice way of dismissing me so she could turn her attention to "the stories." She changed the TV channel to five and turned the volume back up just in time to hear the opening theme song for *The Young and the Restless*.

"Self-acceptance is like oxygen after held breath"

Throughout this research, I worried about whether or not I was ethically responsible and if I was continually guided by my commitment and promise to "do no harm." Had I taken liberties with information that was shared in confidence? Would participants agree with my interpretations of their lives and my portrayal of their experiences? Could I conceal the identities and stories of participants from each other?

The narratives I share acknowledge the nuances and complexities of rural black experiences. I sought to expand, not limit, the representations. I was committed to showing the women in my study as women with problems, not as problemed women. By showing, through stories, the way they cope and resist, I wanted to privilege black women's subjectivity. I know I cannot control how people read and interpret these stories, and I have to be content with knowing I have at least given representation to rural black women.

I reckon with what the representations in Sweetwater say about me as a rural black woman and tenured professor. When I wrote using pigeon-holed stereotypes (of black women as angry, mean, reckless, inherently strong, combative, hypersexual, overly religious, etc.), I was writing myself out of them. While I will always be implicated by the community I grew up in, my departure in my early twenties, and continued and intentional absence from living there permanently since, separates me from its day-to-day realities. While some Sweetwater stories reverberated in my life, others felt foreign as I realize being a child there and being a grown woman there are disparate experiences. As a result, I feel relief, guilt, and shame.

I also struggle with understanding and identifying the most authentic representation of myself. Sweetwater is home and I feel most at home with myself when I am there (Boylorn, 2016; Durham, 2014). Writing and rewriting Sweetwater confirms that I am as much a Sweetwater woman as the women I write about, even though my lived experiences are different from theirs. Our stories and the interconnectedness of our histories—our family and the implications of our legacies—our strength and the inevitability of our vulnerabilities make us mirror reflections of each other. Writing Sweetwater has given me permission to see myself in the women of Sweetwater and for them to see themselves in me. Self-acceptance is like oxygen after held breath.

Overview of Chapters

If ignorance is bliss then my life has been tragic, marked by the realization that despite my attempts to define myself, I am often reduced to what the world says I am. As Goodall prompts in his book *Writing the New Ethnography*, one's personal background and experience creates fixed positions or "personal facts that might influence how you see your data—your age, gender, class, nationality, race—factors that will not change during the course of the study but are often taken for granted and unexamined in the research process" (2000, p. 132). This book considers the impact of those "fixed positionings" and embraces them to tell stories full of knowing and possibility. This book reads as a "subjective position," relying on "self-defining moments, decisions, or turning points" (Goodall, 2000, p. 133) in my life and the lives of research participants who live in Sweetwater.

Black folks' ways of telling are circular, not linear. Accordingly, this book is separated into two parts with an interlude between them. Select chapters are punctuated by a poem, written by Dr. Mary E. Weems, which serves as a personal response and reaction to the preceding story. Weems' poems are "windows" that offer an outsider-looking-in view of Sweetwater culture and relationships. The poems act as symbolic interactions (Blumer, 1969; Denzin, 1992), responding to the rural cultural symbols and landscapes in the stories by connecting my story and the stories of participants with hers. Our complementary and interactive voices offer a unique and layered reading of the text.

Part 1, (DAILY) BREAD, concentrates on the stories collected through interviews with members of the Sweetwater community. Their stories are offered thematically, though not necessarily chronologically, which mimics the way they were told. The stories often fold in on themselves—introducing these women as lovers, mothers, daughters, believers (churchgoers), wives, friends, relatives, and community members. The brief interlude, PORCH PREMONITIONS, introduces Sweetie Pie and Peewee, Sweetwater women who, like the reader, are witnessing the story from the periphery. Their private conversation reflects on the past and makes predictions about the future. Part 2, (ROBIN) BIRD, is part of my autoethnography of growing up in Sweetwater, written in first-person prose. I move back and forth between childhood memories and adult revelations, flashbacks, and flash forwards, to make sense of my experiences as a rural blackgirl and how they are informed by my family, culture, identity, and community. My stories also introduce additional themes of experience.

In Part 3, (BITTERSWEET) ENDINGS, I conclude with a detailed discussion and interpretive analysis of the stories. I discuss how despite collective challenges black women define themselves beyond their circumstances. I focus on what the narratives teach us about rural black women and their strategies of love and laughter to make sense of their lives. I write about what the stories of rural black women in Sweetwater teach us about the intersections of race, gender, sex, and class. Finally, I speculate about how the Sweetwater stories inform our understanding of social justice and how black women respond to injustices communicatively and as a community.

New and Revised Content

In addition to the expanded introduction, the revised edition includes a revision to the interlude, an edited conclusion, and extended appendices. **Appendix A** includes new and additional details about how I gathered and analyzed data, and **Appendix B** documents chapter summaries and themes.

Sweetwater Re/Views is a collection of excerpts from previously published and unpublished responses to Sweetwater, including those featured in a special Sweetwater Forum in the academic journal Departures in Critical Qualitative Research.

Sweetwater Re/Visions is a compilation of my reactions to the reviews, specific responses to queries, and a discussion of how and in what ways I engaged the feedback in the new edition.

The epilogue, **BitterSweet(water)** is a meta-autoethnography about revisiting Sweetwater.

List of Main Characters

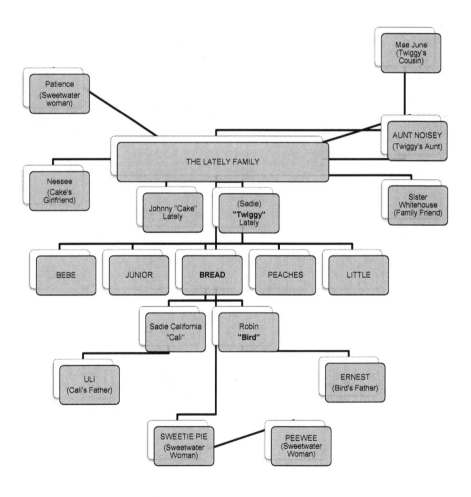

Bebe	Twiggy's oldest daughter, Bread's sister, Bird's aunt
Bird (Robin)	Author; Twiggy's granddaughter, Bread's youngest daughter
Bread	Twiggy's middle child, Bird and Cali's mother
Butter	Bread's best friend
Cake	Twiggy's husband
Cali	Bread's oldest daughter and Bird's sister
Ernest	Bread's husband, Bird's biological father
Junior	Twiggy's oldest son
Little	Twiggy's youngest son
Mae June	Twiggy's cousin and best friend
Neesee	Cake's girlfriend
Noisey	Twiggy's aunt
Patience	Sweetwater woman, distant relative of Twiggy
Peaches	Twiggy's youngest daughter, helps raise Bread's daughters
Peewee	Sweetwater woman
Sweetie Pie	Sweetwater woman
Twiggy	matriarch of the Lately family, married to Cake
Uli	Cali's biological father
Whitehouse	Sweetwater church woman, friend of Twiggy

Part One

(Daily) Bread

countrywomen

church-going and home-staying
women
practicing witchcraft
eating herbs to make them beautiful
and bearable
on the inside
to make up for the outside
self-sacrificing
women loving women
wholly
but not romantically
urgently
desperately
or jealously
like husbands or lovers
who stay long enough to leave a seed
that lingers
like his scent
the smell of sweat and need
stinking like garbage
on closed in porches
traditional beauty was not an option
or a luxury
they could afford
using hair grease for lipstick
homemade soap
and cocoa butter
on rough skin
left everything soft
except knees
elbows
and ankles
late night loving
found them smacking lips
rubbing rough heeled feet
callused with corns

against stiff sheets
recycled from family members
who could finally
afford
them new
you never throw away
anything
that still has use
this was true
of pots, pans,
shoes, and men

Chapter 1

Only people who have lived in Sweetwater all of their life know where Deadman's Road is because there isn't a sign. The dilapidated dead-end sign of a bold arrow marks the middle of the Sweetwater community and points in the direction where most of the black people in Sweetwater live. Mispronunciation and confusion led most people, who at the time could not read or tell the difference, to call it Deadman's Road. Over the years no one bothered to call it any different because the name fit, especially since one of the dirt roads leads to a path of unmarked graves. The younger people in Sweetwater, who found naming a road after some-one's poor fortune ominous, call it the Bottom, not because it is underneath the town, but because it is the only place in the community that only has one way in and one way out.

When black people were free from slavery and could buy their own land and property, many of them moved to the part of town where the land was cheap and chased all of the white people out. Some white people moved to the periphery of the road, for easy escape, while others still own houses there and rent them out to black people. The white church is still in the Bottom, the only church on that road, so black people have to cross the road or go into town to their various sanctuaries, separated by denomination and creed.

The people who have lived in Sweetwater all their lives look past its beauty. The roads are narrow and hugged on both sides by livestock, shacks, trailers, and open space. Stray dogs and hardheaded children can be found wandering the unpaved roads until past the time the streetlights come on, and most everywhere people need to get to in Sweetwater is within walking distance. There are no traffic lights, just stop signs, dirt roads, and intersections. Most residents are unable to say exactly where Sweetwater begins and ends but they share a common idea of "where about" Sweetwater starts and stops, based on their own estimations and assumptions. Most agree that if you travel more than a few minutes driving in any direction you are no longer in Sweetwater. Still others distinguish Sweetwater as Bottom One (Deadman's Road), and Bottom Two (everywhere else).

The stench of the chicken plant can be smelled at least two or three minutes (depending on the weather and time of the day), before you pass the factory in either direction, an aroma so thick the workers sometimes wear it on their skin. It is not a smell you ever get used to, a mixture of sweat, chicken shit, spit, and ammonia. Sweetwaterans know to hold their breath on their way home or right about the time the car is about to tilt on Taylor's curve. Sleeping children wake up in the car, resting their backs in backseats, knowing they are almost home because the smell of rotting meat is so strong.

The river runs alongside Sweetwater on multiple sides. Some people claim the town got its name because the river water is sweet, like honey in cooled off coffee, but no one has ever actually or intentionally tasted the fishy, dank water to test it. Sugar, the dark-skinned and alcoholic wanderer who is as peaceful as he is harmless, has been known to swim naked in the murky river when it's hot outside. Elder ladies in the community roll their eyes at the possibility of a sweet river coexisting with an unclean man. They throw up their hands in disgust saying, "If it was sweet, it ain't now," insinuating that nothing would stay sweet after Sugar's funky ass had touched it.

The houses, usually in a row and at least twenty feet apart, are mostly shot-gun. The rectangular homes have three to five rooms and no hallway, with doors at each end. The front room, generally the largest, doubled as a den during the day and a bedroom at night. The front door stayed locked and was mostly for show, while the back door was used to get in and out the house, sometimes walking through multiple rooms to find a way of escape.

Shotgun houses get their name from the saying that if you fire a gun from either end of the house, the bullet would fly through every room before exiting. It is not uncommon for couples to test that theory in Sweetwater, on restless nights when liquor runs out and jealousy settles in. A lot of people have guns, out of meanness or for protection, and children know not to bother them.

The landscape is surrounded by decaying buildings, weed-overgrown homes, and unkempt yards with wood and trash piles in the back. Junk cars pepper lawns intermittently, sometimes twin cars that unsober men, shade tree mechanics, spend their days "fixing on." They transport parts from one car to the other until one of them is useful enough to drive. Aesthetics are never important with cars in Sweetwater. It doesn't matter what a car looks like as long as it runs. And the bigger, the longer, the wider, the better. In the 1960s cars were broad shouldered like strong armed men, and difficult to steer, which is why most men refused to teach their wives how to drive, out of fear she couldn't hold the car on the road.

Strangers quickly overstay their welcome in Sweetwater and stand out because the people who live in Sweetwater have that Sweetwater look to them and talk with a Sweetwater drawl. They say "finn to" or "fixing to" instead of "about to"; "put on the dog" instead of get dressed up; "make" groceries instead of "buy" them; and "mal-like" instead of "pretend." People who stop in Sweetwater, at the store off the highway, are only there for some cheap gas, cigarettes, peanuts, and a Pepsi-Cola, usually on their way to somewhere else. They don't remember having been there in the first place. Sweetwater is not memorable unless you live there, and when you have always lived there it's the only place you can remember. And you memorize it like an Easter speech, linearly and accidentally. Everybody knows each other, and while liking your neighbors isn't a requirement, you can't help but love somebody who is so close and familiar.

Sweetwater is a town of contradictions, known for its liquor houses, old-time remedies, and religion. The community healer has an herbal cure for everything from period cramps to impotence. For a few dollars and some patience, Uncle Johnny can fix anything that ails you. On the other side of town is a woman who works roots.

Men work for low wages at farms, factories, tobacco priming, or hauling pulkwood. Women do domestic work, tend to children, and clean up after white folk and occasionally work alongside men in factory jobs. Several people make money on the side by selling things out of their home. Every four or five houses down you can buy anything from white lightning, fish plates, and reefer papers, to candy, sodas, and homemade ice cream.

The town is filled with kin and double-kin, many people looking alike in the southern rural way. The women have hard features, and men, even little boys, carry mannish faces and serious looks. Land is passed back and forth between family members, inherited from childless aunts, great-grandmothers who outlived their children's children, and patient planning. With biological family within fifty feet of each side of your own house there is rarely an opportunity for loneliness or privacy. Few people move out of Sweetwater and those who do visit frequently and remain watch-care members of their home churches for an every-other-Sunday excuse to return.

The conversations in Sweetwater are usually conversations about Sweetwater, or Sweetwaterans, or God, or good gossip. Most of the men are just alike but there is a difference in women in Sweetwater. The good ones are churched, or too simple or ugly to be impressive. Good women stay home, except for church services, school, and missionary work. The bad ones, or the ones still young enough to be cute and still naïve enough to think they can convince a man to stay off good looks and good lovin', spend their nights out. The in-between women take turns staying home and going out, depending on the night of the week. Payday Fridays are nights to put on your best clothes and be seen. Saturday nights are for drinking and playing cards. Sundays are for sobering up and praising the Lord, not necessarily in that order. Good women are good cooks, modest lovers, and humble. Many work outside the home, even when it means leaving their children at home to fend for themselves. Good men are the ones who come home at night, bring their check home at the end of the week, and go to church on the occasional Sunday morning.

Everybody in Sweetwater believes in God even if they don't go to church regularly. Everyone has a church home, a place to get married, a place to be buried, and a place to visit on special occasions. Churches and beliefs are usually passed down on your mama's side, so if a mother isn't a churchgoer, her children are prayed for by surrogates in the community who invite them to Sunday school or vacation Bible school.

Summer's long days and cool nights make for outside fun and entertainment. The men in Sweetwater have a community baseball team. Every Saturday from June until September Sweetwater families gather at the ad hoc baseball field in the woods. Mothers, girlfriends, wives, and girl children cheer for their men from the tops of cars and shaded grass while the older women sell hot dogs, fried fish, and cold drinks to the listless fans. Little boys are too easily bored to watch the game, so they play their own version on the dirt, using an extra baseball and thick sticks for a bat.

Winters are different. Tempers are short and nights are long and uncomfortable because the heat is generally stingy, sticking to the ceiling of the room where the potbelly stove resides. The other rooms, usually bedrooms, are vulnerable with broken or unfixed windows, covered with sheets and duct tape that are no match for North Carolina winters. Often, large families sit together in one room for warmth or sleep, fully clothed, three or four in a bed meant for one. There are less distractions in the winter, more fights, less work, more foolishness and frustrations, less love seeking, more lovemaking.

Whiteness is like air, everywhere all at once, even when you were not paying attention, and invisible. Still, Sweetwater land is not divided into the haves or the have nots, or strictly by race, because mostly everyone who lives there has always lived there and understands the unseen lines. There are railroad tracks, but black people live on both sides of them. White people, only seldomly in nicer homes, live on the edges of many roads in Sweetwater, usually next to each other on either side. White people and black people are not scared of each other, but treat each other as if something bad might happen if they actually spoke or touched.

Everybody knows everybody, including their business.

Business

By Mary E. Weems

In our house
business was a grown folks word
time to be seen mama heard
tellin' us to exit room
without words her head
angled Right
hand ready to grab
shoe brush switch
if we so much as slowed down.

At night business came through the walls
stopped us from sleeping
beatings loud as empty bottles
hitting floors just before one Miz so-and-so
after another—
Tellin' everybody's.

Chapter 2

There is not much killing in the Bottom on the outside, but many folk are dying on the inside or killing each other with meanness, spite, and unforgiveness. If it wasn't for the sin of suicide, maybe they would kill themselves. Nobody seemed willing to take that chance. Self-inflicted murder was never immediate or deliberate. It happened slowly and softly—with liquor and bad habits. Unnatural dying happened by accident though there were the stories of women being murdered by drunken boyfriends, fed-up wives putting roots on deadbeat husbands, and men who owed money to bookies being set on fire. The thing about a community as small as Sweetwater is that there is no place to hide your secrets.

White clothes were still on the clothesline when Walter raised his hand at Patience. Towels, bras, socks, panties, and sheets were neatly hanging on the invisible line and held in place with wooden pins. She had put them out that morning, before she went out, and had gotten home too late to bring them in. She hoped the night wind would not carry any of the socks away.

For some reason it was those white clothes still on the line that crossed her mind when his fist pushed against her face that first time. Patience did not hear him coming. Walter had always been a quiet man. It was his stillness that made him so dangerous.

Earlier that day Patience had received a call from home. Her father had called from Sweetwater inviting them for a visit. "Why don't you and Walt come for dinner and a good time?" he'd said. She accepted without asking her husband. She hung up the phone smiling, anxious to visit with her family, whom she saw less often since she had been married. Walter watched and listened from the open door of their humble house and waited. Patience was already getting ready when she first noticed Walter's harsh eyes on her. "Daddy and them frying some fish. Told us to come down."

"I'm not going nowhere."

Patience had learned to look past Walter's meanness. Her attention was on what she was going to wear to cover the pot in her belly. Extra weight and a different hair style were topics her family would find a way to bring into conversation after not seeing you in a while. She wanted to avoid feeling judged and self-conscious. She wanted to camouflage her imperfections under baggy clothes and cocoa butter, but there was limited time. It would take over an hour to get to Sweetwater from the city. They would need to leave soon.

Walter's stubbornness gave him away. She hadn't paid him any mind. Patience stopped in front of him wondering where her white bra was. "What you say, Walt?"

"I said I ain't going nowhere, and you ain't either."

His words came at her with the force of unexpected bad news. The last part, her not either part, sounded softer to her, like he didn't mean to say them out loud. It did not matter. Her consideration of the situation was brief. She *was* going to visit her family.

Patience had not been home in months. It was time for her son, Idgy, to visit with his kinfolk. It was time for her to hug her daddy's neck, and eat her mama's cooking. It had been too long since her last visit and she never declined a direct invitation.

Walter only agreed to live within driving distance of Sweetwater as a stipulation of marriage. He thought the country was too slow paced and that black folk in the country didn't try hard enough to make something of themselves. He did what he could to limit their returns home to scheduled visits during the holidays or for funerals.

"Did you hear what I said?" Walter asked.

"Yes, I heard you," Patience said in her soft-spoken voice. "I heard you say that you weren't going to the country. But do you see that De Ville out there? That's my car! Now I don't know what you doing today, but when I get all of my things and my baby's things together, I'm driving down home to spend the day with my family." Her daddy had given them the car as a wedding gift so that his daughter would always have a way home. Walter resented it.

Later, as Patience stood in the mirror admiring her coconut brown complexion and the lovely way the housedress she had picked out fell loosely below her breasts, her husband stood behind her, undressed. "I just need to get ready now," he said.

By now, Patience had had enough of him. "I don't have time to wait." She gathered her keys and took Idgy by the hand, helping him to the car. She wanted to make it to Sweetwater before the sun sat as high as it would go, and she needed to leave right then to make it. Half-dressed and humiliated, Walter stood at the screen door and watched her leave.

*

Patience arrived home in the middle of the night to a still and dark house. She carried Idgy in the house with both hands and laid his dead weight at the foot of his bed, leaving him there. It was usually Walt who carried him. She was surprised at how strong she was when she had to be.

"Walt?" She called out into the silence and got no response. She only half wondered where he could be while she warmed water on the stove to wash her face, under her arms, and between her legs. When she laid her head on the pillow, sleep was welcome and immediate. She woke up to the sound of a door closing. "Walt?" There was no answer, no proof that she was not dreaming, so she closed her eyes again. Then suddenly and without warning, she felt the weight of a heavy fist.

Walt straddled her between his legs and threw his fists at her. In shock, she kept her eyes open as he struck her, only closing them at the impact of the blows. For some reason, all she could think about were her brilliantly white clothes; only now, in her thoughts the white clothes were stained with her blood, the same way her night gown and bed sheets were.

When he grew tired, Walt collapsed next to her the way he did after sex. She lay still until she was sure he was asleep. Feeling the soreness of her body she remembered the freshly sharpened butcher knife in the top kitchen drawer. She considered going to the kitchen, opening the drawer, grabbing the knife and burying it into Walter's chest while he slept. She had never been hit before, even as a child. She was a change-of-life pregnancy so her parents were too old and preoccupied to beat her.

"You got a daddy," her father had said to her on the day she got married, "and you already been raised. Don't you go let no man try to re-raise you."

Out of habit she returned to her side of the bed and collapsed under the covers. After Walter rested a while, he woke up and started beating her again, turning around and leaning over her half-asleep body like a ghost. This time he seemed sorry, his eyes almost apologetic, his hands almost gentle, as they slapped against her body with an open hand and then a closed fist. The sound of his fists hitting against her was the sound of a fist hitting against an open hand. When he'd tired of beating her he returned to sleep and she turned to face the wall, her pillow soaked with blood, tears, and spit.

The next morning Walter rolled over to make love to his wife and found her stiff and unwilling. She lay there motionless, flinching at his touch, and watching the light outside her window as she waited for it to be over. When he finished she went to the bathroom to wash his touch and her blood from her body. Then, she went to the kitchen to make breakfast.

Idgy was already in the kitchen waiting, wearing the same clothes from the day before. He was a slow learner, born "special" as her mother called it. He was mostly silent and the few words he could speak were always directed at Patience, who devoured them with a mother's pride. Idgy could say "mama," "no," and "help me please" (which sounded like hep me peace). Patience kissed the top of his head, thankful, for once that he could not talk to ask her why her eyes were swollen nearly shut.

She gave her son a piece of day-old fried fatback to chew while she cooked eggs, ham with red-eyed gravy, and homemade biscuits. These were Walter's favorites.

The eggs were in the plate, slightly runny, the way Walt liked them when he walked in like nothing had happened, rolling his eyes over her and inspecting the food. The beds of his fingernails were stained with her blood so she knew he had not washed his hands. He noticed the boy in the corner, not saying anything, and did what he did most mornings and ignored him. Idgy was afraid of Walt and Walt used that terror to control the boy. Now, he figured, he would use that same power to control his wife.

Walt reached in his pants pocket and pulled out a handgun. He put the gun on the kitchen table, between his plate and resting hand. The gun seemed enormous and Patience eyed it suspiciously. She was not aware Walt had a gun. She wondered where it had come from, how long he had it, what he planned to do with it. The gun lay there like an unspoken threat. It reminded her of how a switch or belt instilled fear and forced obedience in children.

She poured well water over the ice in Walter's jelly glass and went to get him coffee. She completed their morning ritual like a record on repeat, moving but not speaking.

"I 'spect you'll know to mind me now," Walt said, drinking the cold water so fast that the ice seemed to sweat through the glass. "I'm tired of you talking to me any kinda way. I intend to be treated with respect."

Patience glared at the gun and then at her son, who was sitting innocently on the floor, grasping the soggy meat with all of his might. She dug a hole in the center of a biscuit on Walt's plate and poured red gravy in the center. Walt grabbed her wrist, spilling hot gravy on her skin.

"Did you hear what I said?"

"Yes, I heard you."

Walt let go of her wrist and dipped the hot biscuit in the extra gravy in his plate, chewing and watching her at the same time. "You better!"

*

The gun was interestingly heavy and slick in tender, soft hands. There was no aim, no premeditation, no thought, no consideration, no malice, no intended harm, but the bullet found its way to the center of his chest, released at close range.

The gun shot cut through the silence and blood spotted the walls, her house coat, the plate of food, and the crying boy in the corner. Patience put the gun back down where she found it, on the table next to the breakfast plate. Walt's body had fallen forward and was heavy on the table. His eyes were open, looking shocked, ashamed, and amazed. Blood met the unswallowed food in his mouth, turning it brownish red and wet.

Patience picked Idgy up off the floor and went to the rotary phone to call home. "Walt dead," she managed matter-of-factly into the receiver. "He beat me so I shot him."

Patience

By Mary E. Weems

First year. I learned to lie
quiet as a corpse right after.
Always worried: Will he wake up
again? Sorry settin' up house
in throat always ready to apologize,
to keep peace I didn't know.

Second year. I got mad once,
trip to the hospital not until
my girlfriend found me
as the doorstop
when she came early
to pick me up for church.

Third year. I was drinking
everything that had a color
to keep from killin' everything I loved
my black eyes still lighting up
like a little girl's
when bouquets with broken flowers
appeared in hands cut on my face.

Yesterday I forgot what year it was
forgot his name
forgot to be
sorry.

Chapter 3

"Lord, did you hear about Patience?" Mae June was talking before she got in the house good and came in making herself at home. She spent as much time at her cousin Twiggy's as she did in her own dollar down house, which was more than 1000 footsteps away. She walked in catching her breath and starting something. She grabbed a mixed matched plate from the cabinet and spooned out some piping hot grits in the center of the plate. Twiggy was cracking an egg in a hot skillet full of pork grease and Cake, her husband, was already sitting at the table, rubbing his hands against his knees as if he was trying to warm them up. Mae June was Twiggy's second or third cousin (they didn't know which or how) and the town gossip. She sat at the table next to Cake, nodding without speaking. "You know she married that out-of-town man with the shifty eyes and done gone plum crazy. Shot his ass dead at the breakfast table."

"She ain't go crazy," Twiggy said, shaking the pan so that grease would slide all over the frying egg. "She got sense. Got his ass back for beating her half to death." Twiggy poured the cooked egg in a plate that was waiting by the stove, fried with the yellow running. "Mae, you want eggs?"

"Nawl, girl, I ain't hungry." Mae seasoned her grits with salt and pepper and tasted a small bite before blowing her spoon to cool them.

"They say she didn't look like herself when they brought her home. Her face was all swole up, eyes half shut. He even knocked the teeth out her mouth," Twiggy said, reaching on the stove for the coffee pot.

"She done been married enough years to be able to take a good beating without going crazy." Mae shook her head at the thought. "Her daddy ruined her by not beating her when she was little. Spare the rod, spoil the child."

Cake was drinking some of the hot coffee Twiggy had poured and thinking about the nonsense Mae June was saying. He was going to say something, but knew better than to get in between woman folk talk.

"And that poor Idgy might as well be a orphan," Mae continued. "Got one parent dead and the other one might as well be dead. I heard they going to lock her ass up in the crazy house and throw away the key."

"Where you get that from?" Cake asked, finally speaking, his hands on the table now.

"I heard it," Mae June said mysteriously, resting her arm on the table and somewhat surprised to hear Cake speak. "Hell, it's better than jail. She might as well be locked up somewhere 'cause wouldn't no other man in his right mind have her, after she done shot and killed her own husband. And Idgy is a handful. He don't talk much."

"You know that boy was born slow," Twiggy said, passing Cake his plate. "Lost some breath when he was first born."

"Well, I heard his ear drum shattered at the sound of that gunshot, so now he is going to be slow AND hard of hearing. Bless his heart."

"You sho' do hear a lot," said Cake.

"Uh-huh," Twiggy agreed.

"And on top of that Walt's family won't allow none of Patience's people, including the boy, at the funeral. They say when they found him he had piss in his drawers and food still in his mouth. They say his eyes was wide open."

"People don't die with they eyes closed no ways," Twiggy said, remembering what her father looked like dead. "Peoples just think that 'cause that's how they look when folks see 'em."

"Anyway, his kin acted like Idgy wasn't no part of 'em, but he look just like Walt. If he could talk, he'd probably sound just like 'em. And if he wasn't slow, he'd probably be just as mean," Mae June said, finishing off her grits.

"You women always got something to say about other folks' business," Cake said, shaking his head at his wife and her kinfolk. He could hear some commotion outdoors and knew it was children but couldn't distinguish which ones. He and Twiggy had five and he hadn't laid eyes on none of them all morning.

Little, the youngest boy, came trotting in near-naked wearing underwear and nothing else. His thumb was in his mouth and he went from his mother's knees to his daddy's. Cake picked him up.

"Where your hard-headed sisters at boy?"

"Out yonder," Little pointed with one hand and kept the other one in his mouth, sucking on his thumb. He was a handsome boy, but didn't favor Cake. He had the kind of sad eyes that made it so Cake or Twiggy would give him anything they could in the world. He had dirt on him from outside, the same color as his coffee-colored skin. Cake lifted his legs on his toes to rock Little while he sat. He watched his mama cook and shook his head when Cake offered him some meat from his plate.

"You still sucking your thumb, Little? You gone be buck-toothed as hell." Mae June pushed her plate forward and smiled.

"Leave my baby alone," Twiggy ordered. She had tried everything from threatening him to bribing him, but Little would not stop sucking his thumb. She told him that he would get picked on at school, but he didn't care. She told him that big boys don't suck their thumb, but he didn't care. She worried the act somehow reflected on her mothering skills. Having a four-year-old child sucking his thumb was as bad as having one still pissing on himself.

"Come, go with me. I got something at my house for that thumb." Mae June lifted Little from Cake's lap and was surprised at how lightweight he was.

"Where you going?" Twiggy asked without looking.

"The po' house."

"You already in it," Cake said, participating in the small talk and goodbye ritual of poor folk, each claiming to be struggling the most.

"Don't piss on my head and tell me it's raining. You make plenty of money Cake Lately." When Cake didn't offer a reply, Mae June took the extra steps to the door. "Well, I'm gone get on up this road. Gone put some homemade hot sauce on Little thumb to keep it out his mouth."

Twiggy turned the stove off and put her plate on the table next to Cake's while she watched Mae June carry Little out of the house. It never occurred to her to get him some clothes or shoes because she knew they would be right back.

"I'da been killed the sumabitch," Twiggy said, returning to the conversation. Twiggy didn't know Patience well, but she would recognize her public, and knew what Patience's voice sounded like.

"And your ass would be locked up, too!" Cake said, sitting in front of a plate of pork brains, molasses, and cold grits. He waited for his grits to get cold enough to cut into pieces before eating them.

"You can't fault a woman for protecting herself." Twiggy sat down in front of her husband and her own plate, reaching for the molasses and pouring it over an open biscuit. Her mouth was watering at the anticipation of the sweet syrup on the fluffy bread.

"She didn't have to kill him, Twig."

"Shit. I woulda quit his ass like a low-paying job."

"And that's what she shoulda done. Just left him alone."

"They say the gun was hissun. He probably intended to use it on her and she turned it around. Serves his ass right."

Cake didn't have an answer and filled his mouth with a biscuit, swallowing and shaking his head at the same time.

"Mama, where do people go when they dead?" Peaches busted in the front door and scooted into her father's lap at the kitchen table. Peaches, the baby girl, was the knee baby. At six years old, her skin was the color of an overripe peach and her hair and eyes light brown. Bread, nine years old, walked in behind her, the screen door slamming shut when they made it into the kitchen.

"They don't go no where. They dead," Twiggy answered.

"See there, Bread, I told you ain't no such place as hell."

"You don't get to say hell. Where you get that from?" Twiggy asked, frowning. Cake ignored his wife's question, knowing good and well if Peaches learned cussin' it was from one of them.

"I got it from Bread!" Peaches said smiling, her eyes glossing over her sister who she hoped was in trouble.

"There is too a hell, little girl," Cake said, saving Bread a beating from Twiggy, and Peaches a beating from Bread.

"Is that where Idgy Carrington's daddy went then?"

"That is between him and the good Lord. Don't you go worrying about it." Cake pulled a plait of his daughter's hair and held it out, measuring it. "Look at how long your hair is, little girl."

"I know Daddy," Peaches said, rolling her eyes. She was too young to know, care, or realize how powerful a long braid was for a little black girl and how proud her father was that her hair grew so long.

"Y'all want something else to eat?" Twiggy asked, her mouth full. She had already fed her children, before Cake got up. After they ate the two oldest left the house before she had a chance to put them to work. Bebe caught a ride up the road to look for mischief, and Junior had been right behind her to pick up glass bottles on the side of the road to exchange for nickels.

"No ma'm," Bread said, wishing there was room on Cake's lap for both her and Peaches.

"Well then, y'all see grown folks talking. Get the hell out of here while we trying to eat."

"Come on Peaches. Let's go to the playhouse," Bread said, leading the way back out the front door. The playhouse was not really a house, but Bread used her imagination, drawing and labeling the rooms in the dirt. Peaches hesitantly but faithfully obliged, hopping off of Cake's lap and following her sister outside.

"It's pay day, ain't it?" Twiggy asked when the children were out of ear shot.

"We need some groceries in this house."

"We'll have some," Cake promised, finishing his breakfast and heading for the door.

Cake

By Mary E. Weems

When I think about cake
I think about a Black man's mouth
kind that opens and closes on mine
everything lips, somethin' sweet
and about me
I think about birthdays
with black surprises and no blown out candles
waiting at a table it took all day
to make
waiting for a man
who came when he got
ready his mouth over me
so fast I couldn't get mad
the crumbs he left
in my bed.

Chapter 4

There was no such thing as domestic violence when Patience killed her husband in self-defense. Husbands and wives fought all the time. It was like a religion and they were faithful to it. Death was intermittent but beating, hitting, kicking, cutting, choking, and cussing was commonplace. The fighting seemed normal and was an expected exchange in intimate relationships. Girls learned that if a boy threatened to kill them or throw them in a ditch, that meant he loved them.

Fighting was just "one of those things" and you learned to live with it. In Sweetwater, people rarely intervened or interfered with public fights. Men often beat their wives out in the open, on front porches, at family gatherings, and even in church vestibules. Some men beat their wives the way they beat their children, with a belt or switch, full force of open hand, and for her own good. They felt it was their right and responsibility as men to discipline their wives and believed that the Bible supported their beliefs. It was the one scripture all the men in Sweetwater knew by heart that wives are supposed to submit to their husbands. When a preacher slapped his wife in the pulpit, people silently wondered what she had done to inspire such anger in a man of God.

There was nothing romantic about how they loved, no sweet around their hearts or softness in their voices. They didn't know how to love and not fight because both feelings came from the same impulse. It was not unusual for women to hit back or pick fights to make sure she was still worth fighting over.

*

Bread covered her head under the sheet, blanket, and bedspread. This is how she slept—in a tiny ball, with her head folded into her chest, her arms wrapped around her knees, and her feet balled up. Every time she moved she would bump into one of her sisters, Bebe on the left, Peaches on the right. They slept on both sides of her in the double bed, closing in on her like secrets and lies.

She used to touch them on purpose to make sure that somebody was there with her but was lately growing tired of the shared and closed in way they lived.

"Be still got-dammit!" This is Bebe, the oldest daughter, who thinks she is grown.

Bebe liked to cuss, liked to be the boss, liked to act like she was the mama when Twiggy wasn't home. Bread knew that Bebe would love to whoop her before she fell asleep and didn't want to give her the satisfaction.

The night before Bebe beat both Bread and Peaches for pissing in the bed. Bebe woke up in a damp yellow circle and immediately blamed her sisters. When they both denied it, she whooped them with two switches stitched together, calling them a "damn lie." It was not until morning that they realized that while they all smelled like piss, it was Bebe who had the pissy draws.

*

Sleep was sweet but temporary. Bread's eyes opened fast and she was facing Peaches, already awake, her hazel eyes full of water. Out of all of the children, Peaches looked the most like their father. Her eyes, giant circles of white with light brown centers, looked just like Cake's when he wasn't drunk. Most days, though, his eyes were bloodshot red and his pupils were so dilated that you couldn't tell what color they were. On days when he was sober and rested he had the most beautiful caramel-colored eyes Bread had ever seen. Bread assumed that it was his white people's eyes that made her mother love him and always take him back. She secretly wished for eyes like Cake's but her eyes were oval and black. Bread often wished she looked more like Twiggy, more like Cake, more like Peaches. She didn't know who she looked like.

Bebe was already up and listening at the door. It sounded like the sky was falling, like the roof was caving in, like the world was coming to an end, but it was just Twiggy and Cake fighting—again. The weekday peace was over.

Bread and Peaches rolled out of bed and followed Bebe into the boys' room and then outside. They stood barefooted in their t-shirts and underwear, throwing rocks in the dark on top of the house. The house was barely as tall as Cake so it didn't take much effort to hit the roof with the debris they threw. The tattered shingles on the tin roof popped as rocks and glass hit against it like hard rain. Throwing rocks was their act of rebellion, turning on the structure that should have protected them. Longing for safety and quiet, they stood defenseless trying to destroy the discourse in the house by going outside of it and picking up symbols of their anger. They threw rocks until the bang against the roof sounded like, "Stop! Stop. Stop. STOP!"

It didn't scare Bread when her parents fought because she was used to it. It was a routine. She was relieved that both Peaches and Little were old enough to not cry anymore. They, too, got used to the fighting, which came every weekend like Sunday. After a long time passed and the exhaustion of interrupted sleep crept back onto their bodies, Junior barged in the house to break up the fight. He knew that it was best to wait until the noise died down. By now Twiggy and Cake were both tired and almost sober. They were looking for a reason to be reasonable, but neither would be the one to give in. Bread peeped in the cracked door and realized that while there were empty liquor bottles on the floor, broken glasses on the table, a lit cigarette still burning in the ashtray, and swollen fists and messy clothes, the room was no different from the aftermath of their lovemaking, which would inevitably follow.

*

Twiggy woke up sore and sober. She had Bengay in the kitchen drawer and a corner of gin in the bottle by her bed so she knew it wouldn't take her long to remedy both wrongs. Cake was asleep beside her, his arm strewn across her chest so she couldn't turn around or get up. With both hands she pushed his heavy arm off her body and sat up in the bed. Cake didn't budge. Sleep cradled him in its arms like a loose woman. She watched him lie there on his stomach, snoring loud enough to wake her children, but she knew they would sleep as much of the day away as she let them. They were up half the night throwing those damn rocks on top of the house like they didn't have good sense. She couldn't remember when they started throwing rocks and she never bothered to ask them why they did it.

She didn't know if she wanted to slap Cake's face or kiss it, so she decided to leave him alone. She knew Cake ran the streets, all men did, but she hated the thought of him throwing it in her face. She had warned him that the next time she heard tell of him being over to that fat, ugly ass Neesee's house that would be his ass. Twiggy always kept her word.

*

Neesee was a big, burly, dark-skinned woman with beady eyes and a round face. She wore blue cat glasses with fake diamonds in the corners and her hair was a blend of perpetual tight curls that needed to be brushed out. The moles on her face resembled polka dots, some big, some small, and she had thick lips that she was always rubbing together like she was blending in lipstick. Her two front teeth were knocked out in a fight with one of her boyfriends, so she didn't smile with her mouth open, but that didn't keep her from smiling. She was far from what you would call an attractive woman, but she had a way with men who already had commitments.

Neesee lived in the trailer park, and even though she didn't have any children of her own she kept other people's children to make a living. Before Neesee took a liking to Cake, Twiggy had dropped her kids off at Neesee's house while she worked. When Bebe came back and said that Neesee had them calling her Mama, Twiggy went back to Neesee's house, called her outside, and cussed her out in front of her children to make her an example. She slapped Neesee's face so hard and so fast that she forgot why her hand was stinging when she walked back to her car. On the way home Twiggy warned her children that she would kill them dead if she ever heard tell of them calling some other woman Mama.

Twiggy would never admit to being jealous of another woman. When she caught Cake with other women, or heard about him being up under somebody else she would step out to be with another man. Damned if she would sit at home like a fool tending to youngins while Cake was out sniffing every tail in the neighborhood. They had married young and both still had some wildness in them. They fell out a lot and fought, but they also liked things in each other they couldn't find in somebody else. She figured that stepping out didn't mean nothing if you end up back together. She knew they would stay together or kill each other trying. She didn't want to kill him though, she just wanted to make him suffer.

She started pouring lye in his food and spiking his liquor with rat poison. She knew that there were three things he couldn't live without: food, liquor, and sex. She figured she would fix him something to eat, let him keep his own stash of liquor in the house, and lay down with him every pay day like always, and he would never suspect her revenge.

"Twig, this liquor taste funny!" Cake had said the week before, his red eyes protruding out of their sockets. It had begun to happen gradually, probably a side effect of the small portions of poison. "Taste it." He held out the jelly-jar-turned-house-glass and Twiggy turned away.

"I don't want no damn liquor, Cake," she said eyeballing the brew.

"But it taste funny. Here drink some and see."

"I said I didn't want no damn liquor. If it taste funny, why the hell you drinking it?" Twiggy took the bottle from Cake's hand and poured it down the drain. "Probably just a bad batch."

Cake nodded in agreement and laid his head in his hands. He swallowed what was left in his glass before passing out.

*

The night before, Twiggy had caught Cake at the liquor house smiling in Neesee's face like teeth and good looks had gone out of style.

Tate Thomas had turned the tool shack behind his house into a liquor house. The house was the size of small room, but on pay day it could hold as many black fools as had money. Every corner served a purpose. The corner by the door with the best light is where you took your money and cup to get a shot or a glass of home brew. The second corner had a side table for playing cards. The other two corners were for socializing. Lopsided tables were spread around the room holding ashtrays and abandoned cups. It wasn't easy for Twiggy to find Cake in the dimly lit room. It was his shitty grin that she recognized and Neesee squealing like a pig, rubbing on his arm like it couldn't keep warm any other way. Before she knew it she hit Neesee upside her head.

Twiggy had Mae June drop her off outside the liquor house because she figured she would drag Cake's drunk ass out after she had a few drinks. She left the kids at home and told them to mind Bebe until she got back. She had put on the dog and walked in like a bandit. Her hair was fixed up in the slick curls it made when she put water and Vaseline together. She had slid her money in her wallet and stuck it in her back pocket like she always did when she went out because she didn't carry a pocketbook and always wore pants. The imprint of the wallet in one pocket and her cigarettes in the other offered the illusion of a curve below her back, where a booty would have been if she had one.

She didn't understand what Cake saw in Neesee. If he was going to step out on her, there were better women around for him to do it with. Decent, better-looking women with some money in their pockets and some teeth in their mouth. When she realized who he was with, her vision got so red she thought she was looking through blood-stained eyes. Before she knew it, she had punched Neesee in the back of the head, while Neesee's face leaned toward Cake like she was sneaking a kiss. Neesee was too drunk to recover before Twiggy grabbed a butter knife from the bar and held it to her throat.

"Twiggy, what the hell?" Cake's words were slurred and spread apart, like he wasn't sure if he was dreaming or seeing things. He stood between the two women.

"You willing to get cut for this bitch?" Twiggy asked, not knowing who she wanted to stab first, her husband or his heifer.

"Put the knife down," was all Cake could say. He had already drank half of his paycheck in liquor, but Twiggy's anger had a way of sobering him up.

Twiggy wished she had a razor blade instead of a butter knife, but at the right angle she could still use the dull edge to cut through skin and possibly to the bone. She had done it before with chicken, using her strength to cut through the edges, leaving the flesh jagged and raw.

Everybody in the liquor house was paying attention to Twiggy. Tate Thomas rushed over to offer his voice of reason. Tate never got drunk with customers because if he did people would slip out without paying and he could always count on a fight breaking out, and it was bad for business. "Twiggy, now y'all gon' have to get out of here with all this now."

"Come on here, Twiggy, fore you get yourself locked up!" Cake was standing in front of Neesee, shielding her from the knife Twiggy was waving in her hand like a flag. He was partly protecting Neesee, but mostly protecting his wife because he did not want to have to bail her out of jail. He started taking steps and pushing Twiggy toward the door. Everyone made room for them without taking their eyes off the scene unfolding before them.

"Bitch, if you don't stay away from my husband Ima kill you dead as hell," Twiggy yelled, as she threw the knife across the room, just missing Neesee's arm. "Mark my damn words."

Cake struggled to get Twiggy in the truck and listened carefully as she cussed him out, threatened to kill him, and warned him as he drove down the road that he had better get all of his shit and get the hell out of the house if he knew what was best for him. She was tired of his shit. Sick and tired. There were plenty of men who would love to take care of her and her children. If he wanted to be with that fat, ugly ass Neesee so be it. He could pack his shit right now. And she wasn't playing this time. He'd better not let her get to her gun. Drunk bastard. She wanted him gone. And he better not wake up her children.

When they got home the lights were on but the kids were in their rooms. They knew better than to be in the front room, which became their parents' bedroom at night, when Cake and Twiggy got home. Cake followed Twiggy in the house and she started pulling his clothes out of the closet and throwing them in a pile. She rested long enough to light a cigarette and wonder where her gun was. Cake was mostly sober now, jonesing for another drink. He didn't feel like getting into it with Twiggy. He was tired, just got off work, had some money in his pocket, and just wanted to enjoy a few drinks before he came home. He couldn't help it if Neesee had a thing for him. She wasn't the best-looking thing in the world, but she was soft to hold and told him what all she would do if he was hers, and it was good to hear. He didn't love her, he just laid with her sometimes, when he wanted to feel something different. He didn't feel like fussing with Twiggy, but he wasn't going to just sit there while she hit him tonight. If he wasn't too drunk he would mostly just grab her, wait for her to calm down, throw things around the room and try to break something she loved or needed, like a souvenir shot glass her sister had brought her from New York or her favorite clay ashtray. He knew Twiggy had a temper like her father and once she was mad, nothing could calm her down but time. The fight lasted until the sky was so black the moon looked white. They were both glad when Junior came in and begged them to leave each other alone.

"Mind your own damn business," Twiggy had said, satisfied that Cake was miserable, bleeding, and sorry, "and get in the bed. You ain't sleeping all day and all night tomorrow."

Moon Looks White

By Mary E. Weems

'Till you take your readin' glasses
off, your teeth out
kiss ancestor spirits
'till you hold your breath
wake up close as sky
run your hand across her face
craters, hollow cheers
places to rest
and pray.

Chapter 5

Despite the foolishness going on in many households, Sweetwater women are devoted to religion. Some people attend church faithfully and with regularity, and others only go occasionally, but everybody believes in God. Even people who don't ever go to church believe in God. Even women who sleep with other women's husbands feel a little conviction on the inside when the loving is over because it is not pleasing to God. When Bread's best friend, Ruth, told her she had a secret to share, Bread never imagined she would hear the whispered words, "I don't believe in God." They had been friends long enough for people to notice them together all the time. Twiggy had called them frick and frack because when you saw one you saw the other. Their friends said they went together like bread and butter, and so they started calling Ruth, Butter. The name fit because Butter was light skinned.

Butter's mother had married Black Charles and moved into his small house with her eight children. Everybody called Butter's stepfather Black Charles because there were two Charles' in Sweetwater who were cousins and the same age. Black Charles is the dark-skinned one and Little Charles is the one named after his daddy (who is called Big Charles). No one ever just said Charles. The prefix was needed to let you know which Charles was being talked about.

"My real daddy used to beat on my mama all the time so she prayed for another husband who would love her and take on somebody else's youngins," Butter explained, "so then she married Black and now he beat on all of us. Why would God get her hopes up like that?"

Bread was startled by her friend's deep-seated disbelief and had never considered the questions Butter asked about how she knew God existed. She had never thought about questioning God and it never occurred to Bread to link God's will with her parents' fighting. That is just what they did. For all she knew, that is what real love made you do. She didn't know any married couples who didn't take their frustrations out on each other, and who didn't take the 'til death do you part of vows seriously. Nobody divorced, and only married twice if the first spouse died.

Unprepared for Butter's questions, Bread didn't have answers. She knew there was a God because she knew. It was all that she had ever known and everyone in her community had nurtured that belief. She had never considered that there were black people who did not believe in God, though she was aware there were different rules and ways to worship.

There are at least thirteen churches in Sweetwater, all different denominations. Methodist, A.M.E., A.M.E. Zion, C. M. E., Presbyterian, Bible Church, Baptist, Missionary Baptist, Pentecostal, Holiness, Pentecostal Holiness, United Church of Christ, and nondenominational churches. Some people even had church in their homes. The denomination determined what kind of Christian you were, and what you could and could not do and still be holy. Pentecostal or Holiness Christians believe the more modest and humble, the closer you are to God. Pentecostal women dress modestly and don't show their elbows or knees, so their skirts are long and their blouses are long-sleeved. Their church services last hours and hours, because they labor until the Holy Spirit comes, no matter how long it takes. They pass the time praying on their knees, speaking in tongues, and shouting to the rhythmic sound of drums. Baptists don't believe in speaking in tongues or prophesying and women know their place, and it is nowhere near the pulpit. No one ever questions Christian beliefs they just figure out what they can live with and do it. Everybody is some kind of Christian.

For the most part people pick up religion because it is convenient. Faith offers unrelenting hope in the face of suffering and oppression. Faith becomes the core of black life, the core of black women's lives. Few conversations take place without sounding like a testimony. "I'm blessed," "I reckon I'll make it with the Lord's help," "You know the Lord works in mysterious ways," "This too shall pass," and "Lord knows," are usual responses to any greeting or inquiry into how a church woman is doing. "God not dead," Sister Whitehouse offered routinely when asked about her health. No one bothered to mention that the sanctified responses were not answers to the questions, they just smile and walk away frustrated and feeling like they don't read the Bible enough.

Bread was careful with her words. She didn't want to say the wrong thing or come across as too holy for her friend to talk to. She wasn't a churchgoer and even though Twiggy and Cake sang in the choirs of their separate churches, they didn't go every Sunday. "I don't know," Bread answered. "The Lord works in mysterious ways."

Butter was silent after that, not convinced or comforted by Bread's words, but not moved to say anything else. To her, her friend didn't sound any different from womenfolk who try to impress each other with church words.

Bread had every intention of keeping the secret, especially from Twiggy, who already thought Butter was too grown acting to hang around.

*

The first time Bread laid eyes on Ray-Ray Carmichael she was playing in the back yard. He rode up in the truck with Cake, looking out the window and jumping out before the truck had stopped all the way.

"Stink-Stink, where your mama at?" Cake wanted to know.

Bread was humiliated that her father was calling her by that nickname in front of a cute boy she didn't know, especially when he knew good and well that Twiggy did not announce, especially to her children, where she was going or when she would be back.

"She gone up the road," was all Bread said. She had watched Mae June's car, barely running, ride down the road, coughing smoke behind it. She knew more than likely her mother was in the car, but she didn't know for sure.

"How long she been gone?"

"Not long."

"This here Ray Carmichael. His daddy the one who just took over the church down there at Antioch."

"It's nice to meet you. You can call me Ray-Ray, that's the name I go by." Bread watched him extend his hand to her and she took it, rubbed her own callused hand against it, and tried not to let on how warm and soft his hand was. She suddenly wished she had soft hands, or at least clean hands.

"Where Junior and Little?" Cake asked.

"I ain't seen Junior. Little is gone with Mama, wherever she at. Peaches went to get us more leaves to play with."

"What y'all playing?" Ray-Ray asked, smiling.

"House!" Peaches yelled, her hands full of dead leaves she had found in the ditch, "Bread gets to be the mama, again."

Bread's eyes told Peaches to shut up but when she looked up and saw Ray-Ray watching her she just smiled. She was always the mama when they played because she was the oldest and she already knew what mamas were supposed to do.

"You're lucky to have brothers and sisters," Ray-Ray observed, "I'm an only child."

"Well, tell your mama I brought somebody by to meet her," Cake said. "The pastor wants to get to know the families in the area and sent his son since he had some other stuff to work on today. I spect he'll come by another time."

"Come on back," was all Bread knew to say. That was the kind of thing that grown folks said to each other when they met someone for the first time.

"I'll probably just see y'all at church tonight. Community Revival at Antioch!" Ray-Ray called back, following Cake to the truck. Bread nodded, but worried that she had not been to church since the last time somebody had died, and she couldn't remember who it was or why she was made to go. Peaches started crying.

"What's wrong with you?"

"I don't want to go to no church," Peaches whined and her eyes filled with water. Even when she was acting like a baby she was a pretty sight. Bread rolled her eyes.

"Well, I do. I need to find some decent clothes to wear."

*

At the revival Bread sat beside Cake because nobody else had wanted to go. Twiggy insisted she had better things to do with her time than sit around with a bunch of fake and phony church folks. Twiggy preferred her church because it only met two Sundays out of the month and left people alone to tend to their own business. To Twiggy you get saved when you get ready to die, and she wasn't in no ways ready to die. She sent Bread wearing a homemade dress that had belonged to Bebe and rebraided her hair in cornrows so she would look halfway decent.

"Act like you got some sense in front of those people," Twiggy warned. "Don't let me hear tell of you showing your ass in church."

"I won't Mama," Bread promised, running out the door to get to the truck before her father left. Cake liked to be on time.

*

Ray-Ray's father, the new preacher, was tall and long-winded. Leaning over the pulpit with deacons sitting behind him in high sitting chairs, he was standing, sweating, stomping his feet, and spitting with every word he said that started with an f. Bread counted. Fix. Foolish. Fire. Faith. Forgiveness. Forgetfulness.

"If you ask him, the good Lord will throw all of your sins into the sea of fff-forgetfulness. But you have to have ffffaith, church!"

Ray-Ray was sitting at the piano with his bible in his lap and his eyes closed. Bread wasn't sure if he was sleeping or praying. His mother, the first lady, sat in the first pew directly in front of her husband so that he couldn't see any of the needy women in the church without seeing her first. She was wearing a huge wide brimmed hat that matched her dress and shoes. To Bread, she seemed overdressed for weeknight church, but it was okay since she was married to the preacher.

When Rev. Carmichael started praying, Bread got tired of keeping her eyes closed and concentrating on the complicated Bible words he was reciting in exhausted breaths. She looked up at her father, whose eyes were closed tight and then looked around the room. Some people were holding hands. Some people were waving church fans in the faces of sweaty-faced babies to combat the body heat and hot breath that hung heavy in the room like the prayer. Some people held their hands high above their heads like they were trying to reach the ceiling. Some people moaned and exchanged "Thaaaaaaaaaaaaaank you Jesuses" across the room like delayed greetings.

The mothers of the church, dressed in long dresses and holding their pocket-books in their laps, sat in the Amen corners on each side of the pulpit, rocking and swaying to the music they made for themselves with collective hums. Thanking Jesus. Saying "Hallelujah" and "Aye-man." The women did everything but stand up and shout, which Bread had wondered about. So far, no one had caught the Holy Ghost. She wasn't sure exactly what that meant, but Bebe had said that when she went to church with Twiggy that the preacher talked a demon out of somebody. She said the possessed woman spit the devil out in green vomit and then got happy. The Holy Ghost made her wallow on the floor, babble incomprehensibly, and holler "Jesus, Jesus, Jesus" while running up and down the church aisle like she didn't have good sense. Twiggy always said that her youngins acted like they had the devil in them, so Bread worried about the Holy Ghost getting a hold of her.

Bread folded her hands together and kept one eye open while she prayed so she could see the Holy Ghost coming and get out of the way. She prayed that Black Charles would stop picking fights with Butter's mama so that it would help Butter believe in God. She also prayed for good grades, good hair, and good luck. Then she prayed that Twiggy and Cake would stop being mean to each other. And right at the end, right before she thought God may have gotten bored or stopped listening, she prayed that God would make it so that she and Ray-Ray Carmichael could be good friends. She knew if she prayed long and hard enough and went to church every Sunday, God would make it happen.

Long and Hard

By Mary E. Weems

Life is an endless
summer rush, afterbirth,
showers, tomorrows, sorrows
furrows, brows of women
who always come when it's time
stay, lay hands, leave after hard nights
of cigarettes, smoke, ashtrays, Black
calloused feet, rooms, fire, water to bless
children, guide fathers, their arms
long enough to hug themselves.

Chapter 6

"Sho' is hot out here." Doughboy, Little's friend from the Bottom, was fanning himself with his hands and sweating like a hooker in church. Doughboy was waiting for Little, who had run in the house to get something, while Bread watched him from the wood plank that led to the backdoor. Doughboy was more stomach than anything else and the only young person Bread knew of that wore glasses. He couldn't see a lick without them.

"Sho' is!" Little said, opening and slamming the door fast, trying not to let the hot air in or the cool air out.

"Ray-Ray Carmichael on his way over here to meet us," Doughboy announced.

"Sho' is!" Little repeated.

"No, he ain't." Bread hadn't seen Ray-Ray since she had been to church revival a month earlier, and didn't expect to see him again unless she went with Cake to church, which she felt less inclined to do as the days went on. The hotter it was the more lazy she felt.

"Yes he is and we's going swimming wit him." Little seemed proud of himself, his permanent teeth crowding in his mouth like broken crayons in the original box.

"Y'all fools can't swim," Bread said, swatting flies and waving to a car that was driving slow on the dirt road.

"We gon' learn, stupid!" Little said, moving closer to Doughboy to get out of Bread's reach so she couldn't strike him for his smart mouth.

Bread knew that Ray-Ray had come from up north and had probably learned how to swim in real swimming pools. Little and Doughboy, bragging and lying and trying to be as good as Ray-Ray had probably claimed that they, too, could swim and that there was a decent place in Sweetwater to do it. Ray-Ray would have never suspected them of lying because he hadn't lived in Sweetwater long enough to know that there was no need to know how to swim because the creeks and rivers were so dirty that nobody would put their feet in, let alone their whole bodies. And Ray-Ray was too good to know that bragging and lying were mostly the same thing in Sweetwater, especially to the children.

"Here he come," Doughboy said fixing his glasses on his face and watching the lanky figure approach the house. Ray-Ray had a straw hat on his head, hiding his hair so you could only see his childlike face and his teeth.

"How y'all doing?" Ray-Ray asked, walking fast until he got close enough for them to see it was him. "North Carolina summers sho' is hot."

Bread didn't say anything, just nodded, to keep from looking at Ray-Ray in the face. She could tell he was already sweating, wetness had saturated his t-shirt under his arms and on his chest. She would have offered him a drink of water but she didn't have time.

"Y'all ready to go?"

Ray-Ray's question was directed at the boys but Bread almost answered, but caught herself. Instead she asked, "Where y'all going anyway?"

"None of your business." Little was afraid of Bread, but knew she wouldn't smack him upside his head in front of company, especially the preacher's son. As the youngest in the neighborhood he wanted to show his friends, especially Ray-Ray, that he didn't take no mess from no girl, especially his nappy-headed sister. Six years old and hard-headed he smacked his lips and stood between Ray-Ray and Doughboy.

"Don't get too big for your britches," Bread said, trying to look disinterested. She didn't really care to know, though she figured she would be the first one Twiggy asked when she got home.

"We going to the creek down by the church to swim. We'll be back after while," Ray-Ray said smiling his wide-gapped smile. At fifteen, Ray-Ray was a few years older than Bread, which she appreciated knowing after she decided she might love him. His almond eyes made up for every other flaw around his face. His hair grew in large, unbrushed, untamed patches, but hid beneath the hat he wore to keep the sun out of his eyes.

Ray-Ray wore a cross around his neck that he reached for periodically, as if to make sure it was still there. Bread imagined Ray-Ray would be a preacher, like his daddy, when he grew up. He already seemed to love God enough.

"You can let Ms. Twiggy know where we went when she get home, but we'll be back long before dark. I'll take care of Little Man."

Little and Doughboy smiled and paused to congratulate each other for being invited on an adventure with Ray-Ray.

"Gimme five!" Doughboy stuck out his hand for Little to hit, "On the black side," he turned his hand over to show his brown skin and knuckles, " [...] stick it in the hole," he made a circle with his free hand that Little pushed his index finger in, "what do you got?"

"Soooooooul!" Little said slowly. Ray-Ray looked at them suspiciously. Curious about their hand game he looked back at Bread and winked. Bread's heart sank and she smiled back and watched them walk away until she could not see the backs of their heads anymore.

*

The ambulance raced past the house around five o'clock in the afternoon, before Cake or Twiggy got home. In fact, it was word that a little black boy had drowned that brought Twiggy home from work early. When she finally got home everybody was outside.

Poolie Boy, a grown man with a boyish face and frame was holding Little and quickly passed him over to his mama. "He fell in the deep end of the creek, Ms. Twiggy."

Little was teary-eyed and still wet. Twiggy wanted to tear Little's ass up for jumping in the creek, but all she could do was pull him into a hug. "They said somebody got drownded."

"Did," Poolie Boy said. "Preacha son got sucked down in the sink hole. They ain't found his body, but can't nobody but God survive being in the water that long."

*

It took days for them to drag the creek and find Ray-Ray's body. By then he didn't look like himself. He had been in the water for so long that everything in him swelled up and his eyes had popped out. Bread secretly wished to find his eyes floating at the top of the creek. She would grab them, put them in her pocket, and roll them around like marbles. She would keep them forever to remind her of Ray-Ray. But the eyes never popped up—Bebe said fish probably ate them.

His funeral was packed because when children die it shakes all sinners awake. People stood shoulder-to-shoulder behind the pews and outside of the church within earshot of the eulogy.

Bread sat beside Cake at the funeral. Twiggy stayed at home with Little, who didn't want to go, didn't want to see what Ray-Ray looked like dead. Bread did. She went to the funeral to see Ray-Ray's face one more time, decide right then and there if she could in fact love him and if she always would. The casket was closed, though, because First Lady Carmichael had threatened to pull him out. She refused to believe that her son was really dead and had been praying and fasting that he would get up out of that casket before they had a chance to put him in the ground. Some people half-believed it would happen and came to the funeral to witness the miracle, but others just wanted to see what Sister Carmichael would do once they laid Ray-Ray's body to rest.

Bread was almost relieved the casket was closed because she didn't want Ray-Ray to be remembered in spectacle. She had seen dead bodies on display in family homes during wakes and was always disappointed. Grown folk would walk around the body talking about the person like they were alive in the room.

"They did a good job with the body," they would say. "He look just like hisself." They would take pictures of the dead body in the casket, sometimes posing next to it or kissing it, to put in family albums. When her turn came to walk past the body she never understood what they said. Dead bodies don't look anything like live bodies. The only body that looked the same, as if he were sleeping in his best clothes, was her grandfather. Twiggy had claimed he died because his bitch of a second wife put a root on him.

Bread didn't get to tell Ray-Ray she loved him and Little was so traumatized that he was afraid to go to sleep, thinking he wouldn't wake up and would die like Ray-Ray did. He refused to take a bath for weeks, saying he was afraid of water. When she couldn't take it anymore, Twiggy whipped him until he got in the wash tub.

"I'm scared I'll get drownded! I'm scared I'll get drownded!" Little yelled hysterically, screaming and out of breath.

"You damn fool, I didn't say to put your head in the water."

"Leave the boy alone, Twig," Cake said, coming to Little's rescue, "He done lost a friend and that hurt him. He can't help it!"

"Well, you wash him then," Twiggy said, losing patience. Cake felt sorry for the boy and lifted him up in his arms, cradling him. He took his time running a warm rag over Little's frail body, wringing all the water out.

Not many nights after that Cake left for work and never came back.

Daddy

By Mary E. Weems

Raised me on lies
like ones you tell little girls
grow up and they don't
his stories refrains
I read in diaries, novels, picture
frames, girl after
curl
up late at night, bedside
prayers for visits, a birthday
card, to see his car parked
in front of our apartment
when I wake up any morning

Daddy, word I didn't learn
to spell until I was thirty-seven
a mental block doctor said,
her pen, dipped in kin.

Chapter 7

Aunt Noisey was a woman of few words. She never talked about the things most present on people's minds about her, like why she looked like a white woman, how she kept her hair so clean without washing it with water, or what happened to her left arm. She was the only person Bread knew with a missing limb, but no one seemed to notice because they were too busy being distracted by her good looks. Noisey was an attractive woman, and one arm or not, she had men lined up at her door begging to give her a few extra dollars and help her take care of her children. She shooed them away with her good arm and shook her head at their simplemindedness. Women saw her as a threat because, while they didn't worry that their husbands would leave them outright to be with her, they wouldn't put it past them to sleep with her out of pure curiosity. Men saw her as broken, desperate, vulnerable, and in need of help, as much for being a woman with no man in the house as for her disability. But Noisey was fully capable of taking care of herself and tending to all of her children alone. Her babies were by different men who had walked out, one by one, when she refused to be their wife.

"I tell you what," she would say, sometimes to herself, sometimes to anybody walking close enough to hear, or nosey enough to listen, "the sun ain't never shone on a man I would marry."

Noisey liked her independence. She liked feeling in control of her life and not having anybody to answer to. She didn't want a man swallowing up all that was good in her life. She felt that marriage was a woman's downfall.

Women were expected to have husbands or children by the time they reached their thirties. Single women past that age were thought of as siddity or simple, or too picky to find somebody in Sweetwater to be with. Women taught each other early how to take care of themselves. Mothers taught their daughters how to keep a clean house by watching them work for white folks, and daughters learned how to tend to children by keeping their brothers and sisters. Learning how to be a wife was different. Harder. Women had to learn that on their own.

Marrying young didn't offer any guarantees. Young love was artificial and temporary. The good feelings only lasted long enough to get a little sugar on the lips or have somebody squeeze the fat on the back of your thighs. And men liked having somebody to talk to. Men loved lying in the lap of a lover while she listened to his dreams and rubbed the worries from his head. This is what they did before they were married. After marriage there were bills, children, and other things to be serious about. Couples stayed together after the happiness was gone because, after so many years passed, people thought of them at the same time, and said their names together as if they were one person instead of two. Twiggy and Cake were no different.

Twiggy never urged her children to get married, especially the girls. But Bebe went to the courthouse with Sonny when she was seventeen and pregnant so that her baby would have his name outright. And Junior dropped out of school and got a job so he could marry his girlfriend before anybody knew she was pregnant. By the time Twiggy was thirty-four years old, in 1965, she was a married single mother with two grandchildren.

*

When women got married in Sweetwater it was rarely for love. Marriage was pivotal, but also damaging. Some women got married because they needed the financial help to take care of unplanned children. There was no contraception, or if there was contraception, no money to buy it, so children were loved and taken care of, but not always welcome or wanted. By the time new parents grew tired of each other they felt trapped because a divorce would cost money they didn't have. It was not unusual for people to be married to one person and living with someone else.

Brown-skinned and holy, Sister Whitehouse was short and enormous. She was always breathing hard, walking slow, and wearing Vaseline on her lips instead of lipstick. She felt that lipstick was for loose, unchurched women.

Bread had never seen pictures but she had heard stories about how Sister Whitehouse had let herself go after she got married, and how she used to have a nice shape. Twiggy said the bigger Whitehouse got, the more saved and sanctified she felt. Twiggy and Whitehouse had gotten pregnant around the same time. Twiggy got married and Whitehouse found a woman who had a remedy for unwanted pregnancies, scraping between brown legs with a metal clothes hanger. After that Whitehouse couldn't get pregnant again and the father of her would-be child married her out of guilt for what he made her do.

Whitehouse's mother had blamed her womanish body and her heathenish ways for getting pregnant so after marriage she hid her "womanish" body behind an unhealthy appetite. She and her husband stayed in their loveless and sexless marriage out of routine. They had been married for nearly two decades but they were almost never at the same place at the same time. They went to separate churches, slept in separate bedrooms, and avoided each other altogether whenever possible. They stayed together because they had always been together and didn't know anything else.

Sister Whitehouse considered Jesus her other husband and to him she was faithful. She was at the church every time the doors were open but was known for church-hopping, going from one ministry to the other every time somebody hurt her feelings. She had recently joined Antioch Church after someone at her former church suggested she lose weight.

At Antioch, everybody had been praying that Twiggy would make it without a husband in the house. After all of those years and all of those children, Cake left her with past due bills and five mouths to feed. Whitehouse stopped by with vegetables from her garden, which, she figured, would help out. She put a reused brown paper bag full of sweet potatoes, cucumbers, corn, and collard greens on the table. The creases in the bag put Twiggy in the mind of an old person's skin.

"Lately, I brought some stuff from the garden," Whitehouse announced as she came in and sat down at the table. She and Twiggy called each other by their last names, something they had picked up from supervisors when they worked together at the chicken plant. Twiggy didn't hug Whitehouse but thanked her, peeking in the bag and putting it on the floor. She was smoking a cigarette.

"Lately, I been dreaming about fish. Two nights in a row." Whitehouse's words were slow. She watched for Twiggy's reaction, but there was none. Disappointed, Whitehouse helped herself to a pickled egg from the open jar on the kitchen table and fell back into the chair, leaning over it with her egg, looking for salt or pepper.

"Well," Twiggy said finally, watching Whitehouse bite the soft boiled egg that was pink on the outside and white on the inside, "it ain't me. I can't have no more chuluns."

"Is that right?"

"Hell, you knowed that." Twiggy blew out the last bit of smoke from the cigarette and put the butt out in the ashtray, "Doctors took out my womb after I had Lil'."

"Well, you don't figure Cake un went around here and got no other woman pregnant, dooya?" Finally, Whitehouse had managed to work Cake's name into the conversation.

"Better not," was all Twiggy would say, rolling her eyes and patting her back pocket for another cigarette. She had not seen or talked to Cake since he left. Some of his things, those that she had not thrown away out of spite, were still scattered around the house. "Hell, what you been doin'? You the one dreamin'."

Whitehouse couldn't remember the last time she had made love to her husband, or any man for that matter. Any late night pantings from her bedroom were her petitions to God. On those rare occasions when she wanted to be held and touched she would beg her husband to put his hands on her, to make love to her, but it happened too infrequently to make a baby, even if her body was able. Twiggy knew that.

Twiggy had not talked to anybody about Cake even though she knew they knew he was gone. The house stayed quiet for days after he left, but it was peaceful. After a few days, Twiggy began to miss his scent. After a few years she forgot what he smelled like.

"You miss having Cake around?" Whitehouse asked.

"After while I did, but as long as he been gone I don't think about it. I fought that damn fool til' I got tired, and I don't want to have to fight no mo. I ain't never gon' have to fight another man like that."

"You love him?"

"I reckon." Twiggy's words were slow and bitter-like. Truth was, if he showed up on her doorstep she didn't know if she would take him back or shoot him dead.

"You gon' get a divorce?"

"I don't need no divorce. I will have a man 'til I get tired of him and then get me another one."

Sister Whitehouse realized that inserting God into the conversation would be hard and then she remembered the point of the conversation. "Well, what about Peaches or Bread? They both got they period, don't they?"

"That ain't nothin'."

"Well," Whitehouse was beating around the bush, leaning back in the chair 'til Twiggy thought it might break, "a girl over to the church got a baby coming. She ain't no older than your two."

"Well there go your fish dream."

"Nol, Twig, I don't believe it is. I don't even know that child's name. How would I be having dreams 'bout somebody I don't even know? Maybe you should check your girls. You know Bebe already had both of hers by the time she was they age."

"You let me worry 'bout my chilluns," Twiggy snapped. "My mama died when I was little and when I was comin' up I was passed 'round from piddle to post. I always said that when I got married and had chilluns they would always have sumthin' to eat, and a place over they head so they won't hafta run from dry place to dry place. And that include any chilluns they have." Twiggy took one last long drag from her cigarette before patting it out in the napkin she was holding in her hand. She held the smoke in her mouth a while, and blew it out in an exasperated exhale. "As long as I got, they got."

Passin'

By Mary E. Weems

Got to be—careful
when you leave
home alone
think you grown—white
painted lines down
roads long as minds
made up, you start
up stairs, lead to a door
a blue face smiling
eyes a code won't translate
to brown, you dress like
somebody else, for success, taxes,
addresses in neighborhoods
that don't check birth, don't question
relatives dark as locs
who just show up
refuse to play—
laugh.

Chapter 8

Bread fell in love when she was eighteen years old and newly out of school. There was nothing extraordinary about the boy, other than that he was not from Sweet-water. His citified ways reminded her of Ray-Ray. It was his smile, bright and magnificent, that caused Bread to feel so drawn to him. He had seduced her by accident, not knowing that all he had to do was look at her for a long time and she would be hooked. His sweet smile, unintentional and automatic when he met anyone's gaze, would make you feel like he had never shown anybody else in the world his teeth before. And that is how Bread felt around Uli, silly, foolish, and like there wasn't anybody else in the world except her. And him.

The broken bottles and her broken heart and her parents' broken marriage and the broken-down cars and the broken windows and the broken fences and the broken-down signs and the broken dreams, and the broken promises of Sweetwa-ter all seemed to mend themselves when Uli was around. He made her life better but she was too young and too naïve to know, at first, that the ache in her chest and the ache in her middle parts might be love, or lust, or a combination of those feelings.

*

With peach fuzz growing over and under his lips, Uli stood in the doorway after knocking. Bread wasn't sure she had ever seen anybody that beautiful in person, up that close. He was tossing a basketball from one hand to the other.

"Y'all want to play some ball?" His words were regular but with a northern accent that made Bread want to keep hearing him talk. She couldn't take her eyes off of his mouth. His voice seemed to come at her in waves and slow motion.

"What you say?"

"Y'all want to play some ball?"

"Y'all who?"

"You and Butter."

"Butter gone to see her real daddy this weekend." This meant Bread didn't have a hanging partner for two days.

Uli didn't look surprised that Black Charles wasn't Butter's daddy by blood. He just stood there like he did in her dreams, not saying nothing, throwing the ball between his hands, daring it to drop.

"Well, you want to play?"

"A'ight," was all Bread could say as she walked out before Uli tried to walk in. Only people she trusted were allowed to come in her house. She worried about how outsiders would judge her based on where she lived. Since Uli didn't live in Sweetwater, he couldn't be trusted not to judge her. She imagined that Uli lived in a real house with both of his parents.

"Where everybody at?" Bread asked once they got to the basketball hoop.

"I don't know," Uli said, and threw the ball to Bread. "I got dropped off on the new road and walked down here."

"Uhm, hm." Bread caught the ball and threw it through the net-less hoop. The homemade goal was pushed against a dead tree and held up with rusty nails. Everybody in the neighborhood played on it.

She looked around her and back at Uli and didn't want to think about what she must look like. She grabbed a fistful of hair and pulled, to give the illusion that her afro was bigger than it was.

"Where you learn to play ball so good?" Uli asked.

Bread hunched her shoulders forward and threw the ball through the hoop again. Uli was impressed, and smiled.

*

Bread lay underneath Uli feeling embarrassed and ashamed. Sex was different from what she expected. It was not romantic. It did not make her feel beautiful, or different, or loved.

They sat in the silence for a while until Uli pulled his pants up, which made Bread feel confused. She hadn't known what to do next so she pulled her panties back over her legs and reached for her shorts. She wondered if this meant he was her boyfriend now.

*

Bread knew something wasn't right. She had been sick on the stomach for days and every time she prayed and checked and then checked and went back to pray there was no blood spots in her underwear. She didn't know a lot about her body but she knew that every twenty-eight days she was supposed to bleed. Something wasn't right.

"What's ailing you?" Twiggy's hand was on Bread's forehead testing for a temperature. "You need to go to the doctor?"

"I'll be all right."

"Gone to the doctor and see what they say." Twiggy slid a ten-dollar bill to her daughter to take with her to the clinic. Bread walked by herself.

*

Uli was sitting on the neighbor's porch, smiling that beautiful smile when Bread walked over. They hadn't seen each other since being naked together in the woods. His smile was no more remarkable than she remembered, but she still thought to herself how she could spend all day just looking at him. He nodded his head to acknowledge her and went right on listening to the lies Bootsy, one of the drunks that walked the road, was telling to the group gathered by the steps.

Bread thought she would feel embarrassed or ashamed around Uli but she didn't. But she didn't feel special either.

"Hey, hey Bread. What you know good?"

"Nothin' Bootsy."

"That's a pretty girl there," Bootsy went on, as if Bread wasn't still standing there. "Don't look nothing like her mama, though."

"Uli, I got something to tell you about."

Uli was still smiling when he stood up without saying goodbye to his friends. They knew he would be right back and wouldn't go far. He and Bread started walking up the road, the opposite direction of her house. He didn't say anything, just waited for her to talk, and she wondered what he was thinking. She stopped walking once they had gotten far enough for no one to hear their voices. She looked at his face and recognized, as if for the first time, how handsome he was. What would he want a baby with her for?

"I'm pregnat." By the time Bread said the words she wasn't sure if she had said them out loud or not. But then the look on Uli's face told her that she had. He just looked at her like she was a ghost, or like she wasn't right there in front of him at all. "Say something," Bread urged, worried.

"What you want me to say?"

"Something." That wasn't entirely true. Bread wanted Uli to grab her shoulders and squeeze them the way he did when she followed him in the woods to see what laying up against him would feel like. She wanted him to tell her that everything was going to be all right, and that he loved her, even if he didn't know it until that very moment, and that he loved the baby too. She wanted him to tell her that he was going to marry her, and buy her a house so she could spend all day sweeping the floor, and trying out recipes, and singing sweet nothings to their baby. She wanted him to tell her how happy he was that she was the one that would make him a daddy. She wanted him to lie if he had to.

"Is it by me?"

Bread was startled by his words. "Yea, it's by you," she said simply, quietly, shame-faced. "I've only done it that one time."

It. In a word she had reduced her moment of awakening to something that made it seem unimportant. By being together they had made something out of nothing. They made a baby out of curious bodies and anxious hands.

Uli looked at her stomach, it didn't look like anything was in it. "What you gon' do?" he asked.

Bread didn't answer out loud, but what she wanted to say was that she was going to have it. Love it. Take care of it. Whatever it is that grown women do when they have a baby out of the blue.

Uli didn't say anything after that and Bread looked at his mouth and wondered if it would ever smile again. "Well, I just wanted you to know."

She started taking steps back toward home and looked back to see Uli still standing in the same place, staring off in the opposite direction. When she walked past the boys, still talking to Bootsy by the porch, she pretended she was invisible and that they couldn't see her pass. She acted like she didn't hear them when they called after her asking where Uli had gone, and if he was coming back.

"I don't know," she said to herself, wondering the same thing.

*

"What the doctor say?"

"It's pus in the blood," Bread lied, eyeballing her mother and hoping she would believe it.

"Puss in the blood?" Twiggy said it out loud while she went over it in her mind, "What the hell is that? Where you get that from?"

"He didn't say."

"It ain't cancer is it?"

"No. He said it'll pass."

"He give you something for it?"

"Said to get some rest."

"Well, get some rest then."

*

"Teeth and tongue in the same mouth and they don't fall out and here y'all is, sisters, and can't get along in the same house. Too many damn women in this house to have peace. Now, you know Bread don't feel good. You just do what the hell I said do." Twiggy's voice carried through every room in the humble house. She had had enough of Peaches' backtalk.

Sixteen and smelling herself, Peaches had been responsible for the bulk of the housework since Bebe and Junior had moved out and Little was always gone somewhere with his friends. Peaches felt that Bread had been playing sick for a day too long.

"You act like Bread is dying or something," Peaches challenged.

"She got pus in the blood."

"Pus in the blood?" Peaches frowned at her mother's ignorance.

"You heard me."

"Every shut eye ain't sleep, and every goodbye ain't gone!"

"Who you talking to?"

"All them youngins you done had and you don't know when somebody pregnat?" Peaches had said it before she realized it, but was satisfied. Women had babies all the time and Bread wasn't nothing special. She had a baby coming and wouldn't call out who the daddy was.

"Bread ain't no pregnat."

"She ain't had a period since it was hot outside," Peaches said.

Twiggy walked to the back room where Bread was sleeping. Bread opened her eyes and stared at her mother with alarm.

"You pregnat?" Twiggy said it as much as a statement as a question.

Tears collected in Bread's eyes and she nodded her head and waited for Twiggy to ask who the daddy was, but she didn't. Then she waited for Twiggy to slap her across her face, but she didn't.

Twiggy's words trailed her out of the room, "Ain"t nothin' to cry about. Peoples have babies all the time. That ain't nothin'."

*

When the baby was born, everybody knew from looking at it that it was Uli's. The yellow baby girl lay in Bread's arms looking like somebody else's child. Bread fell in love with her all at once.

The baby took all of Bread's color and she turned dark, like a shadow was sitting on her face, neck, and hands. Tired and restless, Bread didn't look at all like herself, as if she had literally become another person when she pushed that baby out. Twiggy looked at that light-skinned baby and checked her ears and nail beds to see what color she would end up being. "That's gon' be a pretty baby. She gon' be red as a new penny."

Bread knew that babies were usually named after their daddies, but she decided to name the baby after Twiggy, given that her baby would not have a daddy to speak of.

"What you gon' call her?" "Sadie California."

Sadie was Twiggy's real name and California is where Uli went when he knew the baby was going to be born. California might as well have been on the other side of the world from North Carolina, and as far as Bread was concerned, it could have not been a place at all. She called the baby California to remind herself every time she called her daughter's name that Uli would rather live in California than to live near his child. People usually frowned when they heard the baby's name, like it didn't fit, or they couldn't quite believe it. It was a white girl's name, an old person's name, a city name, it didn't seem to fit a child in Sweetwater. Everyone had a bewildered expression and asked questions out of curious confusion. People seemed satisfied when Bread said she would call her Cali for short.

Twiggy pretended to not be tickled to death that the baby was named after her. The family passed Cali around to find traces of themselves in her. "She definitely has that Bishop chin," they would say, calling out Twiggy's maiden name. "And look at that nose, that's Cake's nose," they would say, seeing something that was not really there.

*

A second daughter, Bird, would come two years later, after Bread met and married a sweet-talking man who told beautiful lies. When Ernest said he wanted to marry her and adopt her child, Bread thought her life could still be salvaged. They were married at the courthouse with no family witnesses, just the white people who signed the papers. There was no church, no gown, and no special vows spoken. It wasn't the wedding Bread had imagined but the man who would be her husband stood in front of her wearing his army uniform, shit colored and dingy, behind his cocoa butter skin. She didn't mind the way he looked because he had an honest face that she couldn't help but pay attention to. His clear skin, long eyelashes, dimpled grin, and way with words made him handsome and charming all at once.

When their daughter was born, Bread knew Ernest was disappointed she was not a boy, but he seemed satisfied that the brown baby looked just like him. Bald-headed and two months early, the baby was small enough to fit in a shoe box. Bread let Ernest's mother, Haddy, name the baby because she had been saving a name for a girl. She named the baby Robin, and even though Bread didn't think the name was extraordinary, after saying it over and over again she liked the way it sounded. When she took the child to Sweetwater, everyone decided they would call her Bird because Robin was a white girl's name.

Ernest loved Bread Lately as much as he was able to at the time. He was too young and too good looking to settle down forever, but he still vowed to have her, to hold her, in sickness and in health, for richer, for poorer, until death did them part. Bread believed him because he seemed to be her last chance of escape. But Ernest had a way of lying like he was telling the truth. He promised he would buy her a two-story house in the city with stairs up to the ceiling, like white folks. He said that he would be faithful to her and once they were on their feet she would not have to work anymore. He said that he was going to take her on expensive vacations to see places in the world she had never even heard of. He was going to make all of her dreams come true. They were all lies. Ernest's promises were copious, but he was used to telling women what they wanted to hear. He talked to Bread in a sweet and low voice as artificial as sugar substitute, and always called her by her real name, Gale. Only people that did not know Bread called her Gale, teachers, people at work, and anyone reading her name off of something official.

Her God-given good name was chosen by her godmother and aunt, who had read somewhere that it meant happy. And with Ernest she was happy. He made her feel special and when he told her he loved her, it sounded like magic. But all the love in the world couldn't keep him from cheating. When they lived together he spent most of his time away from home, and he was not discreet about his indiscretions. Bread was patient but could not compete with Ernest's obsession with adventures, artificial highs, and willing women. One day after work she went home, packed all of the belongings she could fit in her car, and drove home to Sweetwater with her two children. Twiggy met her at the door like she was expecting her, and didn't ask any questions. She swung the door open as wide as it would go so Bread could fit through with two babies in her arms.

Interlude

Porch Premonitions

In Sweetwater, when men fix on cars, smoke cigarettes, and tell lies, with boys watching them from a distance, and girl children sit across from each other touching hands and singing *Miss Mary Mack, Mack, Mack all dressed in black, black, black*, womenfolk foreshadow the future in lustful whispers loud enough for passersby to hear. They sit around from morning 'til evening, rocking in chairs, snapping beans, fanning flies, and dipping snuff. They talk religion, relationships, work, children, secret lovers, and the goings-on of Sweetwater.

Unmarried and unrelated, Sweetie Pie and Peewee live three houses down from the Lately house. Stubborn and set in their ways, they keep mostly to themselves, holding hands behind closed doors, and breathing hard on each other's necks at night. It is almost August so they are burning trash in the trash pile and watching the smoke rise while sitting on the porch catching a breeze. Sweetie Pie wears a housecoat and house shoes at all times while she is at home, and red lipstick. The pink sponge rollers in her hair are daily accessories, promising tight curls for her return to work the next day. She doesn't worry about the smell of burnt garbage hanging in the air and settling on her skin because she will bathe with Clorox and white vinegar before bed, neutralizing the smell of heat, sweat, and poverty.

Peewee is known for knowing things so she does most of the talking. Called mannish for her mannerisms, Peewee keeps her hair cut short and unpermed, and always wears work pants, even on days, like today, when she is off work.

Sweetie Pie rocks herself in the rocking chair and cleans under her fingernails with her longest nail, humming every now and then so Peewee will keep talking and know she is still listening. They don't touch in public, they just talk, and when Peewee initiates a conversation, Sweetie Pie listens.

"You know Weasel dead, don't cha?"

"Sho' nuff? What he die of?"

"That old bitch he married put a root on him. They say his skin shed like a snake before he died."

"No shit?"

"He needed somebody to help with all those youngins."

"He musta been pretty desperate to marry somebody like that."

"She didn't mean him no good [...] and kept a nasty house. I wouldn't eat off a clean plate." Peewee frowns at the thought of an unkept house, and pictures Weasel's dead body laying in a casket in the front room for the wake, "I ain't going to view the body."

"Uhm-hm." Sweetie Pie rubs her legs with both hands, like she is trying to warm them up, and settles into the quiet of Peewee's pause. She doesn't like to talk about death and dying, or the loneliness it leaves. Death had come for everyone she loved except Peewee, and she didn't want death to respond to its name. Instead, she concentrated on the way the hair on her legs laid down under the weight of the Vaseline she put on to keep the mosquitoes away. Then she waited for Peewee to change the subject. "And you know Bread done moved back home with Twiggy with them girls." Peewee says after a while, when Sweetie Pie's silence signaled a request for something else to talk about, something more remarkable than death.

"Damn, didn't she already have a house full?"

"Twiggy ruined her kids, all of 'em always right up under her." Peewee settles in her seat and stuffs tobacco in her mouth between her bottom lip and gums, chewing slowly.

"I knew Bread wouldn't be gone long."

"That marriage sho' ain't last no time, huh? What was it a year?"

"I think two." Sweetie Pie was thinking back to the courthouse wedding nobody was invited to, witnessed by two white people who signed their names on the marriage certificate. "Love is a funny thing, girl. Somebody get your nose open you be ready to follow 'em anywhere."

"I reckon."

"You should know." Sweetie Pie caught Peewee rolling her eyes but didn't say so. If Peewee had her way, they would have moved away from Sweetwater a long time ago, but Sweetie Pie loved living on the land where all of her folks had lived, so Peewee left it alone.

"Anyway, they might get back together after 'while."

"People don't have to live together to be together no way."

"I don't know nobody ever gone and stayed gone, specially round here."

"Cake ain't been back."

"That's different." Peewee doesn't say why at first, thinking about it. "Well, anyway, they got a house full over there now. Can't be acting quare with that many folks living under one roof."

"Quare?" Sweetie Pie smiles to herself, knowing the word has multiple meanings in their community, and knowing that most people wouldn't use the word to describe her and Peewee, even though they did in private.

"Particular. Set in your ways." Peewee explains the word the way she means it and doesn't pay Sweetie Pie's expression no mind. "Too many women and youngins to want things your own way. All that bleeding and crying and fussing, wouldn't be no lasting peace."

"I reckon." Sweetie Pie wished there were more people around to take up some space in the house she and Peewee shared, but doesn't say so. "That little one, the one they call Bird, wouldn't walk 'til they broke crickets on her knees. Was damn near two. Won't walkin' or talkin' or nothin'."

"You know she was born early. Liked to died. Was small enough to fit in a shoebox, they say. She might be slow."

"She got sad eyes like she has seen things."

"Well, she ain't seen nothing yet." Peewee waits to see if Sweetie Pie is finished with the subject and spits in the cup she keeps next to her chair. "Anyway, too many damn women in that house. I hope they don't run each other crazy."

Part Two

(Robin) Bird

a call from home

for reunions, funerals, wedding parties
comes infrequently
I follow the path of dirt roads
leading me to places I once knew by heart
and am known by family name
mother resemblance
*

word of my escape
always gets back
to women who look out of windows
with closed shades & long curtains
with their eyes wide open
and their mouths murmuring whispers of what they see
into a telephone receiver
*

lips on mouth sugar
sincere hugs
church glances and scolds
for not wearing a slip
or stockings
and too-fancy shoes
I take off before standing
for prayer, scripture reading, call to worship
"Can all of the visitors please stand?"
I am suspended in air
somewhere between belonging and visiting
not knowing where I fit
ancient hands
wrap around my waist and squeeze
to see if
I've been
eating enough down there in Florida
still cute as I always was, they say,
with mama's face
& sweet smile
but they don't know where I got that big butt from

must be my daddy's side
who they've never seen
*
on the way home
we pass little houses in silence
in the same place they have always been
and I smile
because in a moment
years collapse together
and it is like I never left
remembering searches in high grass for
four-leaf clovers
& good luck
and holding lightning bugs
between tightly held fists
at night in the hide-and-go-seek summer
mosquito bitten legs
scratched until blood and ash rested on
too-black knees
and old scars
racing to the bathroom
waiting in line
to take a sink bath

Chapter 9

Holding my breath was rehearsed rebellion. I was younger than ten when I started breathing in without breathing out. I would sit on the steps of our trailer, my face resting in my hands, watching women and waiting to see what words would be spoken. The weather and whether or not so-and-so was doing right at home, and whether or not white people were acting a fool on the job, and whether or not their children had good sense, and whether or not there was enough money for bills and groceries, and whether or not they had made good love the night before, or ever at all, and whether or not the preacher preached a good word on Sunday, and whether or not they felt like grinning over crying—all this usually dictated their moods and their words.

Ornery moods meant Cali and I would be sent outside to play bare-footed and in our underclothes until our underarms were wet with sweat, and we could smell the musk rising off our bodies. Instructions to go and take a bath would come to us in the irritated voices of grown women who were too tired to be bothered with dirty children. They would look disgusted at our filthiness and tell us we smelled like dogs.

Cheerful moods meant if I was quiet and still, my presence in the house was tolerated. I could watch soap operas with them. Pick beans with them. Sit close enough to inhale the sweet smell of a freshly lit cigarette. Inside play meant a nighttime bath was not required. Mild-mannered moods meant Cali's presence was not necessary to distract them from their agitation of my presence. She was favored, precious. I was largely ignored.

On this particular day, I am invisible to them and they are laughing. From where I sit, I cannot make out what they are saying, but their smiles are open-mouthed, cheeky, gap-toothed, and gummy, reaching from one side of their faces to the other. Their heads are pushed back and their eyes are sealed shut. I like to see them like this. Full-round and unapologetic. Vulnerable and fragile. Beautiful in their own right and not competitive. Laughing like they don't have a worry in the world, as if being a woman and black and poor makes you free.

My feelings for them are a mixture of envy, resistance, fascination, and curiosity. Sometimes I want to be just like them. Other days I want to escape being the third generation of women living the way we live, out in the woods where everybody knows your name and nobody ever thinks about leaving. I am naïve with little sense of myself as a rural-rooted-black-woman-in-the-making. All I have is Sweetwater and home, which mean the same thing even though Sweetwater is the town, and home is what I call the house I live in. I also have these women, who look right past me because I am too damn much too soon, and they want to concentrate and wrap themselves up in this everything-is-all-right moment, laughing out loud and together because moments like that are too few and far between.

*

The first trailer my mother's family owned was single-wide and the color of fog, dingy-looking with putrid green shutters outlining the windows. In the summer, the doors were always open, and the windows were always lifted because there was no air conditioner, only boxed fans that sat in corners collecting lint and breaking the silence. I would sit in front of the fan, bellowing out songs through the dusty vents, admiring the unnatural way it made my voice sound. This was satisfying until it interrupted TV watching, grown folks talking, or the peace of quiet that an adult demanded, and I would be sent outside "with all that damn noise."

I sat at the open back door, bare legs dangling over the edge of the threshold, my feet feeling the rough exterior of homemade steps made of cheap concrete, lopsided and raggedy. Halfway in and halfway out of the house, I waited for a cool breeze to pass by and give me chill bumps, a delicious distraction and temporary relief from the unforgiving North Carolina summer heat.

Flies snuck in on the shoulders of company and found their way back out through the broken screen. The screen would not close all the way or lock, but it remained linked to the front door like shoulders, offering an illusion of sophistication to our house. No one minded the door anyway, pulling it open and turning the doorknob without knocking. The cinder block steps were steep and dangerous—often taking adults by surprise when they forgot to watch their feet when they walked. I watched closely, secretly hoping to see one of them stumble.

The rooms in the trailer were so small they forced obedience, patience, and familiarity with each other—familial sight, smell, and touch were second nature. You had to touch, often shoulder-to-shoulder and leg-to-leg, when sitting. I didn't mind the unintentional touches, though the older children and adults would often suck their teeth and smack their lips in anger when our situational space closed in, telling me to move. When they would blow out air, I would suck it in and swallow.

*

A garden grew off to the side of the house, next to a ditch, big enough to plant two rows of vegetables—mostly tomatoes and cucumbers, but Cali and I would sneak watermelon seeds in the ground to see if they would grow if we watered them. The watermelon seeds wouldn't grow, but it didn't distract me from digging my hands into the earth until dirt was so deep in my fingernails it would take me days to make them clean. I suspected that the seeds had to be buried deep to latch on, the way a baby did in a woman's womb.

The trees, honeysuckle and pine, would fill the air with a sweet and sour aroma that sank into our skin and lingered like cheap perfume. Patches of wild grass, onions, mushrooms, and dandelions grew amidst clay-red mud and thick tree stumps. Climbing trees was a reasonable pastime before afternoon cartoons, and I would sometimes forget my fear of bugs as I climbed the tree branches, which supported my limber body like strong and wide arms. There seemed to be more oxygen in the trees.

Ditches and dirt piles served as landmarks of where our land started and stopped. The land was tainted with broken glass, plastic soda bottles, trash bags, broken plates, abandoned toys, old shoes, animal bones dragged in by stray dogs, tree limbs, and tree stumps. My uncle's green Thunderbird with no tires, sat defeated on cement bricks, surrounded by other junk. You could see nearly everything from the back door stoop: my aunt's white Cutlass, my grandmother's brown sugar Cougar, a rusted white swing set that became embedded in the tree bark that had once served as shade, and our neighbor's flower garden. A cigar tree grew between ours and our neighbor's yard. I would often sit under the tree and practice smoking with the fake cigars. Nothing, at the time, made me feel more grown up.

Cali and I were the only children in the trailer where we lived with our grandmother, our mother and our aunt and uncle, brothers, and sisters. Three generations in one house was common in our community.

Cali and I were grateful that our room, the one we shared with our mother, had its own bathroom. We would sit at our mother's feet as she smoked cigarettes and sat on the commode, taking turns telling her about our day. If we had bothered each other enough, from not having a place or opportunity to escape each other's company, we would tell on each other, detailing a previously kept secret that would inspire the greatest punishment.

Our mother, beautiful in the way mothers are, sat with us in the dark, the only light coming from the end of her cigarette burning a brilliant bright orange glow as she sucked in. Trapped in the tiny space, we captured her undivided attention because we were temporarily closed off from everybody else in the house. Those moments were like magic.

When the streetlight came on and you could hear stray dogs bark in the distance, we would fall asleep on both sides of our mother's body, daring her to turn toward a daughter, proving (as we feared and suspected) that she loved the other best. I was often the more needy and jealous child, the dark-skinned version of my mother, attention starved and liking the way her hot breath smelled when she breathed on me.

*

Grandma was like a father to us, making us do what our mother didn't enforce and chasing us with switches when we misbehaved. I came to understand the interconnectedness of our lives as women, relying on each other because we were all we had.

*

Ours was the house everyone came to. Our yard was big enough for outdoor reunions when out-of-town family and uninvited neighbors gathered together to pat each other's shoulders, smile wide smiles, and listen to each other tell lies and brag. My favorite memories are of pig pickins. The smell of pork cooking slow on the burner seemed to calm everyone's nerves and ease everyone's spirits. We would stay up all night, the children going in and out of the house, playing hide and go seek and catching lightning bugs in long-throat glass Coca-Cola bottles. Cigarette smoke glowed in the dark and old-school music grooved in the background while I dragged my tired body around to fight off sleep.

Grown men stood in a corner passing joints and whispering while the women sat at the table laughing, lying, and playing spades. They held glasses half-full of brown liquor mixed with brown soda. Almost all of their fingernails were red, and their lips were smothered with shades of burgundy from shared lipstick that had been wiped off accidentally or left on the rim of their glasses.

My summertime memories are filled with company and camaraderie. The house and yard would be full of kinfolk and roguish neighbors who would stop by to play spades in the dark next to a light bulb plugged in to an extension cord. Someone would light some newspaper on fire to keep the mosquitoes away, and my mother was chosen to keep score when they played cards because she had the neatest handwriting. I remember it like it was yesterday, the way beautiful black women with raspy voices were in charge of everything and everybody.

Fireflies

by Mary E. Weems

My eight aunties
hovered over us
at the family reunion
under the same tree
at the same park
for over eighty-five years
all the food, drinks, cakes,
pies, cookies, popsickles, ice cream,
paper plates, napkins, prayers
appearing as if by magic
us kids bringing nothing
but hungry bellies and happy

All have been dead damn near long
as some of us have been alive,
but this year, in the midst of the hottest
July anybody could remember

We talked about them so much
we talked them up outta Heaven
and when it got dark, just before
cousin Mookie
set off the fireworks
all eight of them showed up
brightest fireflies I ever saw.

Chapter 10

Grandma Twiggy was always cooking, always fussing, always moving. She was never young or old, and was intentional in the way she took care of us. She loved us without ever saying the words. Her favorite labor of love was cooking, though it was not without complaint. Nothing irritated her more than my ungratefulness for her gestures at making sure that I never knew what it felt like to be hungry, in the true sense of the word.

"Your black ass would make a preacher cuss," she would tell me after giving me an ear full of grown up words. Knowing a few churchless preachers whose mouths were no more holy than ours, I didn't doubt her, but I still felt inherently bad at the insinuation.

Saturdays were set aside for cleaning the house and making groceries. If we ran out of enough food to make a full meal before the weekend, we had to make do with what we had. The cabinets always had Pet's milk, canned meat, and saltine crackers. Cali and I would split our favorite, Vienna sausages out of the can, or potted meat seasoned with vinegar, salt, and pepper on crackers, until Aunt Bebe told us we were eating cat's tongue.

"You know what you eating don't cha?"

"Ain't nothin' but some little weenies and potted meat," Cali offered back, plopping a whole Vienna sausage in her mouth.

"No it ain't," Aunt Bebe began, "that's cow and cat's tongue. Can't you taste it tasting you back?"

By now, Cali and I are both spitting the food out in the trash can.

"Stop wasting that damn food," Twiggy ordered from over the stove, "y'all been eating it."

The fact that she didn't contradict Aunt Bebe's claims worried us, so when Aunt Bebe continued to tell us about breakfast sausage, brains, and chitterlings, we forgot how good it tasted and refused to indulge in any meat that came in a can or a plastic tub.

After that, our Saturday food options were never appealing to my appetite. Grandma Twiggy could make a meal out of anything as long as she had light bread. Cornbread crumbled into buttermilk, mayonnaise sandwiches with salt and pepper (sometimes with tomatoes or bananas, depending on what we had), and cucumbers marinated in vinegar, salt, and pepper.

"If you hungry, you'll eat what we got." She had chastised me for standing with the refrigerator door open, declaring how I was "starvin' like Marvin." She refused to let me eat the chocolate frosting from the can that I had bought with my own money, because she said it would give me worms. There was nothing else I wanted.

Twiggy was sitting at the kitchen table that was used for preparing food, sitting down to eat, an overflow for company, and card playing.

"I don't want no cornbread or maynaise," I say defiantly.

Cali sat at the table in front of a plate that matched Twiggy's. At ten years old she was big boned and grown-up looking. Her hair was wavy from the roots, making it difficult to manage for different reasons than my thin, fragile locks. Her stomach sat on her thighs and she couldn't cross her legs all the way. Mama worried that she was too big for her age, but Twiggy fed her ritualistically. Cali never turned down the food from Twiggy, even though she knew the buttermilk was homemade, made out of the spoiled white milk that went sour in the refrigerator.

"I don't give a damn if you don't eat," Twiggy took a big swallow of her bread-soaked buttermilk and wiped the thick, white excess from her mouth with her sleeve. "There are chilluns in Africa who would love to have this food."

There were black-eyed peas, another food I disliked without tasting, cooking in the pressure pot on the stove. Twiggy stood up to check the temperamental pot, hissing, sweating, and shaking on the red-hot eye, threatening to jump off and explode. We had been warned to stay away from the pressure pot to keep from getting burned.

I wanted to say that starving children in Africa could have the nasty food they were eating, but I knew better. Twiggy was short tempered and often looking for a reason to send me for a switch. I ignored my bloated but empty stomach, now growling, and went in the living room where our modest furniture, crowded together in the room like it was trying to get out, sat in front of a floor model television. I would sit there and wait for my daddy to come and beg him for Pizza Hut. We always got to eat out when we went with him and he was coming to pick us up. Twiggy had been saying all day that she doubted he would come, but she was also counting on it since she and Peaches had to leave for work by two o'clock. My mother would not get home until after 5 and we were too small to stay home alone.

*

Ernest showed up late like he was on time. All of my anger at his tardiness was lost upon seeing him. Cali and I both were so caught up in loving and missing our father that we never held a grudge. It seemed like he had a different car every time he came. This time he was driving a putrid green Chevrolet Caprice with cigarette burns in the seats but we got in like it was a Cadillac. It didn't matter that the car was old and raggedy or that Daddy was two hours late, he had come and he would keep us out past bedtime to give Mama a break.

"I didn't think your sorry ass would come," Twiggy had said when he pulled up just as she and Peaches needed to leave.

"I promised them I would," Daddy said, as if he had never lied or broke a promise.

My father was a handsome man so my mother didn't seem to mind, in the way other mothers did, the way I looked more and more like him the older I got. His manly features were too abrasive at first. The nose too big. The lips too wide. It would take me years to grow into his face.

I found it appealing that my father never lived in the same place. He moved all the time, taking me and Cali to various places that he "lived" or stayed with pretty women who had pets instead of children and blue water in their commodes.

He treated us like an older brother who gave us attention when it was convenient. His undivided attention was limited to Christmases, birthdays, and every other Saturday, every other month. The older we got, the less frequent his visits.

*

By the time I was in middle school, I had come to resent my father. When I began to experience rejection from boys, and spite from peers I understood how my mother must have felt when my father left her to be with other women. I grew tired of his empty promises and inconsistent interest. Anger made me feel more powerful than pitiful so I was mad all the time.

Twiggy suddenly came to his defense.

"That's your daddy," she would say when I rolled my eyes and poked out my mouth when someone teased me for having his mannerisms, "you better show some respect."

A few years earlier, she had told me she was more of a daddy to me than he was, reaching in her pocket to give me $2 for lunch and ice cream. Back then, she was irritated by the way I minded him and talked back to my mama, the way I blamed my mother for his absence and relished any ounce of his attention. When my feelings reversed, she seemed to feel sorry for my father, as if both of us could not resent him at the same time.

Waiting to See

By Mary E. Weems

Eyes open
One-closed
Brown black as
men in life
I don't
say can you
don't mama
yesterday—blink
retreat images
a Monet
in Black
years—don't count
when every time
sun rises.

Chapter 11

From the outside looking in, it was evident that being in Sweetwater was hard on a man. There were few opportunities for advancement or escape, so men had to rely on mother wit and sound judgment to make it. It was no surprise that the boys chased any opportunity for distraction, be that the bottom of a liquor bottle, between some pretty woman's legs, or smoking dope. Women were forgiving of the vices and somehow took on the scorn of their men, blaming themselves and white folk for black male anger and indifference. Women were prepared to believe anything men said to them, even barefaced lies.

Country boys have honey-dipped tongues and their sweet talk is not all wasted on love interests. They manage to lull all of the women in their life, mothers and sisters, church mothers, and grandmothers included, into believing that every bad thing that befalls them is the result of hard luck or somebody else's fault. It was not uncommon in Sweetwater for grown men to live with their mothers or grandmothers or to go back and forth between multiple households and children. Mothers raised their daughters and let their sons grow up.

I don't remember many men, other than my uncles, whom I saw almost every day in my life. The men in church were ancient. They were handsome if you looked at them long enough and imagined them young. Their faces, like masks, held disappointments and trials. Many of them had been away to war, or out of the state to work, and came back to Sweetwater with either appreciation, resentment, or a mixture of both. For recreation they played sports, drank liquor, made love, picked fights, played cards, listened to blues records, and tried to forget they were the worst things to be at the time—poor and black. Racism and colorism was out in the open, so present that even black folk favored light skin.

Children were particularly worrisome in the summer and autumn months, the change of seasons. It was pneumonia weather, the time of the year when it would be warm outside all day and night, and then the cold air would sneak up on you the next day causing a terrible cold, the worst kind to have when it is hot and humid outside. And the days are longer.

Girl children, who sit gap-legged and wide-mouthed, found sophisticated mischief to get into when it was that hot outside. The women worried because they remembered their own Indian summers, filled with calamity and curiosity. The need to feel grown and rebellious inspired secret meetings at the stumps of trees where neighborhood boys would sit together with sweat collecting at their arm pits and trouble in their eyes. By the time puberty finds them, boys have already started eyeing little girls and women too young to be their mothers. They are not discreet, standing close enough to girls to smell their inside smells and rubbing up against them, as if by accident. The boys seem innocent enough, and pitiful. Their faces are masks of dust with sun-darkened skin coated with dry dirt from too many days of rainless heat. Their teeth, yellow and jagged, have gone too many days without brushing, and baths are considered an inconvenience, so are intermittent. The boys are anxious to be men and feel more grown than their years. They have learned charm from the occasional visits of absent fathers and older boys who say, "Hey there little mama, sho' looking fine" to the grown women who want to feel young, and to girls who want to be grown. The women pretend, at first, to be annoyed at the attention but slowly and surely smile in satisfaction and wait around to hear more. This is why grown women sit around worried about their daughters, because they remember what that was like.

The women in my family would often watch the way I smiled when men offered me any ounce of affection. "Fast ass," they would say, shaking their heads and smirking like my youth put them in the mind of something. "She got womanish ways, Bread. You better watch her!"

They didn't know I was too insecure to be fast. Old men and boys on their way to being men seemed to see past my in-between looks and call me pretty like they were prophesying the future. The boys my age said I was dark-skinned and ugly.

Ugliness was acceptable for men and babies, but never women or little girls, which is why babies with peculiar features were said to favor their daddy's side of the family. No one talked much about looks when it no longer counted, after marriage, or bearing children, or some other arrangement that meant you didn't need to be beautiful anymore any way. Not meeting a particular standard was irredeemable and light skin and good hair, or light skin, or good hair, was enough to forgive any other strange pairing, like beady eyes and missing teeth, or puny lips and no behind.

"Look at her hair!" the women who shared a ride with Grandma Twiggy to work would say of my sister, resisting the urge to touch the perfect ponytails. Everybody knew that it was improper to touch a black girl's hair without permission, especially a child, and Cali had been warned to not let people run their hands through it. "I don't care who it is," Twiggy had said, as if envious women walked around with poison between their fingers, ready to take your hair out like a bad perm. "Niggas be touching your hair and wishing it out!" She never warned me about my hair.

I wanted long hair that flowed forever down my back like Cali's and often blamed my mother for the dilemma. All of the good genes, it seemed, had come out with Cali. Mama felt sorry for me and promised that in time my hair would catch up with Cali's and the other girls in my class. When I sat between her legs for our nightly hair-braiding ritual she would grease my scalp with her fingertips, trying out various hair greases that promised to work like a miracle. She used sweet-smelling oils and grease that smelled like medicine, but nothing worked. She tried the blue and green Dax hair pomade, Dr. Miracle products, Pink Oil Moisturizer, and Doo Gro for hair that won't grow. None of the so-called guarantees ever worked. I was convinced it was my short hair that made me invisible.

"She sho is pretty Twiggy, look just like a doll baby," Miss Sis said, doting over Cali's lightness and looooooooooooooooooong hair. Her dismissal of me might as well have been contempt, "And that's the other one? Looks just like her mama."

Cali was annoyed by the attention, not realizing she should cherish compliments because they came so frequent.

Most of my cousins were the same way. One redbone and the other chocolate colored. With black people you never know. Twiggy said there are so many colors mixed in to colored folk that there is no telling what you'll get. But light-skinned women often expected their children to take their color after them, and didn't hide their disappointment when they didn't.

"That's what you get for messing with that black ass Snowball," Ms. Thomas had told her daughter. Snowball was very dark-skinned, which made his nickname ironic. You would think people would call him Black or Darkie because of his midnight complexion. He didn't seem to mind the name and had it taped to the front of his car, a white Nissan with tinted windows and special seats that went all the way back. He was a good-looking man but that always came secondary to his color. "He nice looking to be so dark," people would say, which was no different from when I was told, "You pretty for a dark-skinned girl," an insult and compliment all in one.

I heard my cousins say that Mary Thomas only dated Snowball to irritate her mama, who was color struck and simple-minded. Ms. Thomas had married the lightest-complected man she could find in Sweetwater to help her make piss yellow babies. She seemed hell bent on keeping that tradition and encouraged her daughters to follow in her footsteps. Mary had said she ain't want no light man. "Two light people together don't look right," Mary had said to Weezie. "They look like they cousins. The blacker the berry the sweeter the juice."

People looked at the baby from afar, shaking their head, "Damn, that baby look like Snowball spit it out. He must have tried to deny it." Old folk said if a man tried to deny a child it will be born his spitting image. They said it was a shame that a little girl had such strong features.

*

I am often afraid that Cali is the preferred child so I find ways to be mean to her. It does not work around adults but when it is just the two of us I can usually manage to pass on some of my insecurities to her. We are outside eating sweet dirt and watching bugs crawl when I tell her she is not really black. "You are orange," I tell her.

She has heard this from me before. The only insult I can throw at her is that she is "yellow as a banana." Not really black like me and mama. It does not do the intended harm. She doesn't care. Being yellow is not a bad thing. When she calls me "Blackie" in return it does more harm than she probably intended. It hurt to be called black. Nobody ever said it but it was understood that there was something wonderful, better, altogether beautiful about being the light, bright, damn near white version of black. I was a pitiful brown-skinned child with ashy knees and rusty elbows. The worse thing I could call my sister was yellow, which made her more beautiful and wonderful than I could ever be. So I decided to pretend that there was something wrong with her since she was the lightest person in the household.

"Your daddy must be white," I said, not knowing what it would mean if he was, but knowing that he wasn't. Her father, Uli, was bright skinned but not white. I had seen him before but not known who I was looking at. He would stop by the house when he was in town, looking like Cali except all grown into his features. He would bring her *Highlights* magazines and thin coats from mail-order catalogs. I was jealous that she got the affection of both her daddy and mine.

"At least I don't have a bird chest!" Cali mocked. When I did not retaliate she knew she had me where she wanted me. "That's why people say you ain't gon' be no good when you grow up," she continued. She knew how to break my heart and in that moment she did it quick and easy, to keep from dragging it out. I pretended not to care, but she knew better. "I wish I was the only child." Satisfied with herself, she watched me to make sure I was ready to cry.

"I ain't studying you," I lied, rolling my eyes and holding back tears.

It Hurt To Be Called Black

by Mary E. Weems

Even now 25 years after
I 'been' grown
dark and lovely words
others have used
when Black and having a 'Fro
have gone in and out
of style and back
when racist White folks
can't say nigger to your face
and have the law back them up
when the cleaning commercial
woman, the new Aunt Jemima
is lighter, wears long braids
and a no-kerchief smile

Dark-skinned women
share the same memory
pass it between themselves
careful not say too much,
or joke, or forget.

Chapter 12

Being popular and pretty is everything to little girls and I was neither. The mere sight of me inspired taunts from neighborhood children who took their insecurities out on me because of my desperate desire to be liked. The girls offered their friendship in exchange for my willingness to be humiliated. They made up games to ensure I always came in last. Who is the prettiest, tallest, lightest, with the longest hair? Their hierarchies always left me at the bottom, the black sheep of the group. The day the game was about beauty marks I felt relieved and worthy of attention.

There were three on my middle left finger, one right below my collarbone, and in my other places I hadn't yet seen. When I realized, during lunchroom conversation, that the dark, sometimes lifted, sometimes flat, perfectly round dark circles on my body were beauty marks I was impressed with myself. I had more on one finger than my so-called friends had on their entire bodies.

"I have beauty marks! See!" I stretched out the third finger on my left hand, begging for approval from the popular girls at the table. They smirked, looking at each other and laughing to themselves.

Isis, the ringleader of the group, grabbed my hand to inspect the finger in question. She threw my hand away after glancing at the darkened marks on my finger. "They aren't beauty marks on you Bird, you're too ugly. Yours are just moles!"

*

"So, so, so your draws
Wash them out with alcohol
Hang them up for Santa Claus"

But there was no Santa Claus that Christmas. By the sixth grade I developed a fascination with dying. My morbidity was a secret but my sadness was put on display like school pictures. I hid evidence in Crown Royale bags I was given when the liquor bottles went empty. When I was younger I would use the bags like a pocketbook, except in public, which Mama would never allow. Now I kept loose change, hair barrettes, a man's handkerchief, a fake gold ring I found, my secrets written on loose-leaf paper, and Tylenol I was saving for my eventual suicide. I hid the bag under the bathroom cabinet behind the wicker basket full of sponge rollers.

I imagined my childhood death would be glorious. Instead of a nuisance or pitiful child I would be remembered as the "poor black girl with so much life left to live." The inside pain came out as migraines and fatigue. When I finally told Mama I wanted to die she looked worried but not surprised. When taking me to the altar of the church multiple Sundays didn't help she made an appointment with a doctor.

The white lady psychiatrist charged $72 an hour. She told me that the reason I wanted to die was because I was depressed. When Mama tells the family I am sick, that I have something called depression, it is a word they are not familiar with. They pass it around like depression is something only white people get, and that now they are afraid I will be contagious, make them get depressed. "Ain't that some white woman's shit?" Twiggy had said, saying the word over and over again trying to make it make sense.

To them I was an odd child. Different. I felt things too deeply. I paid too much attention to details. I cried too much.

"You ain't even been through nothin' yet," Weezie tells me after she hears about my depression, "you wait 'til you get out in the world and you'll really go crazy."

They are suspicious of my diagnosis and don't understand where all the sadness comes from. "She just actin [...] to get attention [...] and watch too much damn TV."

*

Cali is too much of a goody-two-shoes to listen with me so while I hide under the table she goes outside to play ball. The women are drunk off house liquor and rum mixed with Pepsi. Their words are delicious and forbidden, which makes me more anxious to hear them. I listen in silence, our New York cousins talking in their New York accent, and I am mesmerized and hypnotized at once. I recognize some of their words, some slurred from too much liquor and not enough sleep, others hidden behind cuss words that it takes me too many seconds to decipher.

"Honey Don ain't worth a damn, never has been."

"Sorry son of a bitch […] must have a dick dipped in gold."

"He ain't nothin' but a dog."

"A dog don't get mad when you call him a dog. He know it."

"That home-wrecking heifer call the house at least once a week to let her know he just crawled his trifling no count ass out of her bed to go home to hers. Cookie just hang up the phone. I would cuss her ass out and put his ass out."

"She don't know what to do without him. Said he's all she know."

"Yea, and he knows it. He don't want her but don't want nobody else to have her."

"Ain't no man worth that much sorrow."

Honey Don is high yellow with a smile that makes you forget bad things are possible. When he was a little boy his teeth rotted out from eating so much candy so his mama started calling him "Honey," because he would eat anything sweet. Even though his daddy didn't like the feminine nickname attached to his son it stuck. When I first heard it, I did not know if people were saying, "Honey, Don ain't shit" or "Honey Don ain't shit." It wasn't until I heard Cookie say his name in his presence that it seemed more sweet than scandalous.

When I first saw him I was not surprised that Cookie loved him and didn't know how to make herself stop. Cookie, my mama's cousin, isn't ugly, but she's not beautiful either. Average looking and pear shaped, she favors the side of the family that is so mixed together that everybody looks alike, mamas and daddies, sisters and cousins, and aunts and nieces. Cookie is Twiggy's sister's child. She doesn't seem to have much use for children and all but ignored me when she first saw me, after noticing how much I favored my mother and commenting on how I had the body of a slut. "Got the frame for it," she had said walking by.

Cookie's clothes hang loose on her body like she is trying to hide herself. But she smiles big and wide when Honey Don is in the room. His good looks give her something to be proud of. They are an odd couple, the kind that makes people look, stare, and wonder how she got a man like that. The truth is, though, at least according to her sisters and cousins, she doesn't have much.

"He loves her, I guess, in his own way."

"What he loves is her money."

"Girrrrrrrrrrrrl, you know that nigga ain't got a pot to piss in or a window to throw it out of. She his bread and butter. He got sense. He ain't goin' no damn where."

"When a man wants you he will let you know. He will eat, breathe, sleep and shit you. And if he doesn't want you, he will let you know that too."

"If he really wanted to quit her he'd be long gone."

"No he wouldn't. Who else would put up with his pitiful black ass?"

I cross my legs, listening, but getting bored at the repetition of their conversation. I have already heard about trifling no-good husbands. And men with loving so good it will make you act a plum fool. This is always what is said about men. They are wonderful and terrible at the same time.

"He just can't leave her alone."

Honey Don likes to call Cookie his wife and tells the other women who try to take up too much of his time how he has to get home to her. This pisses off the other women, who then call Cookie to let her know what color underwear her husband has on and what he calls her behind her back. This story is familiar. The women sitting at the table laugh a little bit, lie a little bit, cuss for a while, and then say again that Honey Don ain't going nowhere because Cookie lets him get away with doing her wrong. They say men just can't help running the streets and sleeping around. "It's just what men do," they say, "just how men are." I decide that I do not want a man to love me like that, but my father, who is everything to me and the only example of manhood I can use to compare, runs the streets and sleeps around.

*

I linger around the threshold of the wash room and hallway. I know from there I won't be seen, at least for a few minutes, and can listen. The trailer is dim, partly because the sun is going down and partly because the orange curtains make the inside of the house look dark all the time. This is on purpose. Twiggy does not want people to be able to see inside the house.

Aunt Peaches is at the kitchen table playing cards with women she went to school with. They are gambling, playing tonk for fifty cents a hand.

"You gotta watch the dog that bring the bone 'cause it'll carry the bone!"

"Yep, if they'll talk to you, they'll talk about you!" Peaches' warning seemed to be directed at all of the women at once. She held a cigarette halfway in and halfway out of her mouth. She smoked the way most folk drank, socially and in public. She never bought cigarettes or craved them, but she always accepted when someone offered her one. The ashes on the edge of the cigarette were preparing to fall at any moment, but either Peaches didn't notice or she didn't care. She was concentrating on dealing.

I was supposed to be outside since my mama wasn't home because Peaches didn't tend to other folks' children, even though we all lived in the same house.

"Ain't that Bread's youngest?" One of the women asked, noticing my silhouette in the corner as she counted out fifty cents in dimes and nickels.

"Bird, didn't I tell you to stay outside 'til your mama come home?"

I nod my head but don't move my body. I don't know if I am more embarrassed or afraid.

"Come on over here," a woman wearing a head scarf called. "You ain't got to go out no damn doe with bugs biting. Peaches ain't none of your mama no way."

I half smiled as I walked over and sat next to the woman with the head scarf. Her face was filled with indentations and moles. Her fingernails were long, sharp, and pointed like red sticks. Her voice was deep like a man's voice on the telephone.

"Why you so quiet? Cat got your tongue?" The woman seemed curious about me and took a moment to take me all in with her eyes. "A closed mouth don't get fed. How you doing?"

"Fine." I am not sure how to sit at a table of grown folk because I am usually banned. I try not to look up so my eyes watch the ashes from Peaches' cigarette fall on the table but I don't say anything, figuring my aunt wants me to act invisible like always.

"Well, hell, we all fine. Runs in the family." She laughed to herself and winked her eye while she gathered the cards together to shuffle and deal. "We just having us some girl talk."

"What do you want to be when you grow up?" Another woman with coconut-skin asked, raking in her profit with both hands. Her question was predictable for children, along with how old are you, what grade are you in, and do you like boys yet? Still, I am not prepared to answer. I had not expected the women to ask me questions. I was satisfied to just be in their presence, sucking in their air, smelling their funk.

I halfway looked up to see my aunt, finally putting the cigarette out in the ashtray, rolling her eyes at me, resenting me for invading her privacy and good time.

"I wanna be a writer," I say, "and live in a big house with stairs in it." I wanted the three women to close their eyes and see the house with me in their imagination, and help me decorate it with their words, help me fill it up with beautiful things and books.

"You can't make no money being no writer." This is the woman with the head scarf. She looked at me like I had given the wrong answer.

"You ain't gon' be nothin' no way," Peaches said, not meaning to sound as mean as she sounded, but meaning her words. She was too caught up in her own pain to give me false hopes. "Probably end up being the fourth generation to live in this pitiful ass house. And it ain't got no stairs, except to walk in and out."

I wanted to cry but stubbornly held back tears. I wanted to speak up for myself but I knew that talking back would be inviting a heavy hand across my face and a second ass whooping when Mama got home to hear how I had acted grown in front of company. The other women at the table looked at me and felt sorry for me, not because of what Peaches said, but because I had thought otherwise. They expected me to say I wanted to be a mama, or a teacher, or secretary, not a writer. Nobody in Sweetwater was a writer. They looked at me and saw versions of themselves at my age, and felt that I was too attention hungry, too needy, and too much like them to do something different. Being a writer, to them, was a wasted fantasy. I might as well have said I wanted to be white when I grew up.

"Little girl, you just wait," a cinnamon-colored woman wearing bifocal glasses and orange lipstick said. I did not recognize the woman by name but knew her face. She walked the road sometimes, found her way to our house whenever there were a lot of cars in the yard, and that was probably how she had made it to the table tonight. "You gon' be just like me—wallowing around in this dirty ass place trying to make a dollar out of fifteen cents." When the woman smiled all I saw was the huge gap where her teeth should be. Everyone at the table, my aunt and her drunken friends, laughed out loud and I couldn't tell if they were laughing at me or how ugly the woman looked grinning, and how she grinned anyway.

"Oh, no I'm not!" I said defensively, rolling my head and my eyes. I was glad that the women were too intoxicated to notice my sass or I would get a beating for sure.

"Yes, you will," they all said, mostly to themselves and each other, grinning. "Some nappy-headed boy is gon' make you love him so much and so fast that you ain't gon' be thinking 'bout writing. Then, once he uses you up for all you're worth, he gon' leave you so broken that the only thing that will comfort you will be this dingy assed town."

"Sho' is."

"Yea, you get you a lil' bit and you will live in a damn hole as long as you somewhere where you can smell that man and keep up with what he doing."

"Love is a funny thang, ain't it girl?"

"Ain't no boy gon' make me fall in love!" I swore.

The women just laughed, talking more to themselves than to me, shaking their small glasses until they could hear the ice clink against all sides, and then swallowing what was left in the glass in one gulp, together.

"Probably be one of those redbone pretty boys like your mama."

"She always has been color struck and you just like her. Those the ones you got to look out for. Take every piece of money and good sense you got."

They ain't never lied.

Beauty Marks

by Mary E. Weems

All Black women have them
shaded from popcorn color
to deepest earth, their bodies spaces
of love, places for the powerful
to try and leave marks
God makes disappear in the morning.
All Black women have scars
hearts tattooed with countries
in Africa and everywhere
the diaspora
a tragic crap shoot
women-spirits hidden
under gender
marks—stolen babies,
way men take
them, take credit
without askin'.
All Black women have beauty
too many can't see
'cause they too busy
lookin' for it in a man's eyes.

Chapter 13

J was the color of cake batter and honey with a face you would never get tired of looking at. His touch was delightful and the atmosphere of truth in the room devoured the deception. He already knew my secret. My southern drawl gave it away when I got comfortable in conversation and exposed my accent. He smiled when he heard it, his eyes dancing at the thought of me, but not wanting me entirely. We were not from the same place. He was not familiar with red mud and perpetual dirt roads. "Country girls don't have enough ambition for me," he whispered, and I wished I was anything but a country girl.

He liked the way I carried home on my hips though, "country thick" he called it. But the desperation he saw in my eyes, the need for him to rescue me, was too much.

To him, I was just regular, nothing moving in me—nothing about me that could move him to love me.

With closed eyes his hands found and held every curve on my body, making me feel as delicious as the sweet kisses we passed back and forth like lies. The lovemaking was deliberate.

bodies bare
chin to neck
breath on back

held tight
arms
wrapped around
waist
lips touching
near naked
sweat-saturated skin
hot, whole, holy
forehead kisses
breath held
nose to cheek
whispered words
eyes met, staring
an audience of one
mirror reflecting
me kissing
him kissing
me
teeth on lips
sucking
wet
forehead to lips
fingers on hips
lips spread
mouth closed
heart pound
body yearn
inspired lust
kneeled knees
squeezed skin
anxious hands
floating feet
fingernail marks
pushed inside
swallowed moans
tongues touch
legs intertwine
eyes close

arms outstretch
legs open
head bent
gentle deep
fingers overlap
hands clinch
lip ear
heel back
nipple mouth
swallow whole
the smell of rain
back arched
knees bent
heat like a desert
ankles on shoulders
thighs around waist
hands on face

*

He was different from the men in Sweetwater who are half-raised and too easily satisfied. Sweetwater men had mischief in their eyes, and no intention of doing right. Those were the men Mama was afraid I would love. Men who would have a baby by you but not love you. Men who might hit you for the hell of it to see what it feels like.

I pretend we are together in real life the way we are in secret, our bodies touching so that nothing can come between us. While he sleeps I imagine what our babies would look like, and how as a couple we would kiss full on the lips before going to bed, and wake up looking at each other like ourselves in a mirror, recognizing every inch of face. Moon-shaped scars, marks, and moles like Mama.

We do it like our life depends on it. Like my body is breathless and his body is air. Like his body is thirsty and my body is water. Needing and kneading. Wanting and waning. Touching and tousling. He cradles the crevices in my body and pulls me into tender touches and deep exhales. When I finally fall into dreamless sleep, he rises, kisses my forehead, and escapes before I am lucid enough to beg him to stay.

Love Me Tender

By Mary E. Weems

I was born learning
to love other people
Breast fed
and big mouthed
Granny taught me
To get on my knees
before I knew
who God was
Mama too busy finding herself
To look for me
ugly in the mirror.

It took decades
before I stopped
stayed single long enough
to listen
my heart a fist in my chest
until I learned my lesson.

Chapter 14

Women turn to loving God when they get tired of waiting on men to love them, and they turn to men when God's love feels insufficient. The older they get the more frantic and obsessive their love. They trade men and church services until every other night is filled with sin and begging for forgiveness.

Cake-batter-colored men were a beautiful distraction while waiting on God. I had grown up finding men to be unfaithful and unreliable—yet irresistible. Being loved and left seemed an inevitable fate for women. I had never witnessed logical love. Women were never married in a way that made sense. Many of them did not live with or love their husbands. They often only shared children and last names. Unmarried women would claim they were married to Jesus, but his physical absence made their loneliness more palpable.

*

Sunday morning worship at Free Will Church was predictable. Sunday school lessons. Praise and worship. Testimony service. Choir marching. Hands clapping. Singing. Statement of faith. Call to worship. Announcements. Singing. Children's sermonette. Singing again. Offering. Scripture reading. Sermon. Singing. The Holy Ghost. Speaking tongues. The laying on of hands. Tears. Hollering hallelujah. Running. Dancing. Shouting. Fainting. More singing. Getting happy.

I was mesmerized by the source of the sounds, hums escaping red lips covered in cheap lipstick. Church women sat with their arms folded in their lap, and their legs crossed at their ankles, with their pocketbooks hanging on their wrists. The purses, all black with silver clasps, looked just alike so they never set them down, afraid someone might pick up the wrong one by mistake. The gaudy purses were empty except for crumpled-up dollar bills, a house key, Kleenex to pass around in case somebody cried, smelling salts in case somebody fainted, and pictures of great-grandchildren they had to show just in case somebody asked. All of them had on dresses.

Reverend Sam Well had been the preacher for as long as I could remember. His skin, a mahogany mask behind black coal eyes, made him seem older than he probably was. We weren't used to young preachers. Preachers were old, wise, tired, and almost exclusively male, and sometimes good looking. They were preachers on Sunday and worked regular jobs during the week. They had been there, done that, and been back again. They were reformed, born again, and full of God. You couldn't help but love and listen to preachers. Everyone found healing and hope in their raspy voices. "God is good," Reverend Sam Well began.

"All the time!" the church called back, even the small children, because they were used to the ritual and routine, the same every Sunday morning.

The microphone is passed to my mother and I am excited. Her voice is like a soprano blade, cutting people's insides open until all they can do is cry their eyes out. When she sang time stood still, fussy babies stopped crying, sleeping deacons opened their eyes, and bored teenagers stopped passing notes. My mother never sang unless she was at church and that included weddings and funerals.

The tongues sounded off like a siren following her solo, inaudible ramblings elevating to a concert of voices, "Ella-nawnda-bo-sha-ta!" First slow, then fast, the words sprang forth urgently and indecipherable, deliciously falling from the lips of the women who were truly good and who truly believed.

Reverend Sam Well stood in the pulpit behind the huge podium, teasing the congregation with his presence. His robe, his skin, his beard, all black, made it impossible not to notice him on the pedestal. He stood there shaking his head and humming to himself before saying, finally, "Lord, if we had ten thousand tongues we could not thank you enough!" Each word was punctuated by the wails of the organ and the falsettos from the congregation. He was talking to us and God at the same time. The image of white Jesus peered at us from stained-glass windows.

The claps and "thank you Jesuses" started and I could feel the Spirit turning flips in my stomach. The presence of God is intense and urgent and it makes me hot all over, and full. I cry, stand up, wave my fan, twist my hips, and try not to quench the spirit. Weezie has said resisting God is a sin.

*

"If a bird get a hold to your hair or your toe nails you will get a headache or go crazy as hell." Twiggy says this as she collects the hair from the comb only she uses and puts it in the ashtray to burn.

I don't ask how a bird would get a hold of such things, because she has already told me that birds will use anything to make a nest. She keeps her hair and nail clippings together on her nightstand instead of disposing them in the trashcan. She does not take chances.

Old wives' tales dominate our lives. We are superstitious and religious. We know that if it is raining while the sun is shining the devil is beating his wife, if someone has small ears they are stingy, if you put your pocketbook on the floor you won't have any money, if somebody dreams of fish or water it means somebody is pregnant, and a man is supposed to come in your house first on New Year's day because a woman's visit will give you bad luck. We put a coin in the hands of newborn babies when they visit our house to keep from getting rats, and we know that if you drop a fork it means someone is going to come to your house wanting something to eat. When your left hand itches you are getting some mail, if you right hand itches you are getting some money, and if either eye jumps somebody is going to make you mad. Seeing another woman naked is bad luck, letting someone sweep around your feet will keep you from getting married, and if your ears are burning somebody is talking bad about you.

We are told and reminded about these things and believe them as enthusiastically and sternly as we believe in God. We don't think about the contradictions of believing in superstitions and scriptures.

*

Children are not allowed to be baptized until they are at least twelve. We are told we have to be old enough to truly know the difference between right and wrong, and have a relationship with God for ourselves. Before that, we don't have to worry because if a child dies they automatically go to heaven. Any bad choices or behavior of a child is held against their parents. After twelve, though, you are responsible for your own soul and salvation. We have discussed these rules among ourselves at school.

Cali and I don't bother mentioning it to Mama when she pulls us to the altar, one daughter holding each hand, and announces our baptismal date. Cali is almost old enough, but I am not. Because we are both girls, and both hers, we do everything at the same time. We are not asked our opinions because they don't matter. We do what our mother tells us to.

"What is it going to do?" I ask the morning of the baptism. I am nervous about being put under water because I can't swim. I am also afraid of going to hell by accident because I am asked to make promises I can't keep yet.

"You're gon' be born again."

"Born again?"

"Saved. Saved. It just means you're saved." Mama does not have time to tell me everything I want to know. She is busy packing dry underwear and a dress for morning worship for me to put on after my conversion. She is busy trying to remember to put a shower cap in the bag so my hair won't get wet.

"Saved from what?"

"Ask Reverend Sam Well."

She always suggests I ask the preacher when she can't be bothered with my questions about God, but I am too embarrassed to tell him I don't want to be born twice, and I may not be ready to be saved. Cali does not seem nervous or bothered so I mock her ambivalence.

At the church I followed Cali through a secret door in the attic that led to the baptismal pool. Reverend Sam Well was already waiting and we could hear the congregation sounding tired and bored as they sang the hymn "Take Me to the Water." As promised, Mama was waiting at the other side of the pool to dry us off when we finished.

Cali went first because she was the oldest.

"I baptize you in the name of the Father, the Son, and the Holy Ghost." Reverend Sam Well's voice was quieter than when he was preaching. He lowered Cali into the pool and pulled her up. She rose with an all teeth and gums smile. It was my turn. I was concentrating more on holding my breath and not drowning than what Reverend Sam Well was saying. He spoke scripture-sounding words, pushed my whole body under the cold water, and pulled me up to my feet. The entire experience lasted less than a minute. The shower cap I wore to keep my hair dry had not worked and the children's choir robe that I borrowed for my transition was heavy wet. I felt dizzy when I was brought up for air. "Wooo," I said because the water was colder than I expected.

"None but the righteous shall see God," the congregation sang as I clumsily dragged my weighty, wet body to where my mother stood, waiting.

"How do you feel?" Mama asked, helping me out of the soaking wet clothes.

The truth was I didn't feel any different, but I didn't want to disappoint my mother, Reverend Sam Well, or God. "I feel saved," I answered, smiling, lying. "I feel saved!"

I Feel Saved

By Mary E. Weems

When Auntie Ethel called
told mama to have me ready,
as the oldest, on Sunday,
to do something she never explained,
I'd never been to church

Don't remember how old
I was, but felt everything
when a Black woman dressed in white
put a sheet over my head, led me to the edge
of a pool (I can't swim)
so the pastor could dunk me, back first
into water so cold
I couldn't hear a word
He said.

Chapter 15

The day after Thanksgiving, a man I didn't recognize knocked on the door and let himself in. Aunt Peaches and Twiggy greeted him like he was someone they used to know, but didn't anymore. They spoke and smiled, but didn't touch. The man's voice was husky and old, his rounded teeth the color of parchment paper. He did not look like anybody I knew.

"This must be Bread's child," he decided, leaning back into the raggedy recliner chair and then sitting up, when he realized it didn't recline anymore.

"She can talk," Peaches said.

"What's your name?" he asked.

"Bird."

"Bird, huh?" He seemed to be considering whether or not my answer was a lie. "How old are you?"

"Ten."

He smiled and grunted at the same time and I could almost see inside his mouth, thick spit collecting in the corners of his lips. I wanted him to wipe his lips and close his mouth. "I remember when your mama was your age."

I was altogether disinterested in what the man had to say, in the way that I was with all adults who seemed surprised that you had actually continued to grow older and taller when they weren't around to witness it for themselves. I also knew that he was talking more about me than to me—the way adults generally did. I scooted to the front of the television so I could hear the cartoons.

"What you know good?" Twiggy asked the stranger.

"Just got back from up north, got some news to tell y'all, 'bout what I heard while I was up there."

"Bird, get your ass in the back room somewhere. You see grown folks talking." Twiggy pulled a crumpled pack of Salem cigarettes from her back pocket and a Bic lighter from the other one.

On cue I stood up and walked slowly, hoping they would accidentally say something while I was still in the hall, but they didn't. There was complete silence until I was in the room I shared with Mama and Cali and the door was shut all the way. I sat on the floor and pressed my whole body against the wall to try to hear. It was mostly muffled voices, until finally, Peaches hollered out a scream so loud it sent a chill through my body. I knew better than to come out so I waited for the back door to close. It took forty-five minutes.

I eased out of the bedroom and stayed in the hallway and slid down the wall, sitting with my legs stretched out. Eventually, Cali walked in and slammed the door behind her. She could tell something wasn't right and looked at me for answers but only received my hunched shoulders. I did not know what was going on. We sat next to each other, in the hallway, and waited for the adults to speak.

*

"I'm looking for John Lately," Peaches said into the phone. She was surprised at how her daddy's name sounded coming out of her mouth. She had never called his full name, his real name, always said Daddy, always heard Cake or Johnny Cake when anyone referred to him.

Peaches had been calling hospitals in Baltimore, trying to find out if they had admitted John "Cake" Lately. He had been gone for twenty years without coming back or calling, but now he was missing from people who had kept up with where he was.

"He dead." Peaches' words came out slow and angry. She said them like she was speaking in a foreign language, repeating words that she didn't fully understand.

"Where you get that from?" Twiggy wanted to know.

"The woman on the phone said they have his death certificate. He been dead two years next month."

"Two years?" Bread was home now, stunned at the news she got when she walked in the door.

"They said he was just left at the hospital—and no one claimed his body. The records say that the woman with him didn't mention family or children and she didn't want to pay to bury the body so she just left him there."

"What woman?" Twiggy was surprised that even when he was dead she was jealous over Cake.

"I don't know, they didn't say her name—only that it was his common-law wife."

"Common law my ass," Twiggy said under her breath while she listened to Peaches give the rest of the information. She would need to go to Baltimore with proof of being his wife to get his death certificate, and she would need his death certificate to claim his life insurance. She had been struggling with bills and a couple of hundred dollars, which was all the policy was worth, was better than nothing.

Twiggy, Peaches, and Bread sat there, not saying anything. And Bebe, opening the door, broke the silence. Then Little. Then Junior.

"Daddy dead," Peaches announced each time a sibling walked in the door.

"Daddy dead?" They all repeated her words as a question, confused because they were not accustomed to saying Daddy anymore.

"How'd he die?" Little was the first to ask.

"Probably drunk his fool self to death," Twiggy guessed.

"The doctor said he had liver failure," Peaches said slowly. "Said he was a alcoholic, but otherwise in good health. They donated all of his organs, even his skin and his eyes. The only thing they couldn't use was his liver."

"Donated his organs where?"

"To people who needed 'em."

"So you mean to tell me there is somebody, somewhere with daddy's eyes and daddy's skin and daddy's heart?" Bread looked around the room, thinking that Peaches was the only one in the house with Cake's eyes, Cake's skin, and Cake's heart.

"Somewhere," Peaches said finally. "At least that's something."

I thought it was creepy that there were people walking around with parts of my Mama's daddy in them. For a long time I would look at people with eyes like Peaches and wonder if they were his.

"Where is he buried?" Junior wanted to know.

"He won't buried—he was cremated. Burnt up." "So we can't even give him a funeral?"

"Hell, he been dead two years, Junior," Twiggy said and rolled her eyes.

*

Aunt Peaches was the most visibly distraught at Cake's death. For days she stayed in the bed and cried. She was inconsolable. Everybody else went on about their business, going to work, cooking food, tending to children. Hearing that Cake died was like hearing that someone died that you used to know a long time ago. You feel sorry for them but your mourning isn't immediate, the hurt not as significant as if it was someone you were used to seeing, someone you would miss. In every way that counted, Cake had been a stranger, absent from their lives for more years than he had been present, and absent from my life altogether. It was like he had always been dead.

*

On January 1, Twiggy cooked the traditional New Year's meal. Collard greens were supposed to bring money, black-eyed peas brought good luck, and hog jowls brought favor. The next day, while they were still off from work, she was driving up to Maryland with Peaches and Bebe to pick up Cake's death certificate. They needed his death to be official so that she could collect the life insurance, transfer the land deed, and take his name off of the bills. They left in the middle of the night and returned by the time Cali and I made it home from school. I worried that going to where Cake died would make everybody start missing him all over again. No one had laughed or smiled since we found out he was dead. It was as if everybody was feeling emotions but refusing sadness. Twiggy was mad, Peaches cried, Junior was in denial, Little didn't want to talk about it, and my mother was indifferent. Cali and I didn't know how we were supposed to feel because all we ever knew about Cake Lately was that he was gone. Him being dead was no different.

His children needed closure. There were no pictures of him, only stories. Aunt Bebe helped everybody concentrate on what Cake looked like by describing his face and telling us stories about him. "He had eyes like Peaches," she said describing him and helping her brothers and sisters remember. They all sat around the living room, right before the six-hour trip to Baltimore, reacting to their daddy's death and recalling what he was like. They smiled closed-mouth smiles and didn't laugh. "He was crazy about Mama," Aunt Bebe said. Grandma Twiggy rolled her eyes.

*

When the school bus stopped in front of our house the next day Grandma Twiggy's brown sugar cougar was back in the yard and we knew that she and our aunts had made it back home. I had announced in school that my grandfather died. The teachers were sympathetic and patted me on my shoulders. The other children in my class looked at me confused. They didn't know I had a grandfather.

When I followed Cali through the screen door, I was not sure what we would find. Perhaps they would be sitting together in the den crying all over again like they had when they first knew he was gone, or maybe things would finally get back to normal. I was tired of grieving, especially since mustering up tears about a stranger is nearly impossible for a ten-year-old. I had never seen every woman in my family cry at the same time; someone always knew to be strong for the others. I had never seen my grandmother cry at all. Her tears collected in her eyes without falling.

No one was crying when we peeped around the corner. Aunt Bebe's face was suspicious.

"Y'all want something to eat?" Grandma Twiggy called from the kitchen. She was frying chicken drumsticks and there was something simmering in the pressure pot but I couldn't tell what it was.

"Yep!" I said and plopped on the couch next to Aunt Bebe. Having her at our house in the middle of the week was a treat. She was the aunt who always came with treats in her pockets and liked to make us laugh. I figured her fascination with Cali and me was connected to the fact that her children were grown and she only saw us once a week, unlike Peaches, who was stuck with us 24/7.

Cali was the first to notice the clay jar on the coffee table. "Where that come from?"

The jar was deep blue and seemed too fancy for our house. I had never seen it before.

"We brought it back from Baltimore," Aunt Bebe said immediately. She, Twiggy, and Peaches eyed each other and then went back to what they were doing.

"What's in it?" I asked, already touching it and rubbing my curious hands up and down its slick base. It was not unusual for family members to bring back souvenirs from road trips.

"Daddy," Aunt Bebe said.

"Whaaaaaaaaaaaat!?!?"

"His ashes." She continued, "We brought him back from Baltimore."

"Ewh, ewh, ewh!" I threw my hands in the air like they were on fire and watched to see what Cali would do. Before we could move out of the way Aunt Bebe had already grabbed the jar to chase us and the back door would not open fast enough. She ran us all around the yard with the jar, finally catching me, dropping the ashes in the grass and rubbing the residue on my arm as I wailed in agony.

"That's your granddaddy, girl!" She was rubbing the grayish-white powder on my skin and laughing out loud to herself. "He ain't gon' hurt ya."

I hollered like somebody was trying to kill me. I knew I would get in trouble for being loud but I didn't care. I didn't want no two-years-dead-man ashes on my arm.

"Shut your damn mouth!" Twiggy said coming outside. "That ain't no damn Cake. Ain't nothing but some burned up leaves from the trash pile. Hush all that fuss."

By now Aunt Bebe was beside herself laughing. I loved her laugh and it was the sincerity of her chuckles and Cali's return from across the ditch that confirmed it had all been a joke. Five minutes later I still did not find it funny. I was traumatized, half-crying, half-laughing. Cali figured they wouldn't lie about the ashes, especially since no one seemed to mind that half of them had fallen on the ground and gotten mixed up with the dirt. She offered me temporary pity, breathing hard from having run, and grateful that she had outrun Aunt Bebe's short legs. Cali put her hands on her hips and watched Peaches retrieve the jar and refill it with dirt and cigarette ashes. She put the top on it and wrapped some tape around it to keep it from falling off, since the top had chipped when Aunt Bebe dropped it on the ground. We figured they had concocted the scheme on the long ride home and that it was, perhaps, their way of grieving and feeling better. Peaches was laughing and smiling again [...] finally.

"Now y'all hush ya mouth now," Aunt Bebe instructed us as she took the jar from Peaches' hands. "Don't say nothin'. I'm gon' trick Junior, Bread, and Little when they get home."

*

Several years later, I found out that Johnny Cake Lately was not my biological grandfather. I overheard the truth in a whispered conversation. The man who was my mother's real father had lived in Sweetwater all along. I remember his face. Skin like burnt leather. Bald head. Huge hands passing me wrinkled dollar bills from deep pockets. Me, not knowing him, but grateful for the dollar and temporary attention. Toothless smiles on Tuesdays. Tractor pulling on Wednesdays. Fifteen miles per hour on long roads. Muddy overalls and dirty fingernails on Thursdays. Work boots. Tired eyes behind bifocal glasses on Sundays. Dark suits over wide shoulders. He was chocolate brown with a nose like my mama's.

Poem for Mama's Father

by Mary E. Weems

I wish you'd put even a little of you
in my hand with dollars
passed like secret notes in school
Your eyes, bald head
as silent as me looking up
never once wondering why
out of all the little girls in town
you paid attention to me.

Chapter 16

Twiggy always dressed sharp and kept her hair fixed. She didn't wear makeup, except lipstick, which was enough to show off her face. It was the same whether she was supervising housekeepers at the hospital or pulling heads off of chickens at the chicken plant. Her work clothes were dry cleaned and her jeans had a crease down the middle like a dividing white line. Her uniform shirt was the color of potato salad with too much mayonnaise, and she wore a name tag over her left titty. The tag said supervisor, with Sadie Lately on the bottom, because people at work didn't know that nobody called her that at home. At home she was Twiggy, mama, or grah-mah. She would go so long sometimes without hearing her real name that it sounded strange when she heard it, and for a minute she would pause to wonder who was being talked about.

After working twenty years at a factory and another ten years at the hospital, people called her Ms. Lately or Ms. Sadie because she was old enough to be their mama. They respected her, feared her, and looked up to her. She expected the same behavior from her children and grandchildren.

Twiggy never wears anything but pants, with pockets in the back so she has somewhere to keep her pock-a-book, a men's wallet she carries her money and driver's license in. She has never carried a purse or had a checkbook. She pays everything with cash. Money left over after bills are paid and groceries are made is hidden in pillow cases for safe keeping.

Twiggy has never been feminine. She is not soft-spoken, delicate, or dainty. She is not sensitive or sentimental. She prefers boy children, meanness, and independence. You can't help but be tough when you grow up with a mama who is dead because she didn't do nothing but have children and then die doing it, like there is nothing left to do after that. There was nobody there to teach her how to be a woman, wife, or mother so she taught herself, and did the best she could.

*

She tells me, I can do what I want to do when people tell her I've been places I have no business, or wear the wrong thing to church. She encourages my rebellion, tells me I am just like her that way, and smiles. She doesn't think I need to get married if I don't want to, or stay around Sweetwater to listen to people talk shit because they don't have anything better to do. She is stronger than me and doesn't need to leave to be happy. She understands that leaving is the only way I can be happy. She reckons I will go away like her brothers and sisters, get married, make babies, and then come back. But then she worries that I am the kind of woman, men change their minds about after a while. She doesn't know why because I am not hard to look at or get along with. I was raised right and I'm not unclean. But she doesn't believe I should worry about it, and says, "You don't need nobody trying to tell you what to do no way."

We get along better now that I am grown. We have the kind of conversations I was excluded from when I was a child, and I know I have earned her respect. When I tell her I am going away to school she doesn't protest or celebrate. She doesn't ask what I am going to school for or how long I will be gone. She doesn't say she is proud or make a scene. It is as if she knew all along.

In her older age she has become more superstitious. She refuses to say "goodbye" on the telephone or face-to-face. It is as if she fears goodbye means forever so she opts for just hanging up the telephone or saying "see you later." My infrequent visits home yield the same reply when I prepare to leave.

"I'll be back," I promise, kissing her cheek and hugging her neck.

"I'll be here," she says, folding her arms and breathing in before a deep exhale.

*

Quiet as it's kept, women are rarely conscious of their choices as choices in Sweetwater. Their lives are predictable in the way they learn, in the way they love, in the way they are loved back, and the choices that don't seem like choices. To change the circularity of their lives they sometimes have to do something altogether different. To keep from marrying early, loving desperately, and mothering undeliberately, they sometimes have to leave and then come back. To keep from leaving they marry, work, worship, love, and make babies, embracing themselves and the beauty inherent in a place so familiar it reaches back generations. The lure of Sweetwater can draw you in like the arms of a man or woman you once loved and seduce you to stay put. Its pull is seductive. Its reach is long.

Not much has changed in Sweetwater over the years. People still go in and out, but mostly stay in. The community populates itself from the inside and families keep growing, only occasionally managing to escape. People still love on each other and look past faults. People still attend weekly work and worship. People still talk about what goes on behind closed doors and thick shades. People still occupy themselves with other folks' business. People still look for ways to break the monotony of repetitive days. People still choose forgiveness over forgetfulness. People still remember. And they hold on to the way Sweetwater makes them feel.

Part Three

(Bittersweet) Endings

Conclusion

Why Black Women's Stories Matter

The stories in this book include an everyday backdrop of inconspicuous violence, insidious social oppression, and limited options. Sweetwateran women's lives are a combination of ugly myths, debilitating stereotypes, visceral realities, and temporary escapes. Their negotiation of subjugation shows their fragility and vulnerability as well as their strength. It is their shared responses to pain and disappointment, not the conditions that cause their pain and disappointment, that generate their resilience.

The black women in these stories organize their lives in response to life's circumstances. The multiplicative nature of their raced, gendered, and class oppression makes their stories intersectional and involuntary. They confront stereotypes by resisting them, and sometimes adapting to them, because in many ways our environment informs our choices. The self-segregation of *Sweetwater* provides an insulated and isolated space where stories are passed back and forth without restraint. *Sweetwater* is also a place where families recycle bad habits, daughters inherit their mothers' fears and dreams, and romantic love feels fleeting, if not impossible. Davis (2007) says "Black women's collective experience is a cultural performance of survival and resistance" (p. 124), and these stories carry a performative impulse that reinforces what it looks like when women are constantly negotiating how to make a way out of no way, or a dollar out of fifteen cents.

Reconceptualizing rural black women's lived realities urges us to see rural black women's stories as collective narratives of resilience and social justice.

The activism in the individual and collective lives of the women of *Sweetwater* is evidenced through their community engagement, church activities, involvement in schooling and teaching their children, and their participation in local politics. The justice plays out in their resilient capacity to survive courageously under unimaginable circumstances and to live meaningful lives. Social justice requires an engagement and investment in seeking progress, even if it is slow moving and does not look like progress from the outside. These stories matter because they recognize social justice in everyday acts and participatory practices. In *Sweetwater* social justice is inclusive of everyday efforts at endurance, including self-care, prayer, gestures of support, shared child-care, and informal education. They don't just say, they do. They act. They en-act. They re-act.

The performative impulse of black women's storytelling encourages an embodied, rather than ephemeral experience. These stories matter because they stay with you like memories, and ask what happens when injustice becomes normalized and realities are pathologized? While many of the social injustices embedded within these stories are described and understood as simply "ways of life," they are viewed, from the outside looking in, as limitations. These stories ask, how do our communities instill a particular sense of just and right behavior, and how do these expectations translate to people inside and outside of our communities? What does justice look like from the inside looking out? These stories matter because they ask difficult, unanswerable questions.

Social justice moves us toward action and the antithesis of silence. Black communities always have some notion of fairness, and if/when there are no systematic ways to work through injustice, we do so emotionally and interpersonally. And while our negotiations may look like pathologies, it becomes social justice to recognize and identify where the justice and love is—which, as these stories demonstrate, is usually on the margins. Love and justice is on the outside of marriages and the inside of churches. In homes. In hands. In laughter. In escape. These stories identify love and justice in the ordinariness of living. Therefore, the goal of this work is not to further primitivize or demonize black women, but rather to look at how they work out and through concepts of love and justice. These stories matter because they create and chronicle social justice.

Sweetwater makes sense of how rural black women can use (their) stories to respond to the complicated representations of who they are and what they know. Mother wit refers to having natural intelligence, or common sense. Often referenced in rural communities, it speaks to the ways that education is not always structured or deliberate. This book suggests that black women can learn generalizable truths and theorize about their lives through storytelling. Accordingly, nontraditional education is seen as a form of activism, and personal suffering, and tragedies as life lessons. These stories matter because they challenge conventional ways of knowing and offer an epistemological intervention that privileges and centers black women's self-definition.

Sweetwater stories are truthful, they forward discussions of social justice in rural spaces, they contribute to scholarship while privileging black women's lived experience(s), they consider how rural black women make meaning and respond to muteness, they distinguish between everyday talk and conversation, they offer a commentary of the singular and interior lives of rural black women, they tell it like it is, they prioritize the particularities of black women's everyday lives, they embrace and confront stereotypes, they offer multiple perspectives, they are intersectional, they are academic, they are democratic, they contribute to our literacy of black women's lives, they challenge our conceptions of normality, they represent deep realities, they are generalizable, they are generational, they make black women visible, they are authentic, they are demonstrative, they are historical, and they leave a narrative inheritance. Goodall (2005) describes narrative inheritance as the stories given to children by and about family members. I believe that narrative inheritance can also include cultural and community stories, and stories about forbearers that are passed down to leave a legacy. These stories matter because they remind me of who I am, who I belong to, and where I come from.

Sweetwater Re/View(s)

Book Reviews/Book Forum Excerpts

Sweetwater has been taken up in both academic and community spaces, including classrooms, roundtables, book readings, book clubs, signings, lectures, conference panels, and talk backs. This chapter includes excerpts of published and previously unpublished responses to *Sweetwater*, including passages from a book forum in the Spring 2015 issue of Departures in Critical Qualitative Research (formerly Qualitative Communication Research). . The book forum featured solicited book reviews alongside select responses from panels at the 2013 National Communication Association Convention, and the 2014 International Congress of Qualitative Inquiry. The chapter also includes an excerpt from the book review "Kindred Narratives: Reflections of Southern Black Orality in Sweetwater," by Aisha Durham, which was originally published in Qualitative Inquiry (2015) and republished in the Departures forum. "Small Doses," a book review published in The Qualitative Report by Sabrina Cherry, is shared in its entirety, followed by unpublished responses given during a book reaction panel, entitled "Sweetwater along the Potomac" at the 2013 National Communication Association convention in Washington, DC.

The full articles can be obtained by accessing the cited original source.

Sweet Mentoring (Excerpt)
Carolyn Ellis
Carolyn Ellis, "Sweet Mentoring," *Departures in Critical Qualitative Research* 4, no. 1 (2015): 84-85. Reprinted with permission from University of California Press. All rights reserved.

Robin takes my class in autoethnography; she takes Art's class in narrative; she takes all the classes we teach. She writes; she astonishes; she writes more; she astonishes more. She chooses me and Art to be her mentors. We choose her to be our student and our academic daughter. She names me "Mami."

Later, when we talk about why she chose that name for me, she will say, "I come from a community where folk are rarely called by their birth names. Giving people nicknames and shortening their names are gestures of love and respect. I call my biological mother 'Mommie' and my grandmother 'Mama.' I felt that calling you Mami not only acknowledged how special our relationship was to me, but also signified that we were chosen family for each other. Calling you Mami doesn't mean you birthed me, but it does mean you carried me—in concert with the other mothers in my life—through the process of getting my PhD and becoming the woman I am."

Throughout the PhD process, I want to carry her gently—to challenge her to be all she can be, but not push her too far. "You're interested in examining your own experiences," I say, when she is ready to propose her dissertation research. "How do you feel about studying your home community?"

Robin looks enthusiastic and then hesitates. "I am interested in portraying the place I came from, the experience of being there, for me and for the women in my life who were there before me, for me, and who are still there, making a life," she says, "but […]"

I wait.

"But collecting and telling stories from that place, my place, and bringing them to the academy scares me."

I wait, but she doesn't say anything more. So I say, "I always wanted to study my rural community and regret that I never did."

"I want to do it," she says, letting her excitement run full force now, spurred perhaps by my regret. I tell her that together we'll figure out what to say and how to say it, and even more importantly, what not to say and why.

Later she will tell me that in some ways she saw this study as being "our" study, a way for her to "go back home" for both of us. I often found myself experiencing her project vicariously, though I did not tell her so, at least not then.

We meet regularly. Robin tells me stories of growing up in a small, working class and black community in the rural South. They are stories about violence, racism, alcoholism, family secrets, deceit, running around, disappointments, joys, celebrations, and adventures, and the women, always the women, who are there for her. I tell her stories of growing up in a small, working-class, and white community in the rural South—of the area known as "colored hill," of racism, of alcoholism, family secrets, deceit, running around, disappointments, joys, celebrations, and adventures, and my family—the women and men—who were always there for me. Exhausted from recounting the memories, we hug and shed a few tears. She goes off to write, while I sit and stare at the photos of my family tacked on my office wall, considering the similarities (and differences) in my and Robin's experiences. I recall the stories I have written about growing up in the rural South, and inspired by Robin's courage, I consider those I still want to write.

Robin gives me pages, some similar to the ones that follow this introduction. I eagerly take in every word, image, emotion, and scene. I am astounded by her talent, her ability to take her reader into the action and emotions. She makes me feel, taste, hear, and be with the women—and her—as they live through the complexities and mundane details of daily and extraordinary life. We talk of ethics, responsibilities, hurt, and pain as we consider what to reveal and what to conceal, how to tell it, what to tell, how to protect, how to take her academic words back home, how to bring her home life into the academy, for what purpose, and with what result.

"Show, Don't Tell": Redefining Contemporary Black Southern Rurality in Robin M. Boylorn's Sweetwater (Excerpt)

Brittney Cooper and Susana M. Morris

Brittney Cooper and Susana M. Morris, "'Show, Don't Tell': Redefining Contemporary Black Southern Rurality in Robin M. Boylorn's *Sweetwater*," *Departures in Critical Qualitative Research* 4, no. 1 (2015): 107-108. Reprinted with permission from University of California Press. All rights reserved.

Robin M. Boylorn's riveting autoethnographic account Sweetwater feels like home. The women of Sweetwater emerge in these stories with full-bodied voices, full-bellied laughs, and lives rich with love, drama, secrets, and knowing. These women are specific to their own time and place, and yet familiar to the mamas, grandmamas, aunties, cousins, and motley crews of community folk who populate our own landscapes of home. That Sweetwater can tell the story of rural women's lives in North Carolina and signify on our own experiences of Black women's lives in places as seemingly disparate as small town Louisiana and Jamaica reflect the deep resonances of Boylorn's account.

Folks advise aspiring writers to do the following: "Show, don't tell." Now, this may be a way to get writers to narrate experience better or prove a point, but it is also a piece of motherwit we both heard growing up: "I can show you better than I can tell you." In *Sweetwater*, Boylorn has let these women tell it all. And in the masterful ways she weaves the narrative voices and details of these many intertwined lives together, she has shown us everything. Indeed, much of what is most compelling about *Sweetwater* is its firsthand emphasis on black women's interiority. Historically, black women are often overtheorized, pathologized, and talked about rather than heard for what they have to say. *Sweetwater*, however, joins the ranks of other black feminist work that highlights black women's agency and how we make sense of the world ourselves.

We feel like we know our own lives better now, understand the women in our own stories more fully. And this is how work written with a certain aplomb and aptitude for black feminist epistemology sits on the tongue and stays in the mind. Boylorn clearly respects the ways of knowing and cosmologies these rural women have created to understand their lives, loves, and losses. They have their own ideas about what love is, their own understandings and narrations of desire, a communally wrought faith in God, even though there are a few brave dissenters, and their own methods of dealing with grief. However, Boylorn never caricatures the women's lives or choices.

To that end, *Sweetwater* reveals the complicated ways in which black women understand their own identities and their connection to respectability and respectability politics. Boylorn reveals women who skillfully (and sometimes not so skillfully) navigate life and love while adhering to conventional social scripts, outright rejecting these scripts, and more often than not, tipping on a tightrope somewhere in between. The text underscores the dynamic, thoughtful, and tenacious ways of engaging a world hostile to their existence, one in which being black, female, rural, and poor means that their lives are perceived to have less worth than those who do not fit into these marginalized categories.

We know that rural communities and the people who live in them are frequently considered throwaway communities, folk we relegate to a backwater, assured that by leaving them in the past or by forcing them there, we give those daughters who migrate a sure standard by which to mark *progress*. Boylorn's work does not allow us to do that. She refuses us the comfort of a conventional, provincial, or linear narrative wherein the women's stories she shares are simply spectacles for our consumption that will be forgotten once we close the pages of the book. She makes us reckon with the work and lives of women for whom reckoning with all the cards life deals is like breathing.

The critical interventions that *Sweetwater* makes are manifold. Although autoethnographic in nature, *Sweetwater* reminds us of a range of black women's classic literary texts from across the African Diaspora, such as Alice Walker's "Everyday Use," Gloria Naylor's *Mama Day*, Michelle Cliff's *No Telephone to Heaven*, and Edwidge Danticat's *Breath, Eyes, Memory*. These stories are fictional accounts of the children who left and returned home. In that regard, the work blends the tensions of what Carole Boyce Davies calls "migratory subjectivities" we form upon leaving, and the challenges of being a native informant. In this regard, *Sweetwater* contributes both to the scholarship on rural black women's lives and to the record of literary representation of these lives.

Kindred Narratives: Reflections of Southern Black Orality in Sweetwater (Excerpt)

Aisha Durham

Aisha Durham, "Kindred Narratives: Reflections of Southern Black Orality in Sweetwater," *Qualitative Inquiry* 21, no. 2 (2015): 122-24. Reprinted with permission from Sage. All rights reserved.

*This article was also published in Departures in Critical Qualitative Research, Vol. 4, number 1, pp. 110-113.

Sweetwater is a slow cooked auto/ethnography. Each story has a distinct yet complementary character that becomes more layered and deeply textured as the reader stews at home with the folks from "The Bottom." Author Robin "Bird" Boylorn recovers open secrets and recasts the rural apart from its popular and academic constructions that treat it as a lost space where time has stopped or has reversed altogether, or as a less significant place to talk about contemporary blackness, considering much of our collective experience since the great black migration(s) has been defined through the urban, cosmopolitan black masculine. Boylorn blends black vernacular and poetic prose with womanist and feminist epistemologies to concoct a homemade familial narrative that is uniquely Southern and unapologetically black woman-centered.

I can taste *Sweetwater*. It is not so much her description about the aroma of fried fatback and pickled eggs and the lingering ammonia, chicken stench as it is the bittersweet, matrifocal memories she pens about lovers and loved ones fighting to see themselves, to free themselves, to be (good with and to) themselves using whatever cultural tools at hand. One of the tools both Boylorn and other womenfolk use is the word. Boylorn stuffs us with a sensory experience rooted in African diasporic storytelling, which privileges orality, interaction, and spirituality. Through idioms, colloquial references, and poetry, she invites us to take in *Sweetwater* aloud. D. Soyini Madison suggests orality—that connection between sound and rhythm—is important not only to understand black speech but to also to make sense of how we signify and contextualize the world. Boylorn purposefully provides a nonlinear, polyvocal narrative—one that stirs folklore with history, personal memory with transcribed interviews, and the sacred with the secular. (She does so with declarations about being superstitious and religious, and with descriptions of the cussing churchwomen.) This unlikely marriage between black love and hate follows black girls to womanhood where they experience lifetime tussles with wonderful-terrible men. Still, the redemption songs that Boylorn writes is situated in a narrative place of both trial and triumph—a place where black women have been unable to occupy historically. The conversations among Sweetwaterans *within* each chapter are echoed *across* chapters with the integration of "poetic windows" from the city-born series editor Mary E. Weems. Both conversations reflect call-and-response that is also endemic of African diasporic storytelling and performance. Taken together, *Sweetwater* highlights a polyvocal, citational style represented in different writing forms and crafted by a diverse group of women who make up a shared experience of black womanhood.

The Road to Sweetwater (Excerpt)

Christopher N. Poulos

Christopher N. Poulos, "The Road to *Sweetwater*," *Departures in Critical Qualitative Research* 4, no. 1 (2015): 114; 115-116. Reprinted with permission from University of California Press. All rights reserved.

Dusty roads. Poverty. Sweet tea. Dark secrets. Violence. Sweaty brows. Jesus. Lots of Jesus. Sweet Jesus.

Sweetwater.

I've never been to Sweetwater, but I have stumbled across small rural places in the South. I did not linger. I'm mostly a city boy who escapes to Western wilderness, not to rural small towns. I am a product of the big, urban-suburban sprawl of Atlanta and Denver. Sweetwater is not my place.

But now, I think I've been as close to there as you can get without having lived there. I've read Robin M. Boylorn's book.

And this experience triggered a memory.

October 2001. It is my first year at my first real academic job, at the University of North Carolina at Greensboro. I'm standing in my Department Chair's office. His name is Buddy Goodall. You all know him—or, at least, you know his writing. Privately, I am awed by him, though I would never tell him that. He is, after all, an ethnographic rock star. And I'm a rock star wannabe.

Of course, I'm not the only person who thinks this about Buddy.

I'm pretty sure *he* thinks it, though maybe he's a little sheepish about it. Just a little. What I do know for sure is that he thinks of himself as a *writer*, first and foremost. For him, writing is a noble art, a powerful meaning-making enterprise. For him, writing is both search and research. It is a wondrous quest. Writers stir magic into the mystery of life. Good writers stir up trouble, passion, joy, sorrow, anxiety, pain, hope, despair. Good writers move readers. Really good writers move readers to *write*.

On this day, we are talking about our graduate students. I point to a name on the roster of my upcoming Relational Communication seminar.

"What about this one?" I ask.

He glances at the sheet, smiles.

"Ah, Robin. Have you met her?"

"Uh, yeah. Briefly."

"Well, she's a country Carolina girl. A little on the shy side, but she's gaining her voice. Keep an eye on her. She's going places."

He pauses, then: "She's a writer!" he exclaims, with a trace of admiration in his voice.

Now, most of you know that Buddy has left us, has slipped the bonds that held him to this earth. But knowing him as I do, I know at least one thing beyond his reverence for writing. He loved being right. And in Robin's case—was he right!

And I think I know what Buddy saw in Robin's writing. You see, there was a certain something he liked to do in his own writing. Call it diving into the mystery of the ordinary—and finding something extraordinary there. And Robin does that beautifully. Where Buddy did it somewhat sardonically, Robin does it poetically, charmingly, evocatively.

Like I said, Robin finds—or maybe sews, or kneads, or draws, or pulls, or shoves, or yanks, or maybe just stirs up a swirl of extraordinary ordinariness. She takes the ordinary, everyday lives of poor, rural, black Southern women, and transforms them into a remarkable stew of relations, of connections, of the loose bonds of community.

***

And so we enter Sweetwater, this little town on the edge of deeply nuanced, but often overlooked, problems of race and class and gender and poverty—and yes, tragedy. And, while this is a book about expected "big" issues like race and class and gender and poverty, mostly, it's a book about *people in the predicaments of place and relationship.* This life Robin portrays has bumps and dips and puddles and holes and sharp turns, and much unevenness. But somehow, the women of Sweetwater hold on, and they go on, despite the many odds against them.

This remarkable story of ordinary but remarkable people, in the end, reveals, beautifully, the heart at the center of their resilience, the heart that generates their courage, the heart that binds them together and sometimes tears them apart. That is the magic of Robin's writing. I am in this place with these people, in a place I've never been, sitting with them, feeling their joys and sorrows, their struggles and their strains, their hot flaring anger and their stone cold indifference. I feel their resilience. I feel their heart.

Black Girl Strong(er): A Performative Response to Sweetwater by Robin M. Boylorn (Excerpt)

Amber Johnson

Amber Johnson, "'Black Girl Strong(er): A Performative Response to Sweetwater by Robin M. Boylorn," *Departures in Critical Qualitative Research* 4, no. 1 (2015): 117-119. Reprinted with permission from University of California Press. All rights reserved.

> Black girl strong.
> there is no safe space for black girls
> the grass is always greener
> doesn't translate when
> the grass is dead
> the gate is bent
> hovering
> shaded

dirty
covered in trash
memories
junk cars
    and stains
exposed
like sores leaking pus under the sun
black girls have to be strong.

But what makes black girls strong(er)?

my body exposed in her Sweetwater
    her stories are not my own, but my body lives there
    stuck,
    in a space of black girl blues
        trying
        prying
        searching
            for a way out
        into
        a center
        a nucleus
        that i do not belong to
        yet claim as my own
            big city girl knows what it means to be resilient
i wonder though, is resilience enough?
    definition:
    springing back; rebounding.
    returning to the original form or position after being bent,
        compressed, or stretched.
    recovering readily from illness, depression, adversity, or the like
    buoyant

as communication scholars, we know that to experience is never to return to the original.
our experiences change our lives. we cannot undo the bends, the compressions, the stretching. we become strong(er) in our search to resist. we become scholars of "social justice" by recognizing and identifying "where

the justice and love is" —which, as these stories demonstrate, is usually on the margins.

had Robin been only resilient, would we have this body of work?
    this moment to unpack these moments
had Robin been only resilient,
    an adjective resulting in the body's ability to exist despite and beyond circumstance,
        would we be gathered around in this forum,
        talking about what it means to be resilient,
        learning from these narratives
        and theorizing about bodies standing firm in their boots
        no matter the weather?

No.

this book forced me to question resiliency
    to question what it means to be described as being resilient.
        The women laced within the pages are magnificent in their resilience.
        Strong and beautiful in their lived responses to the injustices of life.
        Strong(er) in their willingness to publish these stories as confession, and leave them as inheritance to Bird.
        Robin, the author, is strong(er).
        Strong(er) for leaving them with us.

Robin, and the Women of Sweetwater, and we, are not just resilient
Robin, and the Women of Sweetwater, and we, are verbs
purposefully weaving
our way in and out
of story.
    in to learn
    in to reflect
    out to spread
    out to be active
    out to change.

Resiliency alone is not enough for us. We have to act.
We have to become verbs and move. Be Strong(er).

An Unsettled I: A Response to Robin M. Boylorn's Sweetwater (Excerpt)

Tami Spry

Tami Spry, "An Unsettled I: A Response to Robin M. Boylorn's *Sweetwater*," *Departures in Critical Qualitative Research* 4, no. 1 (2015): 121-122. Reprinted with permission from University of California Press. All rights reserved.

An unsettled I.

My "whitegirlness" is unsettled by this book, unsettling privilege being one of the best reasons for performative autoethnography.

My whitegirlness that feels the bones of systemic and familial racism,

the whitegirl who knows she can and cannot avoid

the presence and absence of embodied race,

who is unsettled by the so little room in our language system

to articulate the complexity of negotiating race with and between selves/others/bodies/cultures.

And the whitegirl who knows she could recede into an apoliticized whiteness

trying to push and push the unsettled back into a body numbed by privilege.

In *Twilight: Los Angeles, 1992*, Anna Deavere Smith notes that we have yet to find a language that speaks the complexity of race while simultaneously creating supportive and productive diverse communities. Cornell West, in writing of the Los Angeles uprising, argues "either we learn a new language of empathy and compassion, or the fire this time will consume us all." I neither trust nor can live without language; but, trust it or not, language will represent me, others, culture, based on its collective will composed by those in various kinds of power at the moment of utterance. Sometimes I am one of those in power. Sometimes not. And so within Smith's and West's complexity, compassion, and fire I think it best to remain an "unsettled I," alarming the whitegirl, magnifying the nerves beneath her freckled melanin.

Because I do not want to engage, as Robin puts it, the "pigeon-holed stereo-types (of black women as angry, mean, reckless, inherently strong, combative, hypersexual, overly religious, etc.)." The stereotypes claw at my own background, where deeply racist aunts and uncles touted these ways of being as evidence for their own refusal to think beyond an ignorance of the other, allowing them to find some class-based solace in relation to their own feelings of sociocultural worthless-ness, as they could easily be—and surely were—profiled as white trash.

And so I find myself situated where any good scholarship should place me, betwixt and between excruciatingly conflictual lived experiences, those exam-ined in *Sweetwater*, and those of my own background; and it is in this liminal and unsettled space, smack dab where Dwight Conquergood would want us to be,6 that I feel more deeply than before the conflicts I have among the shame of my white trash roots, the ways in which that racism might frame the women of Sweetwater, and my own personal/political knowledge that these women's stories are indeed "stories of resilience and social justice."

So I remain unsettled, unnerved, unable to respond without whitegirlness being brought to bear in all of its overt and subtle performances of privilege, sustaining the performativity of whiteness, "a self-reifying practice," writes Bryant Keith Alexander, "a practice that sustains the ability to name, and conversely not to be named, and the power to speak without being chastised while in the process of chastising others." And maybe this racial unnerving is in no small part because of the ways in which the women Robin describes so deeply resonate with the women of my upbringing. Of course, the colors of their skin made the sociocul-turally hued experiences and privileges of their lives quite different.

Family Shame (Excerpt)

Tony E. Adams

Tony E. Adams, "Family Shame," *Departures in Critical Qualitative Research* 4, no. 1 (2015): 124; 125. Reprinted with permission from University of California Press. All rights reserved.

Robin M. Boylorn's *Sweetwater* makes me think about how I have come to live the life I live. I am often ashamed of Danville, IL, a factory and farming town of about 30,000 people, where I spent the first twenty years of my life. I am ashamed of the community's ignorance, drug use, homophobia, and poverty. I am ashamed of my lineage of secret adoptions, mental illnesses, and depression—what Bird's family calls the white person's disease. I am ashamed that I can name the four Black people who attended the Catholic private school with me from kindergar-ten until my senior year in high school. I am ashamed to think about the social conditions that invited me but excluded others who did not look like me from the school. I am ashamed I ever attended such a homogenous, privileged, and preten-tious place. I am ashamed of my family's often-publicly expressed hopes for, not worries about, President Barack Obama's assassination, not because he's a Democrat, but because he's Black. While I have had the privilege to not experience the racial resiliency that Robin describes, her book about home reminds me of the shame I feel when I return to the place I once called home.

***

Since leaving Danville fifteen years ago, I feel as though I have come to survive without my biological family; I have populated my world with friends and chosen family. Maybe this feeling shows my whiteness and maleness bleeding through—I suppose I have learned that my biological family is something I do not need to survive. I do wish I had a Bread and a Cali and a Twiggy in my life and Robin's book makes me want to return to Danville to recognize my family better, but I just can't—I'm ashamed of the ignorance, the drugs, the hate, the poverty. I am ashamed of them. I am also ashamed of my elitist ways.

***

Robin's book shows me that wherever I go, there I am: My past, her past, informs us now, our present, wherever we go, wherever we are. I am my past, my parents, Danville; she is her past, her relatives, Sweetwater. No matter how far I run, no matter how infrequently I visit, I still embody them in my speech, moods, and mannerisms, and in my kindness and ignorance about society.

Hopeful Lament: A Song in Praise of Black Women/Stories

Chris J. Patti

Chris J. Patti, "Hopeful Lament: A Song in Praise of Black Women/Stories," *Departures in Critical Qualitative Research* 4, no. 1 (2015): 128-129. Reprinted with permission from University of California Press. All rights reserved.

CHORUS: (BREAKING) SILENCE

In seeking to share marginalized stories of such a powerful, painful, and perilous nature, Robin's respect for silence, and the potential violence of telling hers and others' experiences, is a critical relational ethic that bears repeating. She reminds me of the lessons I learned while storytelling with Holocaust survivors for my dissertation—stories from different yet somehow connected worlds. In Robin's words, "Telling was murder and I anxiously became a co-conspirator, killing the silence with the story." She reminds me of the words of Sal Wainberg, when he spoke about first telling his story as a Polish hidden child: "The first few times was murder." Through the struggle and risk of telling their stories, however,

Robin and Sal demonstrate that much meaning can be cultivated and found: new perspectives, voices, and memories of oppressive pasts made present; bridges and (broken) windows between generations; resilience and resistance; tools with which to cope and "equipment for living." These are the rewards of narrative inquiry, the fruits of the tree of communication and the knowledge of good and evil that result. This is soul food paying homage to the complexities of situated, lived realities, and the double vision of reflexive auto/ethnography.

BRIDGE: SKELETONS

In her quest to share her and her family's matrilineal story, Robin confronts the dilemma of opening up narrative closets, bravely inviting skeletons to the dinner table. Her resilience and ethic toward suffering remind me of storytelling with my mom, about the abuse she suffered at the hands of her German stepfather, as a Puerto Rican girl in the North East, the "stupid PR" as she was called. I remember the pain of hearing family members speak of oppressions commonly thought unspeakable at home and in dominant, polite society. I want to thank Robin for taking the risk of telling this story.

CHORUS: CRITICAL AUTO/ETHNOGRAPHY

"[…] Like looking in a mirror in a well-lit room. I saw myself fully and accepted and appreciated the culture and community that had helped shape me. Self-acceptance was like oxygen after held breath." Doing the sacred work of storytelling, Robin expands representations—highlighting the tensions, beauty marks, shadows, contradictions, and antitheses—that make up lived realities told intimately, in the way only someone from a studied culture can. Robin tells it like it is, privileging particularities of black women's everyday lives. *Sweetwater* stories are religious in an etymological sense, wherein religion, *re-ligio*, means to link back and connect with the past, to connect one generation to the next. This book is spiritual etymologically too, wherein spirit, *spiritus*, means breath. To breathe in *Sweetwater* stories and the oxygen they create is to be *inspired*. Like her mother Bread, Bird too has a voice "like a soprano blade, cutting people's insides open until all they can do is cry their eyes out." Like a torch singer, Robin's voice is a resonant exclamation, a resilient and hopeful cry that sticks with me, alters me. Her story plants seeds that grow and defiantly throws rocks on cultural roofs. It's a story that exposes personal, collective, theoretical, and methodological possibilities for those of us interested in ethnographically speaking/listening.

More Than Enough

Mary E. Weems

Mary E. Weems, "More Than Enough," *Departures in Critical Qualitative Research* 4, no. 1 (2015): 131-132. Reprinted with permission from University of California Press. All rights reserved.

For: Bird, 24 May 2014

Rushing to this place,
I see Bird surrounded by support
like a cardinal in a house of trees,
the space inside a lecture hall
empty seats filling with women-spirits
whispering.

Each of us on the panel brought flowers
our words a collective bouquet
our individual vibe an original scent
the smells
specific memories from lives both different
and the same.

Sweetwater wets our throats
like Southern tea with sugar and lemon
and we are thirsty for more,
want to walk through these stories
bare feet on red-dirt roads.

Suddenly, the world is a hum
and I'm sitting in the audience
enjoying the looks on faces of strangers
listening with bodies leaning.
I connect to this moment
like I connect to Bird's stories
like I connect to Yardbird's music—story
writing like jazz, in the moment, spiritual,
right on time.

On Sweetwater and the Significance of Black Women Tellin'

Rachel Alicia Griffin

Rachel Alicia Griffin, On *Sweetwater* and the Significance of Black Women Tellin'" *Departures in Critical Qualitative Research* 4, no. 1 (2015): 134-135. Reprinted with permission from University of California Press. All rights reserved.

Privately, I shared with Robin that I felt as though I had a hundred questions to ask and a thousand compliments to offer her as a writer who centers the pride and pain of black womanhood. My compliments greatly outweighing my questions should not imply that *Sweetwater* is perfect or beyond constructive criticism. Rather, I understand articulating wishlists and asking questions as acts of "critical love" that signal rigorous engagement. Reading Robin's work with a critical, loving eye, my wishlist includes wanting to know more about the complex auto/ethnographic decisions she made about who to include and exclude, wanting to hear more about the long-term implications of brokenness in black women's lives—the brokenness imposed by others and reproduced by ourselves, and wanting to see more black female communication scholars cited more often in her work. However, the nature and length of any reader's wishlist should never decry the beauty and power of what is present.

For our panel, I whittled my Sweetwater response down to three questions that I thought trumpeted the beauty and power of Robin's contributions to theorizing black womanhood. Coalescing around voice, agency, and intersectionality, oftentimes understood as bedrocks of US American black feminist thought, my questions read:

1. How did you know that the time had come to tell your Sweetwater secret(s)?
2. Poetry has a powerful presence in your work. What do poems allow you to say that other styles of writing do not?
3. *Sweetwater* broadens the common intersections of race, gender, and class to include region. What do you hope your intersectional foundation is built upon?

These questions importantly center *Sweetwater* as a springboard into future works on black womanhood. However, equally important are the ways that I felt captivated by the personal/political/intellectual pulse of Robin's storytelling, and emotionally beckoned to tell her so. As such, this essay is dedicated to Robin and every black woman, like myself, who has struggled with the dominant imposition of anxiety/fear/pain/suspicion/wariness that oftentimes keeps black women from loving other black women OUT LOUD. Too often we silently assume that we are in opposition/competition; too often we silently wonder if we can be allies and friends; too often we silently feel alone/disliked/ostracized in each other's company; too often we silently celebrate each other's success.

Staging Black Girl Utopias: A Sweetwater Tribute

Ruth Nicole Brown, Durell Maurice Callier, Porshe R. Garner, Dominique C. Hill, Porsha Olayiwola, and Jessica L. Robinson

(Excerpt taken from *Departures in Critical Qualitative Research*, 2015, Vol. 4, Number 1, pp. 137, 138-139.)

Black girls are beautifully complex and their/our living is no different. As such, any articulation of black girl living should be multilayered and equally complex. This performative text deploys performative writing to articulate the complications, struggles, contradictions, and overall beauty of black girlhood and womanhood captured in Robin M. Boylorn's *Sweetwater* and in the labor and praxis of Saving Our Lives Hear Our Truths (SOLHOT). SOLHOT is a space, an experience, a movement to practice a kind of transformative love. By design, SOLHOT encourages the use of time and talent to shape newly accountable ways of celebrating each other while imagining, and reimagining black girlhoods.

***

STAGING BLACK GIRL UTOPIAS

To stake a claim in SOLHOT comes with expectations—expectations to engage in deep digging, unlearning, relearning, self-recovery, and the process of daring to see black girls, black girlhood, black female bodies as beautiful and important. In honor of deep digging, unlearning, relearning, self-recovery, and the process of daring to see black girls, black girlhood, black female bodies as beautiful and important, SOLHOT joins with Boylorn to elucidate the convoluted, beautiful, conflicting, full-of-possibility, and transient realities of black (girls and women) living. The performative text that follows merges words, narratives, and memories prompted by the labor of SOLHOT with the stories, hurts, and lessons of living in and going back to *Sweetwater*. Constructed as a performance on page, the voices, truth telling, and knowledge about black girls and women comes to life, to enact a vision of black girl utopia(s), as provided through the hopes and dreams we collectively envision and stage.

***

As *Sweetwater* shares the experience of change, growth, and love through Boylorn's loving narration, SOLHOT creates texts and performances to share our experiences of growth, love, and most importantly, the beauty of black girlhood as we have known and experienced it together. The following performance script is in dedication to the labor of writing black girl and women stories, to the various truths and contradictions that occupy our lives, and to the brilliance that SOLHOT and Boylorn's Sweetwater exhibit in their tenacious embrace of creativity.

Small Doses (Reprint)

Sabrina T. Cherry

Sabrina T. Cherry, "Small Doses," *The Qualitative Report,* 20, no. 10 (2015): 1626-1628. Reprinted with permission. All rights reserved.

Sweetwater leads us into the multifaceted complexities found in community, love and healing for the women who are a part of that community. The author presents what I consider to be excerpts of day-to-day encounters of Black women living in a small, rural town in North Carolina. Through a variety of short chapters, we are enabled to metaphorically make brief visitations: sitting at the table with each main character—including the author—taking only peeks at their existence. This book will make you laugh, cry, and mourn. For those who have lived in small rural towns in the south, Sweetwater may also call you in to […] remembrance.

I had to read Sweetwater in what I have termed "small doses." The stories resembled so many of those that I witnessed, experienced, heard or wondered about in my own small town that it proved difficult to remember that I was reading someone else's story and not my own. It is because of this intermingling that I preferred to only read three to four pages at a time. Even when attempting to stomach a whopping three chapters in one sitting, I found myself needing debrief time to reflect on my own upbringing and community of rural Black women—what were the differences? Similarities? Painful memories? Unanswered questions? Tragedies? Stories never to be told? These questions and ponderings lingered as I read the entire book—it took me nearly three weeks to read a miniscule 122 pages.

I found Dr. Boylorn's writing to be creative and extremely easy to follow. Sweetwater represented a ripe mixture that incited laughter, tears, long pauses, painful remembrances, and thankfulness. As stated by the author (p. 12) the poems represent neither a closing to the chapter or an introduction to the next, but instead a bridge (or window, as described by the author) marking lives, events, and existence with continuous overlap.

The author closed the Appendix (pp. 117–122) by using a quote from Goodall (2008): "If the text was written in such a way that they could not or would not want to read their own stories, what would be the point?" I hope that the women of Sweetwater found this excerpt of their story as engaging to read as I did.

The author explicitly states the use of black feminist thought and womanism, as well as intersectionality and muted group theories as frameworks for Sweetwater (pp. 4–6), while also acknowledging her role—and accompanying dilemmas—in the collection and presentation of data for this research.

While it is clear to me how muted group theory can be applied to this research, I struggled to find the parallels between the listing provided on page 5 and the stories shared in Sweetwater. Does the mere telling of stories about the lives of Black women orient the work to be defined as grounded in Black feminist thought or womanism? How do the stories we read represent an overlap of gender and oppression? Are there unstated assumptions that should accompany the stories of the women of Sweetwater?

As a novice to qualitative data collection and reporting methods, I was extremely impressed by the time and abundant care that the author took in collecting data and managing to streamline that data into a presentable piece. The author's careful use of narrative inquiry and auto-ethnography allowed me to experience Sweetwater from the perspectives of the observer and community member.

I also appreciate the great detail that was included in the length of time dedicated to data collection, the course of events over which this collection took place, the responses of the participants, as well as various means of protecting their confidentiality. Still I wonder how much data was yielded. How did the author choose what to include and what to omit? Will there be a follow-up piece, perhaps Sweetwater II? What were the common themes? Did the author consider using these themes in a more direct way, such as including them as chapter titles? I would love to know more about the analysis and final presentation process (Author Note: Since the initial writing of this review, a classmate has suggested that I search for the author's full dissertation, which I plan to do).

I started this review by stating how I personally related to Sweetwater by likening many of the stories I read to stories of women I knew or know from my own hometown. Perhaps it is because of this likening that I believe the author has overstated the potential of this book. While Sweetwater does an excellent job of presenting snippets of the lives of Black women living in a rural community—and perhaps a mirroring of the lives of many Black women in rural communities across this country—it only scratches the surface. While I understand and appreciate that a final product that attempted to present all facets of the women's lives would be much too voluminous, perhaps even for a dissertation, I am not sure this sole piece allows one to "look at how they [Black women] work out and through concepts of love and justice in their everyday lives" (p. 116). Did the stories presented in this piece adequately "[suggest] that black women can learn generalizable truths from their personal lived experiences and theorize about their daily lives through storytelling?" If I had not spent the first half of my life living in a small, rural town surrounded by women like the characters in this book, would I conclude what the author has stated? Would I come away from this book with an understanding of how Black women "work out and through" love and justice?

I don't think I would. I think I'd have an introduction to rural life and livelihood for a group of Black women. Perhaps I'd wonder how similar their stories—these stories—are to those of other Black women. I'd question which components are missing—didn't make the final count—such as the presence of church and other rituals like holiday meals or family reunions or funerals that are prominent in the lives of many Black folks. And perhaps I'd wonder how the lives of the Black women from Sweetwater mirrored those of poor women in other parts of the country. However, I don't believe that I'd feel confident in walking away with any conclusive statements or thoughts about the vital components of survival for Black women living in rural communities, particularly in the south.

As I closed the book, I am thankful for authors (artists, teachers, etc.) who find value and make time to tell the stories of Black women. However, I was overwhelmed with sadness at the mere thought of attempting to replicate a similar project in my own town. Who would agree to talk [...] I mean, really talk? What fears would prevail? Would people be honest? How would I protect their confidentiality? Could I write about my own parents and our home? I closed the book with these lingering thoughts. I do not have any answers to the questions I posed to myself.

What I do know is that for those wanting to revisit their childhoods in rural Black, southern communities, budding researchers and scholars exploring narrative inquiry and/or autoethnography or those simply wanting the glimpse the multidimensional lives of Black women across this country Sweetwater is a must read!

In addition to the aforementioned thoughts and sentiments, I'd like to add that I completed my reading of Sweetwater with a deep and profound respect for the author. I cannot begin to imagine what this process was like, but I assume that she felt just as many emotions as the readers glimpse while reading. It is one thing to research and write about those we label as "other," but I imagine that it takes a varying level of strength, courage, and tenacity to write about ourselves. Written with such great vulnerability and transparency makes me appreciate this work that much more!

Unpublished Responses to Sweetwater

In November 2013, at the National Communication Association in Washington, DC, a celebratory panel entitled, "Sweetwater along the Potomac" featured a roundtable of responses, including some of the reflections included in the Sweetwater Forum. However, not all of those responses were published. In an effort to collect the voices and points of view of as many people as possible, I include here some of the previously unpublished feedback from panelists.

What Matters?

Ron Pelias, Professor Emeritus, Southern Illinois University:

Thank you, Robin. Thank you for taking me on your ethnographic journey, for introducing me to Sweetwater and its inhabitants, for allowing me to enter your home. It is a privilege to be in the presence of a writer whose ear is so attuned to your participants' speech, whose eyes take in such telling details, and whose touch is sensitive and firmly placed. I am grateful I can follow you into Sweetwater, can be guided by your careful hand. What a pleasure to be a witness to your telling!

As I travel with you, I watch you move as an ethnographer, using your insider status to reach into the complexities of Sweetwater. You reveal the joys and sorrows of daily living, showing how people make sense of their lives and how they survive. I see your labor—observing, interviewing, participating. I see you working your way into and through stereotypes. I see your ethical struggles and your efforts to do no harm by calling upon pseudonyms, composite characters, and participant checks.

As I travel with you, I watch you move as a writer. You find stories that need to be told and structure them so that readers will be pulled along, want more. You place me in a rich linguistic community, one rich with metaphor and one that can turn a Robin into a Bird. You let me see people at their best and at their worse. And I see you sitting in front of your computer, making choices, good choices, choices that speak to the difficult issue of representation. I see you wanting to be fair to all involved, to tell the truth as you see it, to help those inside and outside Sweetwater to understand. I see you realizing that each choice opens one door while closing others.

And now, because I want to keep learning from you, I am hoping that you will speak about what may have fallen away as you opened one door and closed others, particularly in regard to issues of representation. You mention, for example, that your interviews 'ranged in time from one to four hours each' (p. 120). As you turned their interviews into third-person omniscient narratives, did you feel the loss of their first-person narratives? Did you feel that the use of third-person omniscient narrative and your own first-person narratives run the risk of giving you too much narrative control? Did you play with letting different characters be the narrator of different chapters and if so, what did that choice offer?

Another example of an issue of representation is that the reader never is quite sure what is true to experience and what is true in experience. You say, for instance, that you 'found a way to honor and maintain the words they used to describe their lives by writing stories based on the situations and circumstances they shared, using (when possible) their word-for-word accounts in the retelling' (p. 122). I trust this claim, but I leave the book unsure when I am in the presence of fictive or actual speech. I wonder if it matters?

The Same and Different

Brenda J. Allen, Professor, University at Colorado Denver

I was moved and fascinated by the similarity and familiarity of black women's experiences in Sweetwater—a rural, poor, southern community where Bird was raised in the 80s, and those in Brick City—an urban, poor, northern community (projects) where I was born and raised in the 50s and 60s. These demonstrate the significance of intersections of race, class, and gender, as well as the related pervasiveness of white supremacy while also illuminating the persistence of various aspects of culture, such as language, ritual, disciplinary practices, etc.

Knee baby, Long hair ("good hair"), grown folks talking, White people's eyes, Water and Vaseline, Show your ass, Too big for your britches, Womanish, Dreaming about fish [means someone is pregnant], Smelling herself, check ears and nail bed for skin color, Miss Mary Mack Mack Mack, Food, chittlins, potted meat, Vienna sausage and crackers, Cornbread, mayonnaise sandwiches, Pressure cooker, Big boned, Fast ass, Ashy knees, rusty elbows, I ain't studying you, Beauty marks, Dick dipped in gold, Burnt hair or birds nest superstitions.

I was disappointed that background/supporting information/theories/perspectives for the research barely and superficially referenced the powerful body of similar scholarship by and about black women in the field of communication. The book contributes wonderfully to that work to corroborate Houston and Scott's (2006) assertion that 'Black women are not a monolith and Black feminist scholarship can reveal the variety of language and communication choices, styles and strategies that inform everyday interaction' (Houston & Scott, 2006, p. 409). Because I suspect (indeed I hope) that the book will be widely read, I lament the missed opportunity to share and celebrate generations of black women **communication** scholars whose work also contributes to *Sweetwater's* goal 'to determine how black women use narratives to cope and communicate about their experiences and as acts of social resistance' (Boylorn, 2013, p. xxi).

Question:

The narratives imply a strong heteronormative culture that seems devoid of GLBTQ-identified residents. Please comment on sexual identity politics in Sweetwater.

Weaving Stories: The Potential for Black Women's Narrative Performance

Olga Idriss Davis, Associate Professor, Arizona State University

The dissertation-turned-book-inspired ethnography of Robin Boylorn is a gift of Story. It is a compelling examination of the lives of poor, rural African American women at the precipice of life and challenge. Their personae are clear, embellished only by their lived experience of love, loss, regret, and resilience. The performative voice is impressive and is waiting to be realized; revealing the complicated meanderings of lives lived by Black women in a community of other mothers, aunties, and children. The lives, which often bear the brunt of a marginalized social narrative that has brushed away their stories and their voices as though they were leaves on a field during a brisk, Fall day.

While this study offers a new lens to explore the interior of rural Black women's lives, it is a reminder that situating Black women's stories within the social, political, cultural, and performative milieus is not novel. Black women's stories have always been there, as Barbara Smith noted, and black women have always theorized our experiences, but in ways that are counter-intuitive to Western sensibilities and culture. This ethnography constructs a cultural body of struggle and survival from the continuum of Black women's storytelling—a history that is often lost and forgotten. Yet the array of Black women's stories have always been there—situated in the everyday lives of our existence. The book offers a point of entry—a place Paula Friere calls "situationality"—a historical awareness of critically reflecting on one's own experience the narratives within the story, and critically acting upon it through the transformative space of performance. Weaving these stories creates yet another performance—an opportunity that together they become a dialogue, a critical act, a political intervention, a performance of self-reflection by which a historical continuum crafts what it means to experience blackness in an instance of existence. It then has the potential of becoming a generative autobiographical performance—that has the potential to explore the intersections and divergences of lived experiences; placing special interest in blending and bleeding the experiences that often magnify difference and create division. Moving forward, this project needs to locate the intersectionality of the personal and the professional in the character of Bird—in navigating a Black woman's identity in the professoriate.

Sweetwater Re/Vision(s)

Author's Response to Re/views

I made an effort, in this revised edition, to consider the feedback I have received, both in the form of book reviews and responses, class discussions, conversations with participants, and reconsiderations after teaching and re-reading the book. In this chapter, I take up the generous feedback from reviews of the first published version of *Sweetwater*, and respond to implied and direct questions in their essays. I react and respond to re/views of *Sweetwater*, considering the critiques and appreciation of the work as an opportunity to further imagine how *Sweetwater* topics and themes can be taken up in the classroom and the living room. I am interested and invested in the ways *Sweetwater* creates visibility and voice to (rural) black women while simultaneously offering a counternarrative for those who find similarities in the stories beyond race and gender. Accordingly, in addition to providing my personal responses (revisions) to reviews, I also put the re/views in conversation with each other, finding adequate answers to questions in the feedback of other scholars.

One of my biggest concerns about *Sweetwater* is linked to intentional choices I made about whose story I was going to tell. *Sweetwater* is intended to represent a group I felt was un(der)represented in scholarship. As a rural black woman, I wanted to create a text that would not only resonate with black women, but reflect the shared experiences of rural black womanhood. As a storyteller, I was committed to doing this through narrative. The risk with writing a book about rural black women in/for the academy is that it can be interpreted as only for rural black women in the academy. This conundrum is consistent with research about marginalized populations. We are used to reading about them marginally, but what happens when they are centered? People who are white and/or men may feel alienated, left out, or disinterested in reading about "black women and narratives of resilience." While I was confident that black women, even those who were not rural themselves, would understand and connect with the black women characters in the book, I was less sure how nonblack audiences would receive it.

In the review, "Small Doses," Sabrina T. Cherry (2015) has similar concerns, doubting that she would come away from the book with an understanding of how black women work out and through love and justice if she, herself, was not a black woman with similar experiences. She says, "I don't believe that I'd feel confident in walking away with any conclusive statements or thoughts about the vital components of survival for Black women living in rural communities, particularly in the south." (p. 1627)

In contrast to Cherry's skepticism that *Sweetwater* was instructive of black women's survival strategies, H. L. Goodall, Jr., who wrote the Foreword, and Chris Poulos (2015), who writes the review, The Road to Sweetwater, argue that *Sweetwater* gives them insight and entry into the lives of rural black women that they would otherwise not have access to. While the novelty of stories about growing up a black woman in the South is inevitably more substantial for non-black women readers, other reviewers, including white scholars with similar small town backgrounds and black scholars who grew up in northern cities with southern influences, felt resonance and camaraderie with the characters and characterizations.

As an "autoethnographic ethnography," *Sweetwater* does not intend to be THE story, only A representative story. *Sweetwater* was written to give voice to the participants, but also to instigate and provoke similar and/or related stories, or even stories that are entirely different from *Sweetwater* women. Reviewers, including Carolyn Ellis, Tami Spry, Chris Poulos, Chris Patti, Tony Adams, Ron Pelias and H. L. Goodall reflected on the ways that *Sweetwater* not only informed them about the lives of black women in rural communities, but it also exposed how they are implicated by the narratives through their ignorance of these women's experiences, or through the whitened spaces they themselves have inhabited, rendering black women invisible.

In An Unsettled I, Spry (2015) talks about the uneasiness she feels, as a white girl, reading *Sweetwater*, even though the women of *Sweetwater* are not unlike the women she grew up around. Spry's race consciousness and recognition of the significance of racial difference allows her to reckon with the apprehension she feels while using it to reflect on her own story. For Spry (2011), one of the main purposes of performative autoethnography is to unsettle privilege, and *Sweetwater* helps her recognize privilege in new and uncomfortable ways. She sees engaging *Sweetwater* as an opportunity to "unnerve her whitegirlness" and participate in conversations that require reflexivity, not only about race difference, but about class sameness (see Frankenburg, 1993).

In The Road to Sweetwater, Poulos (2015), speaks of literal and metaphorical roads to(ward) and away from *Sweetwater*, not unlike the roads Goodall describes in the Foreword. Poulos states,

> I've never been to Sweetwater, but I have stumbled across small rural places in the South. I did not linger. I'm mostly a city boy who escapes to Western wilderness, not to rural small towns. [...] Sweetwater is not my place. But now, I think I've been as close to there as you can get without having lived there. (p. 114)

Poulos feels the book offered him access and insight, which allows him to focus on the humanity of the people in *Sweetwater*. He summarizes the book as being essentially about *"people in the predicaments of place and relationship"* (p. 116). I appreciate that he does not distinguish a difference between black people and white people, instead centering the sameness of shared experiences that all people have in common, regardless of where we are from.

Spry and Poulos' responses to *Sweetwater* are heartening for me, because while they don't dismiss or disregard the importance and inevitable influence of issues of race, gender, and class, they recognize that the lessons we learn from *Sweetwater* are about what makes us all, regardless of our differences, human, fallible and redeemable. They also make claims about what these stories allow them to know about the survival and strength of black women in the South.

*

Cherry (2015) asks about what is missing from the book, "such as the presence of church and other rituals like holiday meals or family reunions or funerals. [...]" She wonders, as a new qualitative researcher, how I made decisions about what to leave in and what to leave out. She asks, how much data was yielded? How did the author choose what to include and what to omit? Will there be a follow-up piece, perhaps Sweetwater II[1]? What were the common themes? Did the author consider using these themes in a more direct way, such as including them as chapter titles? I would love to know more about the analysis and final presentation process.

The book focused on the mundane and everyday "lived experience" of black women, which means I sought, through interviews and observations, to record the particularity and ubiquity of their lives. I wanted to know about the things they did every day or remembered in repetition from their childhood. I wanted to know what stood out to them and why, and in what ways those things shaped who they are and how they see themselves. I was also interested in the specificity of those things as it related to their rural identity and the small community they lived in. When you are focusing on day-to-day experiences, extraordinary occasions (like birthdays, Christmases, Thanksgiving dinners, etc.) are often left out. What stood out, however, were the experiences that punctuated their daily existence, and the coping strategies they adopted to make sense of sudden or unexpected death, absence, violence, and poverty. For example, the most memorable Thanksgiving talked about was the year Bread, Peaches and Bebe learned their father had died. It was, therefore, the memories of receiving that delayed news, not the ritualistic meal, that was described in detail in the interviews, and therefore in the narrative.

The common themes in the book included church and religiosity, family dynamics, food, female friendships, romantic relationships, intimate partner violence, gender scripts, equity, emotional (in)justice, mental illness, colorism, and survival. All of these themes, and others, show up in the lives of the women in *Sweetwater*, through their conversations and narratives. However, while I believe that *Sweetwater* contains themes of black women's survival, a shortcoming of the first edition was perhaps a lack of specificity in naming them. The themes are embedded in the narrative and subjected to interpretation. My intention was to allow the reader to identify themes organically based on their reading and personal experience. However, some readers were disadvantaged by being expected to read between the lines and understand the (raced/classed/gendered) implications of themes, sometimes without context. In this new edition of the book,

---

1   My next book, *Blackgirl Blue(s)*, (forthcoming, Routledge) is an autoethnographic echo of Sweetwater, picking up where the story leaves off, theorizing blackgirl (one word) as an identity marker, and introducing blackgirl (one word) autoethnography as a method of resistance and affirmation.

I add a second appendix (Appendix B) to discuss themes, inviting the reader to think through additional topics represented in the stories. I also summarize the narratives and expand the analysis to more explicitly discuss and speculate about the themes and their relationships to black women's lives in general, and rural Southern black women's lives in particular.

Details on how I collected and analyzed data is included in Appendix A, which details the method I used to conduct the research. Appendix A has been revised to include more details about what information was used, yielded, and why, and how the interviews and data were analyzed and translated to stories, which responds to Cherry's query and Ron Pelias', who wondered in his response,

> As you turned [their] interviews into third-person omniscient narratives, did you feel the loss of [their] first-person narratives? Did you feel that the use of third-person omniscient narrative and your own first-person narratives run the risk of giving you too much narrative control? Did you play with letting different characters be the narrator of different chapters and if so, what did that choice offer?

I used third-person omniscient narratives to summarize the first-person accounts I collected through interviews. The third-person omniscient allowed me to tell multiple stories at once, and to synthesize accounts when there was significant overlap or similarity in the stories told. Third-person also gave me the necessary distance, as a writer, to tell the stories of the women, in their own words, and then my own story, in my own words. The autoethnographic narratives are first-person, for that purpose, which allows me to take ownership and responsibility for the "I" in my story, which were written in response and in relation to the participants. I did not feel a loss of the first-person accounts in the translation to third-person because I held myself accountable to curating a discernable narrative that privileged and held in tact the words and gestures used during the interviews. In re-telling stories that were told to me, I documented details such as the way words were spoken, the mannerisms I observed, over time, from participants, and how they were described in order to fold them into the narratives. The stories I tell from a third person point of view are intended to be somewhat objective in order to offer a more distanced and observational perspective, but are inevitably influenced by my own bias, conscious and unconscious editing choices, and the decisions I made to weave the stories together, thematically. My intent was for the participants to recognize their stories and their words, but to also recognize the universality of their experiences.

While I recognize the problematics and tensions of a researcher having too much authority or narrative control, it was an inevitable necessity for me to story *Sweetwater* from an omniscient perspective. Because I was translating multiple interviews, with multiple people, into one story, I had to write it in a way that would allow various characters to emerge, sometimes only once, for the purposes of thematic storylines. However, because of the number of characters, I did not attempt to isolate individual narratives based on the participant, or transfer the role of the narrator to multiple participants. That choice would have allowed for a more authentic snapshot of individual women, but it would have also exposed them, which would have jeopardized my commitment to external anonymity and internal confidentiality.

*

Carolyn Ellis' review concentrates on relational ethics, which is closely associated to issues of yielded information. In her reflection, Ellis (2015) shares our collaborative discussions about *Sweetwater* at the dissertation phase,

> We talk of ethics, responsibilities, hurt, and pain as we consider what to reveal and what to conceal, how to tell it, what to tell, how to protect, how to take her academic words back home, how to bring her home life into the academy, for what purpose, and with what result. (p. 85)

Ellis is my academic mother/mentor and was my dissertation advisor. Together we discussed and negotiated the ethics of writing *Sweetwater* and on what terms. The goal was to construct a narrative that had verisimilitude and veracity, did not compromise the confidence or confidentiality guaranteed in the informed consent protocol, and protected the participants, their relationships in the community and outside of it. This was particularly complicated because of my positionality as a (former) member of the community and researcher. I relied on reflexivity and intentionality to make ethical and moral decisions about the stories, collapsing details and camouflaging characteristics so that I could tell the representative stories without implicating or outing members of the community. I also did several informal, off the record interviews, which yielded data, but often without the same structured consent as the formalized, recorded interviews, which meant I had to make case-by-case decisions about whether or not some information was intended to be included in the book.

*

Other reactions to *Sweetwater* considered the theoretical framework and whether or not *Sweetwater* was successfully and theoretically supported. Cherry (2015) states,

While it is clear to me how muted group theory can be applied to this research, I struggled to find parallels between the listing provided [...] and the stories shared in Sweetwater. Does the mere telling of stories about the lives of Black women orient the work to be defined as grounded in Black feminist thought or womanism? How do the stories we read represent an overlap of gender and oppression? Are there unstated assumptions that should accompany the stories of the women of Sweetwater? (p. 1626)

The introduction of *Sweetwater* argues that "theories are embedded in our experiences and the questions that emerge from our curiosities about the world we live in," (Boylorn, 2013, p. 4). The introduction also suggests that theories are stories and/or that stories are theoretical. An examination of black women's lives as stories necessitates that we consider their stories and what their stories tell us as inherently analytical. I expand my explanation and description of black feminism (and/or womanism), intersectionality theory, and muted group theory in the revised introduction, but I want to explain how and why these theories are present in many, if not all, of the *Sweetwater* narratives.

As a black feminist, scholar activist, I don't think it is possible to engage black women's lives without a black feminist analysis. In that way, I do think that the mere telling of stories about the lives of Black women is grounded in black feminist thought and/or womanism. I believe this claim is supported by the definition of black feminist thought, which recognizes and privileges the storied experiences of black women, particularly those who are unfamous. *Sweetwater* stories are also intrinsically womanist. While I would not argue that all scholarship about black women is womanist, *Sweetwater* is a womanist text because it embraces the creativity and acts of resistance of everyday black women (Phillips, 2006). I personally consider Alice Walker's womanism and black feminism to be synonymous, but even if the theories are separated, they are both connected through *Sweetwater* narratives, which consider black women's ways of knowing and cultural traditions. *Sweetwater* narratives also celebrate womanish ways, resilience, and strength.

Intersectionality is largely understood as an identity politic and/or an account of power (Collins & Bilge, 2016; Cooper, 2016; Crenshaw, 1991) that attempts to explain how marginalized identities are stigmatized and oppressed and experience specified subjugation as a result. Intersectionality claims that standpoints and experiences of oppression cannot be separated. The race, class, gender, sex, sexual orientation, religion, ability status, age, education, and marital status of *Sweetwater* women, as well as the systems of oppression attached to them, including racism, classism, sexism, heterosexism, ableism, ageism, and elitism (including religious elitism) inform their understanding of their lives and the world.

Their experiences cannot be divorced from their positionalities, which are shaped according to the circumstances they were born into. Intersectionality is as embedded in these narratives as it is in their lives.

Similarly, while gender oppression cannot be separated from the oppression *Sweetwater* women experience being black and poor, their gender inevitably informs their experience. Gender oppression is discussed and reiterated throughout the book, in narratives, dialogue, and analysis. In particular, gender and oppression is demonstrated through the ubiquity of heterosexual romantic relationships, which required and reinforced gender roles and scripts about how men and women were supposed to relate to each other. Women experienced oppression and disadvantages because of sexism and were simultaneously forced to adopt masculine-identified traits such as independence and meanness for survival, in the absence of men. Scenes from the community, church, and individual households, as well as general descriptions of how *Sweetwater* men and women are socialized to conduct themselves show the fragility of femininity and the necessity of women's independence.

Muted-group theory functions similarly by showing that dominant groups determine how and/or if non-dominant group experiences are communicated. Black, working-class women are often silenced and their voices, when heard, are erased or distorted by overarching storylines designed to make them indiscernible, even to themselves. Muted group theory can be applied as a way to understand why the stories of rural black women are missing or underrepresented in scholarship, and what is (potentially) lost as a result of that absence. *Sweetwater* un-mutes these voices and magnifies them.

I believe there are two ways to read *Sweetwater*. When read for pleasure, I have no expectation that a reader would have prerequisite knowledge or interest about qualitative methods, ethics, textual analysis, black feminism, or narrative theory. Those readers will likely skip the framework and start reading from the Prologue or Chapter 1, focusing on the narrative/s and reading *Sweetwater* to learn about and from its characters. I suspect that Southern women raised in similar communities connect to the stories by comparing the experiences in Sweetwater to their own. When read academically, I assume readers have some background, knowledge or curiosity about narrative theory, ethnographic and autoethnographic method, and black women's studies. An academic reading of *Sweetwater* would require an understanding of how to interpret texts through analysis (including identifying themes), and an engagement of relevant or applicable theories. Academic readers would learn from the book's content and consider what theories help explain the storylines.

*

Cherry (2015) finally states, "I am not sure this sole piece allows one to 'look at how they [black women] work out and through concepts of love and justice in their everyday lives,'" as the book claims. She also wonders if the stories adequately "'[suggest] that black women can learn generalizable truths from their personal lived experiences and theorize about their daily lives through storytelling?'" (p. 1627)

In their review "Show, Don't Tell," Brittney Cooper and Susana M. Morris (2015) note,

> Indeed, much of what is most compelling about *Sweetwater* is its firsthand emphasis on black women's interiority. Historically, black women are often over-theorized, pathologized, and talked about rather than heard for what they have to say. *Sweetwater*, however, joins the ranks of other black feminist work that highlights black women's agency and how we make sense of the world ourselves. (p. 107)

Aisha Durham (2015) says of *Sweetwater* in Kindred Narratives,

> Boylorn recovers open secrets and recasts the rural apart from its popular and academic constructions that treat it as a lost space where time has stopped or has reversed altogether, or as a less significant place to talk about contemporary blackness, considering much of our collective experience since the great black migration(s) has been defined through the urban, cosmopolitan black masculine. Boylorn blends black vernacular and poetic prose with womanist and feminist epistemologies to concoct a homemade familial narrative that is uniquely Southern and unapologetically black woman-centered. (p. 110)

In Black Girl Strong(er), Amber Johnson (2015) states,

> "our experiences change our lives. we cannot undo the bends, the compressions, the stretching. we become strong(er) in our search to resist. we become scholars of "social justice" by recognizing and identifying 'where the justice and love is'— which, as these stories demonstrate, is usually on the margins. (p. 118)

The reactions of Cooper and Morris (2015), Durham (2015), and Johnson (2015) reinforce the impetus to read *Sweetwater* as a commentary on black feminist intervention, love, resistance, and social justice. These are generalizable truths.

*

Rachel Griffin (2015) poses three questions in *On Sweetwater and the Significance of Black Women Tellin'*. I include them below, with my responses:

1) How did you know that the time had come to tell your *Sweetwater* secret(s)?

I think I had been writing versions of *Sweetwater* for the entirety of my graduate education. Once I began writing autoethnography, in 2001, I started writing pieces of *Sweetwater*, without knowing it. My thesis project, Finding Voice: African American Women in the New American South (2003), was my prequel to *Sweetwater*, and my next book project, Blackgirl Blue(s) (forthcoming), is an extension of *Sweetwater*.

The impetus for telling the stories was in reaction to their absence in the literature I read as a student. I wanted to create scholarship that would make rural black women (in the academy and in their community) visible. I wanted to explain why their voices, stories, and lives mattered.

I also wanted to deaden the fear associated with telling our stories. As a black woman, especially a rural black woman, I was taught from the time I was child that "what happened in the house, stayed in the house," and that warning-declaration stayed with me my whole life, and it made my experiences feel isolated in a way they were not. By telling my *Sweetwater* stories and secrets, putting myself (and my family/community) out there to be consumed and critiqued, I was also liberating myself and others whose stories and experiences were locked in shame and silence.

I don't' think I made the conscious decision to tell my *Sweetwater* secrets, they insisted on being told, little by little, over time.

2) Poetry has a powerful presence in your work. What do poems allow you to say that other styles of writing do not?

Poems come when the story I am trying to tell has absences and pauses. Poems are shortened breaths, abbreviated prose, and lyrical lamentations. Poems allow me to express myself in fewer words while taking up more space on the page. Poems let me be creative and play with language without playing by the rules. Poems, for me, are short stories (see "countrywomen" and "a call from home").

Poetry opens up the possibility of how I can tell a story, and it leaves gaps for the reader to fill in. I love poems because they allow me to say so much without saying much at all, and poetry reminds me to consider the orality of my writing. Poems, like stories, are meant to be spoken out loud, so I am intentional about how and when to include them.

I use poems in *Sweetwater* to synthesize a scene or summarize a setting. They are also useful and beautiful interventions or starting points. Poems or poetic language can be used to bridge difficult stories, and/or instigate poetic responses. Mary

E. Weems' window poems, which are included after select chapters throughout the book, were written as respites between chapters, and reflect the resonance she felt from her own memories/experiences.

3) *Sweetwater* broadens the common intersections of race, gender, and class to include region. What do you hope your intersectional foundation is built upon?

I think regionality, in the domestic US, is an overlooked, but important factor in identity politics and discussions of intersectionality. Where we are from influences how we understand the world we live in, and how far and wide that world feels. When factored alongside race, gender, and class, region dictates taken-for-granted truths, and experiences that privilege the elite and silence the oppressed. I hope *Sweetwater* encourages additional considerations of region as a significant factor to discussions of difference, diversity, and representation.

*

Other reviews did not ask questions, but they inspired them. For example, Tony E. Adams' review, Family Shame (2015), chronicles the ways Sweetwater reminds him of his relationship to his home community and family. While he focuses on the "shame," he feels about where he is from, and what he characterizes as his "elitist ways," as a result of his education and escape, Adams' response also challenges the benefits of "going home," by discussing the personal, ethical, and emotional suffering that can happen when home communities are not safe spaces. His ambivalence about returning home, even for intermittent visits, is in contrast to my enthusiasm about visits home, even before I began my research.

As an openly gay man, Adams finds the small-minded, racist, homophobic tone of his small hometown to be dangerous and unwelcoming. His review reminds me that the circumstances for my return to Sweetwater were subjective and privileged because of my relationship to my family. Adams challenges me to consider how my return home may have been different if I identified as nonheterosexual? It also reminds me that I chose Sweetwater as a site because of access and familiarity. My family's ongoing presence in the community gave me credibility, but it also provided me with insularity and safety that I would not have had if I visited a neutral or unknown community to collect black women's stories, or if I was estranged from my family who were my primary participants. Context matters, and returning home to collect community or family narratives is not a (physically or emotionally) safe option for everyone.

Cooper and Morris (2015) talk about *Sweetwater* as a story of homeplace, representative of the varied yet interconnected experiences of black women across the diaspora, and the familiarity of characters that are reminiscent of their own women kinfolk. They recognize the cultural complexities and contradictions *Sweetwater* women must negotiate while honoring and honing in on generational and traditional ways of knowing from their own childhoods and experiences. They suggest that black women's epistemology make them inherent storytellers whose identities and realities are often inconsistent with external expectations and representations. They see *Sweetwater* as a necessary and welcome intervention of ethnographic scholarship that joins fictional literary work by black women writing about people who leave and then return home.

I am honored at the generous comparisons Cooper and Morris make between *Sweetwater* and classic black women's literary texts, many of which have inspired my work over the years. The recognition of the ongoing and historical conflicts black women experienced with leaving home, staying at home, or going back home reinforce the complicated relationship we often have with home. Their words remind me that I carry vestiges of *Sweetwater* with me and it "shows" even when I don't tell.

*

Durham (2015) conceptualizes *Sweetwater* as a "slow cooked autoethnography," (p. 122) which beautifully reckons with the time and patience it takes to layer a narrative so that each intricate and intentional detail is discernable. She recognizes the deliberate choices of the written word and the powerful potential of the spoken word, saying *Sweetwater* beckons to be taken in "aloud" and out loud, which is how I experienced her review, sitting down and listening to myself say the words, later hearing her words in her voice while I watched. I understood our lives, our blackgirl stories, made us kinfolk without biology. Through Durham's eyes and words *Sweetwater* expands beyond central North Carolina, up and down dirt roads, walk ways, riverbanks and sidewalks. Her review includes a consideration of the window poems Weems writes to stretch *Sweetwater* tapestries from rural roads to urban cityscapes. Durham wraps her Virginian stories around mine, held together by Weems' words, offering a serenade that centers the balm of female friendship, forever love, and poetic possibilities.

Durham was not the only scholar who used poetry and performative writing to write about *Sweetwater*. Johnson's (2015) poetic response theorizes black girlhood as a verb and black woman friendship as a site of healing and wholeness. She defines strength, not in the sense of infallibility, but as an extension of resilience. She challenges us to consider what action is required, alongside an ability to recover, for black women's survival. She asks, "what makes black girls strong(er)?"

(p. 117), implying that we must do more than just be, we must act, lessons offered through the lived experiences reflected in the book.

Weems' (2015) poem, More Than Enough, chronicles her immediate response to a *Sweetwater* Celebration panel, wherein she identifies communal strength and the support she witnessed from the audience. Both Weems and Johnson challenge us to (re)consider the implications and limitations of black women's supposed strength and need for affirmation.

Chris Patti's (2015) Hopeful Lament is a lyrical song script, broken down into a chorus and bridge. In this song for *Sweetwater*, Patti considers the significance of silences in storytelling, and the importance of giving reverence to the painful memories that shape the stories we tell. Reflecting on his experience collecting the stories of Holocaust survivors, and his memories of hearing family stories from his mother, he reminds me that storytelling is risky, but necessary. He also reflects on the personal and communal implications of critical autoethnography attaching *Sweetwater* stories to spiritual awakening, saying,

> *Sweetwater* stories are religious in an etymological sense, wherein religion, *re-li-gio*, means to link back and connect with the past, to connect one generation to the next. This book is spiritual etymologically too, wherein spirit, *spiritus*, means breath. To breathe in *Sweetwater* stories and the oxygen they create is to be *inspired.* (p. 129)

*

In Staging Black Girl Utopias: A Sweetwater Tribute, Brown, Callier, Garner, Hill, Olayiwola, and Robinson offer a symphony of moments, movements, melodies and words, putting *Sweetwater* in conversation with the movement of Saving Our Lives, Hear Our Truths (SOLHOT), the blackgirl honoring brainchild of Ruth Nicole Brown. SOLHOT's purpose of celebrating and territorializing blackgirlhood is consistent with ethic of *Sweetwater* and its commitment to hearing and telling blackgirl (woman) truths. It is a privilege to have *Sweetwater* in conversation and dialogue with SOLHOT.

I need to set the scene. We are gathered in a lecture hall at the University of Illinois for a panel on *Sweetwater* and I am invited to the front of the room. My chair is situated with the presenters on each side of me, and I feel surrounded by solidarity, mutual respect, and reciprocal appreciation. I hold my breath and listen. I exhale and experience.

The performance and soundtrack blends their lyrics with occasional lines from *Sweetwater* and I am overtaken with the inability to distinguish the difference between our blackgirl truths and secrets, shames and lies, our stories. I am centered by a wall of black bodies, collaborating and reflecting on the importance of work that, like *Sweetwater*, reminds blackgirls that they are capable of anything, everything.

The artists introduce *Sweetwater* as an ode to blackgirlhood, a shout out to their own storied truths, and a way of re-thinking our rural roots.

The choreographed dance ends with asking audience members to contribute by writing down what *Sweetwater* taught them. I feel anchored. Affirmed. Visible.

Tears melt into the lap full of notes I am given, *Sweetwater* prophesies and promises.

*

In an earlier *Sweetwater* Panel, at the National Communication Association in Washington, D.C., panelists Ron Pelias, Brenda J. Allen and Olga Davis wondered, in different ways and for different reasons, about issues of representation, both in terms of how and why characters were represented as they were and what counts as a truthful (or problematic) representation of marginalized groups. Allen and Davis expressed disappointment in what they believed to be a lack of representation of black women communication scholars in the theoretical framing and grounding of *Sweetwater*.

I was committed to questioning and challenging representations of black women with *Sweetwater*, and I also hoped to expand representations of black women in the cultural imagination to include rural black women. I did this by absorbing some of the negative traits of rurality, and crafting new interpretations of old representations of black womanhood. It was a complicated endeavor to simultaneously challenge and embrace stereotypic illustrations of black women, but that work is consistent with my other autoethnographies (Boylorn, 2008, 2013a, 2014).

Sweetwater presents black women who are mean, kind, godly, worldly, educated, sophisticated, formally uneducated, street smart, sassy, independent, needy, sexy, prudish, and more. There were, however, some representations that were missing, including queer and lesbian women (Sweetie Pie and Peewee, in Porch Premonitions, are intended to be read that way, but the brevity of their exchange makes them easy to overlook). I intentionally wrote their relationship as innuendo, because that is how it would have been interpreted in Sweetwater. There were no out lesbian relationships in the community, though they likely existed, as open secrets.

One participant, who at the time of the interview was in her seventies, and would have attended college in the 1950s, spoke about her ignorance about the existence of lesbians. She said that while she was aware that men could love and be with other men, because of their presence in her family and community, it never occurred to her that women could be "that way." It was not until she went away to college, and had a roommate who identified as a lesbian, that she realized how sheltered she had been in *Sweetwater*. And she speculated, that even though it wasn't openly talked about or admitted, there had likely been closeted lesbian couples and/or queer women in *Sweetwater* when she was growing up.

While I did not envision *Sweetwater* as a traditional or communication-specific text, the focus on black women's communication practices deserved greater emphasis and explanation for how black women communicologists have engaged and theorized black women's lived experience and communication practices. To remedy the absence of depth in the original publication of *Sweetwater*, an expanded, though not exhaustive, section on Black Women's Communication is included in the introduction. Additional black women scholars, in Communication and other disciplines whose work preceded and informed *Sweetwater*, have also been added to the Bibliography.

In addition to recognizing *Sweetwater*'s place in a long tradition of black women storytelling and storytellers, Davis distinguishes *Sweetwater* as a book with performative potential. Davis (2008) defines performance of care as "a ritualized experience of transforming oppression into strategies for struggle and survival" (p. 178). In her review of *Sweetwater*, she states,

> The book offers a point of entry—a place Paula Friere calls "situationality"—a historical awareness of critically reflecting on one's own experience the narratives within the story, and critically acting upon it through the transformative space of performance. Weaving these stories creates yet another performance –an opportunity that together they become a dialogue, a critical act, a political intervention, a performance of self-reflection by which a historical continuum crafts what it means to experience blackness in an instance of existence.

Davis' structure helps me see *Sweetwater* as a collection of experiential performances that house memory, history, and possibility. *Sweetwater* stories, as she suggests, work together in dialogue as a call-and-response between intergenerational black women who see themselves in them.

*

Writing *Sweetwater* was as much about who I was becoming through the process of writing the stories, as it was about the stories themselves. I am grateful for the opportunity to see *Sweetwater* through the eyes of others, respond to questions and constructive criticism, and reconsider the choices I made in the first draft.

Appendix A: Method(ologies)

How (And Why) I Collected Data

Methods are means or techniques for conducting research;
they are one's plan of action for getting a particular research task done.
Methodologies, on the other hand, are the underlying principles,
assumptions, and rules that inform methods.
Methods are tools; methodologies are world views.
–Marsha Houston, 2000, p. 675

Zora Neale Hurston says that "research is a formalized curiosity. It is poking and prying with purpose" (Walker, 1979, p. 49). I conducted research nonconsecutively for three years. I poked and pried by using various methods including autoethnography, ethnography (participant observation), interactive interviewing, informal focus groups, and traditional archival research to collect stories and other information about the small town referred to in this book as Sweetwater, North Carolina. I interacted with participants and joined them in their various daily activities during the summer months of 2006, and holidays, vacations, and various trips to the research site from the early spring of 2006 through the spring of 2008. I did extensive observation during events where the extended and immediate family joined to reminisce and tell shared stories about their experiences. This happened particularly during Christmas and New Year's gatherings in 2006 and 2007, a fiftieth birthday celebration for my mother in 2006, a birthday celebration for my grandmother in 2006 (where attendees were invited to share a memory of growing up), and following Sunday dinners.

I was an "involved observer" (Clark, 1989/1965). Kenneth Clark describes an involved observer as a researcher who has a personal history and connection with the people in the community they are studying. Like traditional participant observation I was required "to be a part of what [was] being observed, to join in the lives of the people while at the same time seeking to understand them and the forces which mold them and to which they respond" (p. xxx).

I participated as an insider in the community—attending church services, going to the store and post office, picking up children from school, visiting the homes of community members, sitting on the porch and having conversations with passersby, watching the local news and soap operas so as to have a foundation for common conversations among the women, and witnessing gossip and woman talk between women in much the same way I did as a child (though now I joined the conversation instead of interrupting it). I went about my normal routine during visits home, only this time with more open eyes. Because I was "Bread's daughter," back home to "do research" for school, no one seemed to be distracted by my presence or bothered by my questions.

Given my interest and curiosity about the lives of rural black women, I began by reviewing research, reading novels, and viewing films on rural black women in the South and conducting archival and historical research. At the county library, I uncovered archives of old newspaper articles, census reports, history books, maps, research studies, and community diagnoses facilitated by graduate students at a nearby university, transcribed narratives and lectures given by community historians for the local historical society, and pamphlets and brochures that highlighted places of interest in the county. During interviews, I was given wedding and funeral programs, bookmarks, pictures, church directories, tributes, and books written about the community and/or affluent members of the community. Within a few weeks of being in the field, I began to make arrangements to begin formal interviewing procedures.

I aspired to conduct conversation-based research that encouraged participants to share their stories openly. The interviewing was sometimes unstructured and informal. They told. I listened. They spoke. I wrote. At other times, I shared my own stories and memories of growing up in Sweetwater, at which point our voices and experiences came together during the interviews—making them relaxed and interactive.

Interactive interviews encourage a reciprocal exchange between the researcher and the participant that closes the hierarchal gap and encourages dialogue, mutual investment, engagement, and vulnerability (Ellis & Berger, 2001; Ellis, Kiesinger, & Tillmann-Healy, 1997). This method of interviewing proved beneficial because it allowed me to connect with the participants and identify places of commonality between our experiences during the interview process (Anderson & Jack, 1998; Ellis & Berger, 2001).

I began the interview process by explaining the significance of my research, going over IRB [Institutional Review Board] documents, and expressing my gratitude for the women's willingness to participate. I watched them half listen to me, seemingly anxious to get on with the telling part. They sat patiently, as I talked about the logistics of my study and my devotion to their privacy. They watched and waited for my mouth to stop moving and then they scribbled their names on the signature line of the consent form. Though I had followed many of them, with my eyes and feet, around their houses, yards, and across kitchen tables, the "formal" interview began with suspicion. Their eyes moved from me, to the pages of questions and notes placed in front of me, to the digital recorder sitting between us like an intentional divider, separating our sameness.

Sometimes it would take a while for them to speak after the first question. I asked them to introduce themselves by telling me broadly about their family and background. One woman watched for the red light on the recorder and at its urging sat up straighter, looked forward, and spoke with an eloquence and deliberate tone that implied she was being both visually and audibly recorded by the tiny device and its red eye. When I suggested a more "authentic" stance she relaxed into a comfortable slump, still occasionally, as if on cue, sitting up and looking ahead as she recalled her story. Continuously aware of the recorder, she used her "telephone/work/white" voice to continue our conversation. She seemed anxious to answer questions correctly and cautious to answer questions discreetly.

Another woman spoke more freely. I went to her as she was waking from a nap and lay down next to her. She sleepily recounted a childhood memory of her father sneaking peaches home in his pockets from his job at the hospital cafeteria, stealing something he couldn't afford to buy. He would have a peach for each of his children and she said it was one of the few things they did not have to share. She remembered how delicious the peaches tasted, how happy she always was to see her father, and how odd she felt to have that specific and vivid memory.[2]

---

2   This story was so profound I used the name/pseudonym Peaches to tell this woman's story in Sweetwater.

Another woman sat across from me with the plate of food she offered upon my arrival sitting before me, getting cold, as she watched me take small bites, chew, and listen. I had already eaten before my arrival but as a native country girl I knew she would be offended if I refused the food she had prepared. My plate was an assortment of orange, green, yellow, and pink: yams, cabbage, corn, and pork.

Still another participant sat in a comfortable chair watching me watch her, crossing her legs, investigating my responses to her responses, and apologizing for a ringing phone that frequently interrupted her telling.

Others were intimidated, changed by the recorder, watching it curiously, suspiciously, and saying very little when the recorder was on. One woman seemed paralyzed by the formality of the recorder. When it was not in sight, she was generous with language and stories, but the recorder silenced her. Its presence somehow stole her voice and ability to speak freely. I realized that, with her, I had to record our conversations, her stories, in my head. As a researcher, I would memorize her words until I could steal away and jot them down. This seemed to make her more comfortable, though I have no way of knowing if she realized that when I was "observing" her, I was "recording" her.

The first time the recorder faded into the background was when I interviewed a group of women simultaneously—family members—who remembered together, layering their voices and memories on top of one another for me to sort through. I tried to take notes but their expressions and presence distracted me. I watched as they remembered together and reminded each other of traumas they had shared, and laughed about things that used to make them cry. Their voices competed, struggled, as if the person who said it the loudest or who spoke last was telling the greater truth. Their voices began to merge and I knew it would be difficult to distinguish them later, impossible to separate them when transcribing. I realized that not only could I not hear them but they couldn't hear each other. They were speaking to hear themselves speak; they were speaking to hear their own story, spoken out loud, against the others. It became clear to me that as characters of each other's stories and witnesses to each other's lives they understood the unspoken things that I was trying to interpret, and I could not "get" it all because I hadn't been there. But being in their presence during their remembering helped me to recognize the significance of their exchange, which was less about what they were remembering and saying and more about how they were remembering and sharing, together. They were speaking their legacy and I was hearing and inheriting it.

I began with my immediate family, recording their memories of growing up in Sweetwater and concentrating on their expressions and experiences as black women in the community. I also brought people together in groups to observe their interactions. I observed what people said and did and how they interacted, making note of how I perceived the interactions and what effects they had on me as a researcher.

Interviews were conducted in the homes of participants, in cars during brief trips, over the telephone, and while on long walks. Most of the interviews were one-on-one though there were some occasions when two or more participants were involved in a single interview. Most participants were interviewed multiple times over two years, but everyone was interviewed at least twice. The interviews ranged in time from one hour to four hours each. Each first interview began with me asking the women to tell me about their family background, education, occupation, and other information about parents, grandparents, and forebears. Beginning there, each woman shared what she remembered, careful, and cautious at times to hold on to parts of her life story that she had perhaps never said out loud. The stories they shared and the experiences they revealed uncovered realities of their lives, and the lives of community members ranging from the everyday to the extraordinary. Subsequent interviews usually picked up where the earlier ones left off, allowing participants to reflect on what they had previously shared, incorporate details they may have remembered since our last meeting, and elaborate on starting points introduced in earlier exchanges.

Interviewees included ten women (myself included) who were raised in Sweetwater or currently reside there. The ages of participants ranged from twenty-seven to ninety-five at the time of the study. The current economic situations for the participants varied according to their occupations and livelihoods. As a student, my income was taken from student loans and scholarships while another participant was fully economically independent, having secured a "good-paying" and professional job after graduating from college. Only three of the women were currently married and living with their husbands on whom they were mutually and financially dependent, while the two older women, widows and retired, relied on social security, savings, inherited money, and the assistance of family members. Another participant, retired from working for the state for twenty years, collected disability and joined her income with two of her children who all shared household expenses.

As for education, two participants did not complete high school, four were high school graduates, two were college graduates, and one attended college though did not complete a degree. I completed a PhD shortly after leaving the field.

Some of the most useful interviews were unscheduled and spontaneous (sometimes with unsolicited participants in passing). Following these conversations and observations, I would jot down notes as soon as possible after they happened (since audio recording was either impossible and unavailable or inappropriate given the circumstances). Information was not gathered exclusively from interviews, however. In addition to conversations with participants, I also immersed myself into their everyday lives (Geertz, 1973).

Once the "official" research and data collection was completed, I continued to gather notes and make observations during subsequent visits home to the community. During later visits, however, I began to focus more on my personal relationship to the community, the characters, and my personal feelings about my identity and surroundings.

I knew traditional methods and procedures of data collection would fail to contribute to a view of the day-to-day realities these women experience. I was disinterested in a demographic or quantitative analysis of rural black women's lives but rather wanted an intimate portrait of their everyday lived experience. I was interested in their emotions, fears, hopes, and desires. I wanted to learn how they understood and resolved conflicts in their daily lives, and how they negotiated their relationships in the midst of poverty, joblessness, educational and gender inequalities, alcoholism, drug addiction, crime, and abandonment. The women did not focus on themes as they spoke (I was able to recognize and identify themes from their stories later) but rather concentrated on their memories, thinking backward and talking forward, telling me about their past while also sharing their hopes for the future. It seemed to help them to view their lives as a story, the telling of which helped them understand their experiences. I was writing as a method of inquiry (Richardson, 2000) while they were telling as a method of understanding.

By making the participants narrators of their own experiences, I focused on their communication choices and selection of words. I found a way to honor and maintain the words they used to describe their lives by writing stories based on the situations and circumstances they shared, using (when possible) their word-for-word accounts in the retelling. For example, I created scenes and settings based on the specificity of their memories and the details shared in their interviews.

There were some stories I yielded in order to protect participants. While I was committed to telling a full story, some stories were not needed or did not need to be attached to individual women. I was more concerned with representation than designation, especially because of my commitment to protecting the privacy and anonymity of participants. Creating composite characters allowed me to tell stories without attributing them to individual women. In those cases, I created a composite character or collapsed details from multiple interviews to tell a generic story about the community at large, allowing Sweetwater itself to absorb narratives too difficult to attribute to an individual.

I concentrated on the narratives that had resonance and that represented resilience. Resilience was the overarching theme of all of the stories. When I looked at the individual interviews, as a whole, each woman had exhibited resilience in their lives, despite their circumstances.

All of the Sweetwater stories are true. Everything written about happened. In many cases, the stories told themselves. I honed in on particular details from the interviews, allowing the participants' responses to set the scenes or create the setting for individual stories. I also had the benefit of overlapping stories/memories, in some cases securing multiple perspectives of the same event.

All of the stories from the interviews did not make it to the dissertation or the book. The data had to be coded thematically, analyzed theoretically, and then curated into a discernable, reasonable, somewhat chronological story that made sense. In many ways, the story dictated what was included and what was left out. But there were other considerations when translating the data to narrative. Some of it was redundant. Some of it was not provocative or important. Some things were intentionally left out to preserve relationships and/or privacy. Some things were cut or edited out during the revision process. Other stories were not included because they didn't fit the overall narrative, weren't evocative or compelling enough to move the stories forward, and/or didn't have a theme consistent with the conversations of at least two other women. It was important for me to have Sweetwater stories be relevant to Sweetwater women. Ultimately, I had to decide what the story was and what the storyline was based on the information I had collected. Then, I needed to tell that story.

My research methodology, as demonstrated in the introduction to this book, privileges lived experiences and stories. I relied on grounded theory to determine what theories were most salient to the lives of Sweetwater women based on the interviews and data. While I was committed to a black feminist analysis all along and expected narrative theory to inform my understanding of black women's storied lives, intersectionality and muted group theory emerged organically as theoretical frameworks from the themes and consistencies in the interviews. I coded field notes, and transcriptions of interviews to identify recurring themes that dictated the focus of the narratives I would later write. Topics that recurred across multiple interviews and with at least three women became themes and the basis of chapter narratives in the first part of the book. I later used intersectionality and muted group theory, alongside black feminist thought/womanism, to help explain the participants' stories. In particular, black feminism reiterated the relevance and scholarly potential of the everyday and ordinary experiences of black women. Intersectionality accounted for the multiple, and oftentimes layered ways these women's identities influenced their circumstances. Finally, muted group theory was useful because of the repeated insistence by many of the participants that their story was not worth telling or being heard.

After coding the interviews and notes, I identified themes, collected all corresponding answers, and then wrote them as poems and stories, using, when possible, pieces of each interview. The themes, which would later become the focus of book chapters, included domestic violence, gender performance, religiosity, sex/uality, black men, failed romantic relationships, colorism, fatherlessness, poverty, sudden death or absence, mental illness, and race/racism. I noted that the terms and language I used to summarize or describe the events in the narratives were different than how they may have been described or summarized by participants. Because coding was part of my methodological process, and I sought to analyze the stories thematically, I began thinking about what the themes meant before I wrote the stories. I did not share my speculations with participants during the research process, nor did I ask or expect participants to analyze their own stories.

I used almost everything shared with me in interviews. With the exceptions of stories I was asked to withhold, or stories I did not feel comfortable telling, I used as much raw data as possible. Because of my interest in everyday experiences, I incorporated even mundane details and descriptions into the narratives. Even those things shared as memories or stories that were heard but could not be confirmed as truth were blended into the community narratives. I included everything from smells participants described to nicknames they were called. It was important to me that the stories reflect their experiences. I blended characters and characterizations into composite characters, but carefully crafted stories that would be discernable and have verisimilitude to community members.

The written stories shift between a third-person omniscient perspective that allowed me, as the narrator, to have access into the private thoughts and hidden events of characters, and a first-person account that offered me the opportunity to talk back to the stories. The stories show how the participants talked about and made sense of their lives and my personal experiences as a cultural and community member.

During the writing stage, I listened to and transcribed recorded interviews, reviewed field and journal notes, wrote personal narratives from memory, and translated the interviews into poetry and short stories. I felt that by writing stories it would give the participants an opportunity to participate in the process beyond being interviewed. By telling stories, to which they would later respond, I was making their lives, framed academically, accessible to them.

There are consequences to pursuing unconventional representations of research. When defending her decision to write an interview as a poem, Laurel Richardson (1997) explained the importance of giving a representation of participants' lives close to their lived experience. For me this means scholarly jargon or dispassionate prose would relinquish the voices and contaminate the experiences of the black women in my study, making them unrecognizable. It would be useless and futile to collect their experiences with the hope of magnifying and centering their lives if they themselves could not benefit from or translate the meaning. If the text were written in such a way that they could not or would not want to read their own stories, what would be the point (Goodall, 2008)?

Appendix B

Sweetwater Summaries

The narrative chapters of Sweetwater are numbered and not named. I wanted to expand, not limit, what the stories teach and tell us about black women, their communication practices, their relational negotiations, and their resilience. Because I expected each reader to have a separate relationship to Sweetwater based on their own lived experiences and background, I decided not to identify survival strategies and themes, in an effort to allow them to surface through reflection and discussion. This appendix offers brief chapter summaries in order to introduce the corresponding chapter themes. The themes included here are not exclusive or exhaustive, but outline the most observable topics addressed in the chapters.

Part 1: (DAILY) "BREAD"

The opening chapter of Sweetwater introduces the town and situates its race and class politics, alongside its demographic makeup. Sweetwater is described as a self-segregated community wherein black folk are bonded by biological kinship, religious faith, socioeconomic circumstances, and proximity. Chapter 1 describes what Sweetwater is like and what it is like to live there.

Chapters 2 through 4 discuss the ubiquity of intimate partner violence and infidelity in marriages, how romantic relationships are shaped and understood, and the persistence of alcoholism/substance abuse. In Chapter 2, Patience, a Sweetwater woman who moved away, kills her husband after he beats her. In Chapter 3, Twiggy is introduced, reinforcing assumed or preferred gender scripts for marriage and family. Twiggy sides with Patience's self-defense while her friend places the blame on Patience. Their conversation reinforces the problematic gender training that happens in most households.

In Chapter 4, we see the conflation of domestic violence, substance abuse, infidelity, and class politics. Twiggy and Cake's relationship is used to explain why couples fight, why they cheat (on each other), and why they stay together. Cake's infidelity, which he does for softness and "something different," implies that Twiggy is too hard and harsh, reinforcing the standard stereotype of the Sapphire or "angry black woman." Twiggy's infidelity, which she does in retaliation and defiance, reiterates that sex is used as sedation and distraction, like a drug, and as a way of making up after an ass whoopin.

Chapter 5 focuses on the role of and reliance on religion, faith, and prayer in the lives of churchwomen, and how religiosity sustains them despite their circumstances. The chapter also offers commentary on the performance of Christianity, the prevalence of belief, and the connection between church attendance and sanctimony. Bread is intrigued with the preacher's son and considers her salvation, which is nestled somewhere between ambivalence and fear.

Chapter 6 returns to Bread's infatuation with Ray-Ray, and closes with a reflection on death and endings. The themes of death and departure are reconciled by themes of romantic and maternal love. The chapter also makes claims about the influence/s of Sweetwater masculinity.

Chapters 7 and 8 focus on romantic relationships, unplanned pregnancies, and the negotiation of marriage. Unplanned pregnancies, not love, are the impetus of many marriages in Sweetwater. In Chapter 7, Twiggy's Aunt Noisey and her intentional singleness is used to discuss the role and expectation of marriage for women, and the consequences of not marrying. Many women get married because of the expectation that women get married and have children, or get married because they have children. A fish dream, which is a premonition of pregnancy in Sweetwater, implies the possibility of another marriage.

In Chapter 8, Bread falls in love, becomes pregnant, and gets married. The chapter also concentrates on the relevance of names, what they mean, what people are called, and how the community collaborates to accept or reject a given name, replacing it with a nickname. We learn that Twiggy's real name is Sadie, Bread's real name is Gale, and why Bread named her daughter California. Robin/Bird is also born.

PORCH PREMONITIONS/INTERLUDE

The interlude is intended to act as a partition between Part 1 and Part 2, centering Bird's narrative, which will be the focus of the second part of the book. In it, Sweetie Pie and Peewee, who can be simultaneously read as platonic friends and/or lesbian lovers, gossip about the goings-on of Sweetwater in between the end of Part 1 and the beginning of Part 2.

The ambiguity of Sweetie Pie and Peewee's romantic relationship was intentional. It was important for me to write the possibility of their relationship and the inevitability of their existence into the story even though none of the interviews suggested same gender loving relationships in the community. By presenting them as queer, I give visibility to a story that would have been intentionally invisible and silenced during that time.

Part 2: (ROBIN) "BIRD"

Chapter 9 introduces Sweetwater and homeplace through the eyes and perspective of young Bird, the author. Shifting to first person, I set the scene as an amalgamation of childhood memories centering home life and my feelings of isolation and abandonment. I reflect on the women in my family and my relationship to them, while describing the scene and setting of Sweetwater in the mid-1980s.

Chapter 10 is about food, stubbornness, and fatherlessness. I talk about my father being attentive and loving when present, but mostly absent. I also reflect on my grandmother as a father-figure.

Chapter 11 is about beauty politics and colorism, and the rituals of courtship, how men and boys learn to seduce young girls, especially those who are not traditionally beautiful and who, like me, lack self-esteem.

In Chapter 12, depression and mental illness are introduced, alongside black women's everyday talk, warnings about seduction, and reasonable dreams. Intergenerational dialogue is used to establish bonds, reiterate relationships, share secrets, and express joy. I reflect on how being invited into a grown woman dialogue was both affirming and disconfirming.

In Chapter 13, I flash-forward to a future moment of intimacy and infatuation, describing the inevitable heartbreak the women prophesied in the preceding chapter.

Chapter 14 focuses on religion and God. In this chapter, I talk about the contradiction of Bible belief and superstitions, and the confusion of childhood faith. I also describe church rituals and expectations, and how religious devotion is an alternative to romantic relationships.

In Chapter 15, Cake reenters the storyline following his premature death. Revelations of his passing inspire identity crises and confusion for family members, myself included, though I did not understand them at the time. I reflect on the legalism of death and the move from grief back to laughter following the death of a family member who was also a stranger.

The final chapter, Chapter 16, returns to Twiggy, the main character whose story, legacy and family centers the entire narrative. In a passing conversation, I announce my plans to leave Sweetwater, as she confirms her intentions to stay. The chapter concludes with an explanation of Sweetwater's inevitable pull and familiarity, and what makes it the same place it had been generations before.

RECURRING THEMES

Parallel narratives told in Parts 1 and 2 include the following recurring themes:

- Intimate Partner Violence (Part 1 focuses on physical abuse, while Part 2 concentrates on emotional and psychological violence)
- Gender/Sex (Black masculinity and the performance of black masculinity is considered in both narratives, concentrating, most specifically, on the harshness of men and ill-intent toward women. This is also related to misogyny, sexism, and gender scripts)
- Religion/Church (This includes prayer, church services, gospel music, baptism, and faith)
- Sex and Sexuality (Specifically its relationship to unplanned pregnancy and/or premature marriage)
- Colorism (The preference and benefits of light skin is present in both Parts, but most explicitly discussed in Part 2)
- Father Absence (generationally)
- Black Men (This theme includes the ways black boys are reared to reiterate problematic performances of black manhood)

- Failed Romantic Relationships (Resulting from infidelity, separation, divorce, abandonment, and rejection)
- Social Class (Specifically, working-class identity and the shift to middle-class due to educational attainment)
- Unexpected Death and/or Abandonment
- Mental Illness/Depression (While this is not explicit in the first part, it is alluded to and implied. In Part 2, it is specifically named)
- Race (While the stories are centered on the experiences of black folk, "Whiteness is like air, everywhere all at once…" p. 21).

Epilogue: BitterSweet(water): A Meta-Autoethnography

When I wrote *Sweetwater*, I never imagined it would be read beyond the few hundred people who may have stumbled upon my dissertation looking for something else. I never expected it to become a book. I never thought my book would sit on people's coffee tables. I never knew my words would be taught in classrooms. I am honored that what began as an attempt at understanding my community, and thereby myself, has inspired and instigated other stories and considerations of place-specific autoethnographies.

Shortly after *Sweetwater* was first published I revisited the community to talk to people who were interviewed about their impressions of the book. I planned to use their feedback to consider what, if any, follow up projects I would pursue, related to *Sweetwater*. Three of the nine women I interviewed passed away between the time I completed my dissertation in 2009 and published the book in 2013. When I approached the other women I interviewed about *Sweetwater*, only a few of them were interested in talking about the book. While I initially felt their ambivalence may have been a result of dissatisfaction with how they were represented, I later realized that three of them had not read the book and had no interest or intention in doing so because they did not have the luxury of time or interest in pleasure reading. One woman read the book but felt intimidated discussing it with me, saying she would feel more comfortable if she read it again before we talked. Once she re-read the book and agreed to a discussion, I had the opportunity to reflect on *Sweetwater* with three of the original women interviewed. I also talked about *Sweetwater* with other members of the Sweetwater community who read the book and were marginally, if not collectively and generationally, characterized in the text.

They all expressed pride that the book existed. For them, *Sweetwater* was a personal diary they didn't write themselves, recounting their innermost thoughts and remembrances. They said it brought back memories and dredged up feelings that had been long buried or hidden. *Sweetwater* helped the women think about themselves, each other, and their community in new ways. The book urged them to appreciate their heritage, recognize the legacy of their lived experiences, and critique circumstances that were oftentimes beyond their control. It made them feel proud. It made them feel conflicted. It made them feel exposed. It made them feel seen. Sweetwater gave them visibility and voice.

When asked about what, if any, representation was missing from the Sweetwater stories, two women indicated that while there were stories about women loving God, there was not a story about the woman in our community who had broken barriers in the black Baptist church, emerged as a leader in a male-dominated space, and who lived, off and on, in Sweetwater throughout her life. The woman they were describing was a woman I was unable to interview because she had been diagnosed with Alzheimer's disease and was subsequently admitted to a custodial care facility in a nearby city. She did not appear significantly in the stories the interviewed women told[3], so it was only in retrospect that they understood her story as being representative and important. She was known, broadly, as Aunt Bertha, even though she was not our biological aunt. She was my grandmother's cousin.

Aunt Bertha died in the summer of 2014, at the age of 92, after living several years with a degenerative disease that rendered her unable to remember herself. Her obituary boasts her various accomplishments, including being ordained as a minister in 1970, founding her own church in her home in Sweetwater, and becoming the first woman pastor in the Deep River Missionary Baptist Association, the second in the state of North Carolina to have a woman pastor. She was a trailblazer, a visionary, a woman of God, and a community member invested in the lives of elderly citizens. Largely self-taught, she earned her GED at age 57, and went on to attend community college where she received bachelor degrees in theology and the arts. She later enrolled in the Master of Divinity program at Shaw University when she was 60.

---

3   I did, however, reference Aunt Bertha, in summary, when talking about church women generally.

As I work on the revision of Sweetwater, I regret not being able to collect Aunt Bertha's stories in her own words. Her illness, at the time of my data collection, prevented her from being a viable candidate, vulnerable and therefore unable to be give consent. I am also grateful that I was able to collect the stories of my grandmother, who now, 84, suffers symptoms of dementia alongside diabetic blindness. She is less the version of herself she was when I was growing up, less the person I write about in Sweetwater. My grandmother still tells stories sometimes, but they are less coherent, oftentimes skewed by confusion and mixed memories. I feel simultaneously grateful and guilty when I think about the stories I gathered, and the ones my grandmother can only now recall during fleeting moments of lucidity. My mother, whose children my grandmother helped raise, is now my grandmother's primary caregiver. Their roles have reversed but their stories remain interconnected and circular.

These days, when I come to Sweetwater it is markedly different. Many people I associated with the community are no longer here, having moved away or passed away. The touchstones of my childhood remain, including the trailer I grew up in. The house looks different. Paint and wallpaper hide the paper-thin faux-wood walls underneath them where, as a child, I pushed my ear against to listen to conversations I was forbidden to witness. The floors are covered with years-old, overworn burgundy carpet and laminate floors that don't need vacuuming. There is new furniture, old plates, new doors, old pans, new windows, and old family albums. There are no pictures of us on the walls, just sayings and scriptures, prophesies and promises, and images of white Jesus in nice frames, overlooking what has always been and perhaps always will be.

The stories in Sweetwater were intentionally focused on experiences growing up in the community, which means there was less focus and consideration of growing old there. Aging in a small community has particular challenges related to health care access, financial resources, and physical aid and assistance. If I were to write another story for Sweetwater it would consider those things, and how Sweetwater women age in a community with shifting circumstances. The new story would be bittersweet, documenting the latter years of life, slow-moving illnesses, intergenerational caretaking, intermittent memories, and a new relationship to stories, from the tales we tell to pass the time to the legacies we leave to tell about our lives. Bitter and sweet.

As I move forward to work on my forthcoming book, Blackgirl Blue(s), I take the bittersweetness of Sweetwater, the absences and pauses, the gaps and the secrets, the laughter and the pain, and prepare to tell another side of the story, picking up where Sweetwater leaves off.

Postscript

Three of the nine women I interviewed are now deceased. Collectively, they lived over twenty decades. I selected them to participate in my study because they lived extraordinary lives and were leaders of/in their communities and families, and because their lives remained grounded in rural roots. They were engaged citizens, wives, mothers, educators, healers, friends, and survivors. They lived consciously, courageously, intentionally, and fully. They lost loved ones over the years and resurrected them through the narratives they told. I am honored to have that same opportunity to bring them back to life through storytelling.

*

Ms. M.,
her name, calm waiting
her Mama's last child
full of memories and strength
known for making
black woman's history
educated but not high minded
proud but not arrogant
an activist, educator, and politician

*

Butter
to my Mama's Bread.
tears
chasing pain
remembering
hard things not often spoken.
The room filled
with best-friend laughter
between grown women
who share childhood and secrets

*

Aunt H.,
alive almost 100 years
Greensboro-born
brown-skinned brown-eyed girl
chosen by high yellow, green-eyed, boy
married at 17
in the country
mother of 14 babies
a beautiful wonder

Bibliography

Adams, T. E. (2011). *Narrating the closet: An autoethnography of same-sex attraction.* Walnut Creek, CA: Left Coast.

Adams, T. E. (2015). Family shame. *Departures in Critical Qualitative Research, 4*(1), 124–126.

Adams, T. E., Holman Jones, S., & Ellis, C. (2015). *Autoethnography: Understanding qualitative research.* New York: Oxford University Press.

Alexander, B. K. (2012). *The performative sustainability of race: Reflections on black culture and the politics of identity.* New York: Peter Lang.

Alexander-Floyd, N. G. & Simien, E. M. (2006). Revisiting "what's in a name?": Exploring the contours of Africana womanist thought. *Frontiers, 27*(1), 67–89.

Allen, B. J. (1998). Black womanhood and feminist standpoints. *Management Communication Quarterly, 11*(4), 575–586.

Allen, B. J. (2002). Goals for emancipatory communication research on Black women. In M. Houston & O. I. Davis (Eds.), *Centering ourselves: African American feminist and womanist studies of discourse* (pp. 21–34). Cresskill, NJ: Hampton Press.

Anderson, K. & Jack, D. C. (1998). Learning to listen: Interview techniques and analyses. In R. Perks & A. Thomson (Eds.), *The oral history reader* (pp. 157–171). New York: Routledge.

Ardener, S. (1978). *Defining females: The nature of women in society.* New York; Wiley.

Ardener, S. (2005). Ardener's 'muted groups': The genesis of an idea and its praxis. *Women and Language, 28*(2), 50–54.

Atkinson, Y. (2000). Language that bears witness: The Black English oral tradition in the works of Toni Morrison. In M. C. Conner (Ed.), *The aesthetics of Toni Morrison: Speaking the unspeakable* (pp. 12–30). Jackson: University Press of Mississippi.

Bambara, T. C. (Ed.). (1970). *The Black woman: An anthology*. New York: Washington Square.

Bambara, T. C. (1992). *The salt eaters*. New York: Vintage Books.

Banks-Wallace, J. (2000). Womanist ways of knowing: Theoretical considerations for research with African American women. *Advanced Nursing Science, 22*(3), 33–45.

Beale, F. (1970). Double jeopardy: To be Black and female. In T. C. Bambara (Ed.), *The black woman* (pp. 109–122). New York: Signet.

Bell-Scott, P. (2015). Debunking Sapphire: Toward a non-racist and non-sexist social science. In A. Hull, P. Bell-Scott & B. Smith (Eds.), *All the women are white, all the blacks are men, but some of us are brave: Black women's studies (2nd ed.)* New York: Feminist Press.

Blauner, R. & Wellman, D. (1973). Toward the decolonization of social research. In J. A. Ladner (Ed.), *The death of White sociology* (pp. 310–330). New York: Vintage.

Blumer, H. (1969). *Symbolic interactionism: Perspective and method*. Englewood Cliffs: Prentice-Hall.

Bobo, J. (1991). Black women in fiction and non-fiction: Images of power and powerlessness. *Wide Angle, 13*, 72–81.

Bobo, J. (1995). *Black women as cultural readers*. New York: Columbia UP.

Bochner, A. P. (1994). Perspectives on inquiry II: Theories and stories. In M. Knapp & G. R. Miller (Eds.), *The handbook of interpersonal communication* (2nd ed., pp. 21–41). Thousand Oaks: Sage.

Bochner, A. P. (2002). Perspectives on inquiry III: The moral of stories. In M. Knapp & J. Daley (Eds.), *The handbook of interpersonal communication* (3rd ed., pp. 73–101). Thousand Oaks: Sage.

Bochner, A. P. (2014). *Coming to narrative: A personal history of paradigm change in the human sciences*. Walnut Creek, CA: Left Coast Press.

Bochner, A. P. & Ellis, C. (2016). *Evocative autoethnography: Writing lives and telling stories*. New York: Routledge.

Borum, V. (2006). Reading and writing womanist poetic prose: African American mothers with deaf daughters. *Qualitative Inquiry, 12*, 340–352.

Boylorn, R. M. (2006). E pluribus unum (out of many, one). *Qualitative Inquiry, 12*, 651–680.

Boylorn, R. M. (2008). As seen on TV: An autoethnographic reflection on race and reality television. *Critical Studies in Media Communication, 25*(4), 413–433.

Boylorn, R. M. (2013a). Sit with your legs closed: And other sayin's from my childhood. In S. Holman Jones, T. Adams, & C. Ellis (Eds.), *The handbook of autoethnography* (pp. 173–185). Walnut Creek, CA: Left Coast.

Boylorn, R. M. (2013b). *Sweetwater: Black Women and Narratives of Resilience*. New York: Peter Lang.

Boylorn, R. M. (2014). A story & a stereotype: An angry and strong auto/ethnography of race, class, and gender. In R. M. Boylorn & M. P. Orbe (Eds.), *Critical autoethnography: Intersecting cultural identities in everyday life* (pp. 129-143). Walnut Creek, CA: Left Coast.

Boylorn, R. M. (2014). My daddy is slick, brown, and cool like ice water. In J. Wyatt & T. E. Adams (Eds.), *On (writing) families: Autoethnographies of presence and absence, love and loss* (pp. 85–94). Boston, MA: Sense Publishers.

Boylorn, R. M. & Orbe, M. P. (Eds.). (2014). *Critical autoethnography: Intersecting cultural identities in everyday life*. Walnut Creek, CA: Left Coast.

Boylorn, R. M. (2016). On being at home with myself: Blackgirl autoethnography as research praxis. *International Review of Qualitative Research, 9*(1), 44–58.

Boylorn, R. M., & Adams, T. E. (2016). Queer and quare autoethnography. In N. K. Denzin & M. D. Giardina (Eds.), *Qualitative inquiry through a critical lens* (pp. 85-98). New York: Routledge.

Bradley, D. (1984, January 8). Alice Walker: Telling the Black woman's story. *New York Times Magazine*, 25–37.

Bradley, R. N. (2016). Beautiful Ones Fiction. Transition, 120, 61–78.

Bradley, R. N. (2017). *Boondock kollage: Stories from the hip hop south*. New York: Peter Lang.

Brown, R. N. (2009). *Black girlhood celebration: Toward a hip-hop feminist pedagogy*. New York: Peter Lang.

Brown, R. N. (2013). *Hear our truths: The creative potential of black girlhood*. Urbana, IL: University of Illinois Press.

Brown, R. N., Callier, D. M., Garner, P. R., Hill, D. C., Olayiwola, P., & Robinson, J. L. (2015). Staging black girl utopias: A Sweetwater tribute. *Departures in Critical Qualitative Research, 4*(1), 81–88.

Brown, T. F. (1997). I got your back: African American womanist theory. *The Other Side, 33*(5), 71–72.

Cannon, K. G. (1988). *Black womanist ethics*. Atlanta: Scholars Press.

Christian, B. (1987). A race for theory. *Cultural Critique, 6*, 51–63.

Christian, B. (1997). *Black feminist criticism: Perspectives on Black women writers*. New York: Teachers College Press.

Clark, K. B. (1989). *Dark ghetto: Dilemmas of social power* (2nd ed.). Hanover, NH: Wesleyan UP. (Original work published 1965.)

Clarke, C. (1983). *Narratives: Poems in the tradition of black women* (2nd ed.). New York: Kitchen Table.

Cleage, P. (1990). *Mad at Miles: A Blackwoman's guide to truth*. Southfield, MI: Cleage Group.

Cleage, P. (1993). *Deals with the devil: And other reasons to riot*. New York: Ballantine Books.

Cliff, M. (1996). *No telephone to heaven*. New York: Plume.

Clifford, J. & Marcus, G. E. (Eds.) (1986). *Writing culture: The poetics and politics of ethnography*. Berkeley, CA: University of California Press.

Coles, R. (1989). *The call of stories: Teaching and the moral imagination*. Boston, MA: Houghton Mifflin.

Collins, P. H. (1986). Learning from the outsider within: The sociological significance of Black feminist thought, *Social Problems, 33*, 14–32.

Collins, P. H. (1998). *Fighting words: Black women and the search for justice*. Minneapolis: University of Minnesota Press.

Collins, P. H. (2009). *Black feminist thought: Knowledge, consciousness, and the politics of empowerment*. New York: Routledge. (Original work published 1991.)

Collins, P. H. & Bilge, S. (2016*). Intersectionality*. Malden, MA: Polity.

The Combahee River Collective (1982). A Black feminist statement. In G. T. Hull, P. B. Scott, & B. Smith (Eds.), *All the women are White, all the Blacks are men, but some of us are brave: Black women's studies* (pp. 13–22). Old Westbury, NY: Feminist.

Conquergood, D. (1985). Performing as a moral act: Ethical dimensions of the ethnography of performance. *Literature in Performance, 5*(2), 1–13.

Cooper, B. (2016). Intersectionality. In L. Disch & Hawkesworth, M. (Eds.), *The Oxford handbook of feminist theory* (pp. 385–406). New York: Oxford University Press.

Cooper, B. (2017). *Beyond respectability: The intellectual thought of race women.* Urbana, IL: University of Illinois Press.

Cooper, B. & Morris, S. M. (2015). "Show, don't tell": Redefining contemporary Black Southern rurality in Robin M. Boylorn's Sweetwater. Departures in Critical Qualitative Research, 4(1), 107–109

Cox, A. M. (2015). *Shapeshifters: Black girls and the choreography of citizenship.* Durham, NC: Duke University Press.

Crenshaw, K. (1989). Demarginalizing the intersection of race and sex: A Black feminist critique of antidiscrimination doctrine, feminist theory and antiracist politics. *University of Chicago Legal Forum*, 138–167.

Crenshaw, K. (1991). Mapping the margins: Intersectionality, identity politics, and violence against women of color. *Stanford Law Review, 43*, 1241–1299.

Dance, D. C. (Ed.) (1998). *Honey, hush! An anthology of African American women's humor.* New York: W. W. Norton.

Danquah, M. N. (1998). *Willow weep for me: A black woman's journey through depression.* New York: Ballantine.

Danticat, E. (1994). *Breath, eyes, memory.* New York: Vintage.

Davis, A. Y. (1983). *Women, race & class.* New York: Vintage Books.

Davis, O. I. (2007). Locating Tulsa in the souls of black women folk: Performing memory as survival, *Performance Research 12*(3), 124–136.

Davis, O. I. (2008). A visitation from the foremothers: Black women's healing through a "performance of care"—from African diaspora to the American academy, *Women Studies in Communication, 31*(2), 175–185.

Denzin, N. (1992). *Symbolic interactionism and cultural studies: The politics of interpretation.* Cambridge: Blackwell.

DeVeaux, A. (1990). Where did you grow up/where born?/how did you get to the place you are now? In M. H. Washington (Ed.), *Black eyed susans & midnight birds: Stories by and about black women* (pp. 173–179). New York: Anchor Books, Doubleday.

Dews, C. L. & Law, C. L. (Eds.). (1995). *This fine place so far from home: Voices of academics from the working class.* Philadelphia: Temple University Press.

Didion, J. (1976, December 5). Why I Write. *New York Times Book Review*, 17–18.

Doughtery, M. C. (1978). *Becoming a woman in rural black culture.* New York: Holt, Rinehart & Winston.

Du Bois, W. E. B. (1918). *The souls of Black folk: Essays and sketches.* Chicago: A. C. McClurg.

Durham, A. S. (2014). *Home with hip hop feminism: Performances in communication and culture.* New York: Peter Lang.

Durham, A. (2015). Kindred narratives: Reflections of Southern Black orality in Sweetwater. *Departures in Critical Qualitative Research, 4*(1), 110–113.

Ellis, C. (1995a). Emotional and ethical quagmires in returning to the field. *Journal of Contemporary Ethnography, 24*, 68–98.

Ellis, C. (1995b). The other side of the fence: Seeing black and white in a small, southern town. *Qualitative Inquiry, 1*(2), 147–167.

Ellis, C. (2004a). *The ethnographic I: A methodological novel about autoethnography.* Walnut Creek: AltaMira.

Ellis, C. (2004b). *The ethnographic I and intimate journalism.* Communication and Methodology, 175-182.

Ellis, C. (2007). Telling secrets, revealing lives: Relational ethics in research with intimate others. *Qualitative Inquiry, 13*(1), 3–29.

Ellis, C. (2009). *Revision: Autoetnographic reflections on life and work.* Walnut Creek: Left Coast.

Ellis, C. (2015). Sweet Mentoring. *Departures in Critical Qualitative Research, 4*(1), 81–88.

Ellis, C., Adams, T. E., & Bochner, A. P. (2011). Autoethnography: An Overview. *Historical Social Research, 36*(4), 273–290.

Ellis, C. & Berger, L. (2001).Their story/my story/our story: Including the researcher's experience in interview research. In J. Gubrium & J. Holstein (Eds.), *Handbook of Interviewing* (pp. 849–875). Thousand Oaks, CA: Sage.

Ellis, C. & Bochner, A. P. (2000). Autoethnography, personal narrative, reflexivity: Researcher as subject. In N. K. Denzin & Y. S. Lincoln (Eds.), *Handbook of qualitative research* (2nd ed., pp. 733–768). Thousand Oaks, CA: Sage.

Ellis, C., Kiesinger, C. E., & Tillmann-Healy, L. M. (1997). Interactive interviewing: Talk about emotional experience. In R. Hertz (Ed.), *Reflexivity and voice* (pp.119–149). Thousand Oaks, CA: Sage.

Etter-Lewis, G. (1991). Black women's life stories: Reclaiming self in narrative texts. In S. B. Gluck & D. Patai (Eds.), *Women's words: The feminist practice of oral history* (pp. 43–58). New York: Routledge.

Evans-Winters, V. E. & Love, B. L. (Eds.), *Black feminism in education: Black women speak back, up, and out.* New York: Peter Lang.

Fine, M. (1994).Working the hyphens: Reinventing the self and other in qualitative research. In N. K. Denzin & Y. S. Lincoln (Eds.), *Handbook of qualitative research* (pp. 70–82). Thousand Oaks, CA: Sage.

Fine, M., Weis, L., Weseen, S., & Wong, L. (2000). For whom? Qualitative research, representations, and social responsibilities. In N. K. Denzin & Y. S. Lincoln (Eds.), *Handbook of qualitative research* (2nd ed., pp. 107–131). Thousand Oaks, CA: Sage.

Fisher, W. R. (1987). *Human communication as narration: Toward a philosophy of reason, value, and action.* Columbia: University of South Carolina Press.

Frankenburg, R. (1993). *White women, race matters: The social construction of whiteness.* Minneapolis: University of Minnesota Press.

Franklin, D. L. (2000). *What's love got to do with it? Understanding and healing the rift between black men and women.* New York: Simon & Schuster.

Frederick, M. F. (2003). *Between Sundays: Black women and the everyday struggles of faith.* Berkeley: University of California Press.

Geertz, C. (1973). *The interpretation of cultures.* New York: Basic Books.

Giddings, P. (1984). *When and where I enter: The impact of Black women on race and sex in America.* New York: Perennial.

Gilkes, C. T. (2001). *If it wasn't for the women.* Maryknoll, NY: Orbis.

Goodall, H. L. (2000). *Writing the new ethnography.* Lanham, MD: AltaMira.

Goodall, H. L. (2004). Narrative ethnography as applied communication research. *Journal of Applied Communication Research, 32*, 185–194.

Goodall, H. L. (2005).Narrative inheritance: A nuclear family with toxic secrets. *Qualitative Inquiry, 11*(4), 492–513.

Goodall, H. L. (2008). *Writing qualitative inquiry: Self, stories, and academic life*. Walnut Creek, CA: Left Coast.

Griffin, R. A. (2015). On Sweetwater and the significance of Black women tellin'. *Departures in Critical Qualitative Research, 4*(1), 133–136.

Gumbs, A. P. (2016). *Spill: Scenes of black feminist fugitivity*. Durham, NC: Duke University Press.

Gumbs, A. P. & Martens, C. (Eds.). (2016). *Revolutionary mothering: Love on the front lines*. Toronto, Canada: Between the Lines Books.

Gwaltney, J. L. (1980). *Drylongso: A self-portrait of Black America*. New York: Random House.

Hanbrick, A. (1997). You haven't seen anything until you make a black woman mad. In K. M. Vaz (Ed.), *Collecting treasures: Oral narrative research with black women* (pp. 64–82).Thousand Oaks, CA: Sage.

Hannerz, U. (1969). *Soulside: Inquiries into ghetto culture and community*. Chicago: University of Chicago Press.

Harley, S. (Ed.). (2002). *Sister circle: Black women and work*. New Brunswick, NJ: Rutgers University Press.

Harris, T. (2003). *Summer snow: Reflections from a Black daughter of the south*. Boston: Beacon.

Harris-Perry, M. V. (2011). *Sister citizen: Shame, stereotypes, and Black women in America*. New Haven, CT: Yale University Press.

Hecht, M. L., Collier, M. J., & Ribeau, S. A. (1993). *African American communication: Ethnic identity and cultural interpretation*. Newbury Park, CA: Sage.

Holman Jones, S., Adams, T. E., & Ellis, C. (Eds.). (2013). *Handbook of autoethnography*. Walnut Creek, CA: Left Coast Press.

Hooks, B. (1981). *Ain't I a woman: Black women and feminism*. Boston: South End.

Hooks, B. (1989). *Talking back: Thinking feminist, thinking Black*. Boston: South End.

Hooks, B. (1992). *Black looks: Race and representation*. Boston: South End.

Hooks, B. (1993). *Sisters of the yam: Black women and self-recovery*. Boston: South End.

Hooks, B. (1999). *Remembered rapture: The writer at work*. New York: Henry Holt.

Hooks, B. (2001). *All about love: New visions*. New York: Perennial.

Hooks, B. (2009). Returning to the wound. In *Belonging: A culture of place*. New York: Routledge.

Hooks, B. & Mesa-Bains, A. (2006). *Homegrown: Engaged cultural criticism*. Boston, MA: South End Press.

Houston, M. (1992). The politics of difference: Race, class, and women's communication. In L. F. Rakow (Ed.), *Women making meaning: New feminist directions in communication* (pp. 45–59). New York: Routledge.

Houston, M. (2000). Writing for my life: Community-cognizant scholarship on African-American women and communication. *International Journal of Intercultural Relations, 24*(5), 673–686.

Houston, M. (2002). Triumph stories: Caring and accountability in African American women's conversation narratives. In M. Houston & O. I. Davis (Eds.), *Centering ourselves: African American feminist and womanist studies of discourse* (pp. 77–98). Cresskill, NJ: Hampton Press.

Houston, M. (2004). Multiple perspectives: African American women conceive their talk. In R. L. Jackson (Ed.), *African American communication & identities: Essential readings* (pp. 157–164). Thousand Oaks, CA: Sage.

Houston, M. & Davis, O. I. (Eds). (2002). *Centering ourselves: African American feminist and womanist studies of discourse.* Cresskill, NJ: Hampton.

Houston, M. & Kramerae, C. (1991). Speaking from silence: Methods of silencing and of resistance. *Discourse & Society, 2*(4), 387–399.

Houston Stanback, M. (1988a). Feminist theory and black women's talk. *Howard Journal of Communications, 1*(4), 187–194.

Houston Stanback, M. (1988b). What makes scholarship about black women and communication feminist communication scholarship? *Women's Studies in Communication, 11*(1), 28–31.

Hull, G. T., Scott, P. B., & Smith, B. (Eds.). (1982). *All the women are White, all the Blacks are men, but some of us are brave: Black women's studies.* Old Westbury, NY: Feminist.

Hurston, Z. N. (1990). *Mules and men.* New York: Perennial Classics. (Original work published in 1935.)

Hurston, Z. N. (1995). *Dust tracks on a road.* New York: Harper Perennial. (Original work published in 1942.)

Hurston, Z. N. (1998). *Their eyes were watching God.* New York: Perennial Classics. (Original work published in 1937.)

Jackson, II, R. L. (2004). (Ed.), *African American communication & identities: Essential readings.* Thousand Oaks, CA: Sage.

Joas, H. (1987). Symbolic interactionism. In A. Giddens & J. Turner (Eds.), *Social theory today.* (pp. 82–115). Cambridge: Polity Press.

Johnson, A. (2014). Negotiating more, (mis)labeling the body: A tale of intersectionality. In R. M. Boylorn & M. P. Orbe (Eds.), *Critical autoethnography: Intersecting cultural identities in everyday life* (pp. 81–95). Walnut Creek, CA: Left Coast.

Johnson, A. (2015). Black girl strong(er): A performative response to Sweetwater by Robin M. Boylorn. *Departures in Critical Qualitative Research, 4*(1), 117–120.

Johnson, E. P. (Ed.) (2013). *Dwight Conquergood, Cultural Struggles: Performance, Ethnography, Praxis.* Ann Arbor, MI: University of Michigan.

Jones, C. & Shorter-Gooden, K. (2003). *Shifting: The double lives of Black women in America.* New York, NY: HarperCollins.

Jones, J. L. (1996). The self as other: Creating the role of Joni the ethnographer for Broken Circles. *Text and Performance Quarterly, 16*(2), 131–145.

Kelley, R. (1997). *Yo' mama's disfunktional! Fighting the culture wars in urban America.* Boston: Beacon Press.

King, D. (1995). Multiple jeopardy, multiple consciousness: The context of a Black feminist ideology. In B. Guy-Sheftall (Ed.), *Words of fire: An anthology of African-American feminist thought.* New York: New Press.

Koch, T. (1998). Story telling: Is it really research? *Journal of Advanced Nursing, 28*(6), 1182–1190.

Kramarae, C. (1981). *Women and men speaking: Frameworks for analysis.* Rowley, MA: Newbury.

Kramarae, C. (2005). Muted group theory and communication: Asking dangerous questions. *Women and Language, 28*(2), 55–61.

Ladner, J. A. (1971). *Tomorrow's tomorrow: The Black woman.* New York: Anchor Books.

LaPaglia, N. (1995).Working-class women as academics: Seeing in two directions, awkwardly. In C. L. Dews & C. L. Laws (Eds.), *This fine place so far from home: Voices of academics from the working class* (pp. 177–186). Philadelphia: Temple University Press.

Lorde, A. (2007). *Sister outsider.* Berkeley, CA: Crossing. (Original work published in 1984.)

Love, B. L. (2012). *Hip hop's li'l sistas speak: Negotiating hip hop identities and politics in the new south.* New York: Peter Lang.

Madison, D. S. (1993). "That was my occupation": Oral narrative, performance, and black feminist thought. *Text and Performance Quarterly, 13*(3), 213–233.

Madison, D. S. (2012). *Critical ethnography: Method, ethics and performance* (2nd ed.). Thousand Oaks, CA: Sage.

McLaurin, I. (Ed.) (2001). *Black feminist anthropology: Theory, politics, praxis, and poetics.* New Brunswick, NJ: Rutgers University Press.

McLaurin, I. (2001). Theorizing a black feminist self in anthropology: Toward an autoethnographic approach. In I. McLaurin (Ed.), *Black feminist anthropology: Theory, politics, praxis, and poetics* (pp. 49–76). New Brunswick, NJ: Rutgers University Press.

Moraga, C. & Anzaldúa, G. (Eds.). (1983). *This bridge called my back: Writings by radical women of color.* New York: Kitchen Table Women of Color.

Morris, S. M. (2014). *Close kin and distant relatives: The paradox of respectability in Black women's literature.* Charlottesville, VA: University of Virginia Press.

Moynihan, D. P. (1965). *The Negro family: The case for national action.* Washington, DC: Government Printing Office.

Naylor, G. (1993). *Mama Day.* New York: Vintage.

Orbe, M. P. (1998a). *Constructing co-cultural theory: An explication of culture, power, and communication.* Thousand Oaks, CA: Sage.

Orbe, M. P. (1998b). From the standpoint(s) of traditionally muted groups: Explicating a co-cultural communication theoretical model, *Communication Theory, 8*(1), 1–26.

Osborne, B. L. (1996). *A generational analysis of survival strategies of southern rural black women.* MA Dissertation, Florida International University. United States–Florida. Retrieved June 25, 2008, from Dissertation & Theses: Full Text Database (Publication No. AAT 1382616).

Patti, C. J. (2015). Hopeful lament: A song in praise of Black women/stories. *Departures in Critical Qualitative Research, 4*(1), 127–130.

Payne-Jackson, A. & Lee, J. (1993). *Folk wisdom and mother wit: John Lee an African American herbal healer.* Westport, CT: Greenwood.

Phillips, L. (Ed.). (2006). *The womanist reader.* New York: Routledge.

Phillips, L. & McCaskill, B. (1995). Who's schooling who? Black women and the bringing of the everyday into academe, or why we started The Womanist. *Signs: Journal of Women in Culture and Society, 20,* 1007–1018.

Pini, B. (2004). On being a nice country girl and an academic feminist: Using reflexivity in rural social research. *Journal of Rural Studies, 20,* 169–179.

Plummer, K. (Ed.). (1987). *Symbolic interactionism: Vol. 1. Foundations and history.* Brookfield, VT: Edward Elgar.

Plummer, K. (Ed.). (1991). *Symbolic interactionism: Vol. 2. Classic and contemporary issues.* Hauts, England: Edward Elgar.

Poulos, C. N. (2009). *Accidental ethnography: An inquiry into family secrecy.* Walnut Creek, CA: Left Coast.

Poulos, C. N. (2015). The Road to Sweetwater. *Departures in Critical Qualitative Research, 4*(1), 114–116.

Richardson, L. (1997). *Fields of play: Constructing and academic life.* New Brunswick, NJ: Rutgers UP.

Richardson, L. (2000). Writing: A method of inquiry. In N. K. Denzin & Y. S. Lincoln (Eds.), *Handbook of qualitative research* (2nd ed., pp. 923–948). Thousand Oaks, CA: Sage.

Scott, K. D. (1995). Identity and ideology in Black women's talk about their talk: A report of research in progress. *Women and Language, 13*(1), 8.

Scott, K. D. (2000). Crossing cultural borders: 'Girl' and 'look' as markers of identity in Black women's language use. *Discourse & Society, 11*(2), 237–248.

Scott, K. D. (2002). Conceiving the language of Black women's everyday talk. In M. Houston & O. I. Davis (Eds.), *Centering ourselves: African American feminist and womanist studies of discourse* (pp. 53–73). Cresskill, NJ: Hampton Press.

Scott, K. Y. (1991). *The habit of surviving: Black women's strategies for life.* New Brunswick, NJ: Rutgers University Press.

Scott, K. Y., Muhanji, C., & High, E. (1999). *Tight spaces: An expanded edition.* Iowa City: University of Iowa Press.

Scott, P. B. & Johnson-Bailey, J. (Eds.). (1998). *Flat-footed truths: Telling Black women's lives.* New York, NY: Henry Holt.

Shange, N. (1991). *The love space demands: A continuing saga.* New York, NY: St. Martin's Press.

Shange, N. (1997). *For colored girls who have considered suicide when the rainbow is enuf.* New York: Scribner.

Smith, A. D. (1994). *Twilight: Los Angeles, 1992.* New York: Doubleday.

Smith, B. (1983). (Ed.). *Home girls: A Black feminist anthology.* New York: Kitchen Table Women of Color.

Smitherman, G. (2000). *Black talk: Words and phrases from the hood to the amen corner* (Rev. ed.). New York: Houghton Mifflin.

Spillers, H. J. (1987). Mama's baby, papa's maybe: An American grammar book. *Diacritics, 17*(2), 65–81.

Spry, T. (2001). Performing autoethnography: An embodied methodological praxis. *Qualitative Inquiry, 7*(6), 706–732.

Spry, T. (2008). Systems of silence: Word/less fragments of race in autoethnography, *International Review of Qualitative Research, 1*(1), 75–80.

Spry, T. (2011). *Body, paper, stage: Writing and performing autoethnography.* Walnut Creek, CA: Left Coast.

Spry, T. (2015). An unsettled I: A response to Robin M. Boylorn's Sweetwater. *Departures in Critical Qualitative Research, 4*(1), 121–123.

Stack, C. (1974). *All our kin.* New York, NY: Basic.

Stack, C. (1996) *Call to home: African Americans reclaim the rural South.* New York, NY: Basic.

Tate, C. (1985). (Ed.). *Black women writers at work*. New York, NY: Continuum.

Taylor, J. Y. (1998). Womanism: A methodologic framework for African American women. *Advances in Nursing Science, 21*(1), 53–64.

Tolich, M. (2004). Internal confidentiality: When confidentiality assurances fail relational informants. *Qualitative Sociology, 27*(1), 101–106.

U.S. Census Report. (1995). *Urban and rural population: 1900 to 1990*. Retrieved June 30, 2008, from http://www.census.gov/population/censusdata/urpop0090.txt

Vaz, K. M. (Ed.). (1997). *Collecting treasures: Oral narrative research with Black women*. Thousand Oaks, CA: Sage.

Wagle, T. & Cantaffa, D. T. (2008). Working our hyphens: Exploring identity relations in qualitative research. *Qualitative Inquiry, 14*, 135–159.

Walker, A. (1973). *In love and trouble: Stories of Black women*. New York, NY: Harcourt Brace Jovanovich.

Walker, A. (Ed.). (1979). *I love myself when I am laughing... and then again when I am looking mean and impressive: A Zora Neale Hurston Reader*. New York, NY: Feminist.

Walker, A. (1983). *In search of our mothers' gardens: Womanist prose*. New York, NY: Harcourt Brace Jovanovich.

Walker, A. (2003). Everyday use. In *In Love and trouble: Stories of black women*. New York: Harcourt.

Wallace, M. (1999). *Black macho and the myth of the superwoman*. New York, NY: Dial. (Original work published in 1978.)

Weems, M. E. (1997). *White*. Kent, OH: Kent State UP.

Weems, M. E. (2008). *An unmistakable shade of red and the Obama chronicles: Poems*. Huron, OH: Bottom Dog Press.

Weems, M. E. (2010). *I speak from the wound in my mouth: Public education and the imagination-intellect*. New York, NY: Peter Lang.

Weems, M. E. (2015a). *Blackeyed: Plays and Monologues*. Boston, MA: Sense Publishers.

Weems, M. E. (2015b). More than enough. *Departures in Critical Qualitative Research, 4*(1), 131–132.

West, C. (1993). *Race matters*. Boston, MA: Beacon.

Williams, S. A. (1986). Some implications of womanist theory. *Callaloo, 27*, 303–308.

Wilson, E. (1983). *Hope and dignity: Older Black women of the South*. Philadelphia: Temple UP.

Wood, J. T. (2005). Feminist standpoint theory and muted group theory: Commonalities and divergences. *Women and Language, 28*(2), 61–64.

Woodson, C. G. (1930). *The rural Negro*. Washington, DC: Association for the Study of Negro Life and History.

Worth, S. E. (2008). Storytelling and narrative knowing: An examination of the epistemic benefits of well-told stories. *Journal of Aesthetic Education, 42*(3), 42–55.

Wyatt, J. & Adams, T. E. (Eds.). (2014). *On (writing) families: Autoethnographies of presence and absence, love and loss*. Boston, MA: Sense Publishers.

ROCHELLE BROCK & CYNTHIA DILLARD
Executive Editors

Black Studies and Critical Thinking is an interdisciplinary series which examines the intellectual traditions of and cultural contributions made by people of African descent throughout the world. Whether it is in literature, art, music, science, or academics, these contributions are vast and far-reaching. As we work to stretch the boundaries of knowledge and understanding of issues critical to the Black experience, this series offers a unique opportunity to study the social, economic, and political forces that have shaped the historic experience of Black America, and that continue to determine our future. Black Studies and Critical Thinking is positioned at the forefront of research on the Black experience, and is the source for dynamic, innovative, and creative exploration of the most vital issues facing African Americans. The series invites contributions from all disciplines but is specially suited for cultural studies, anthropology, history, sociology, literature, art, and music.

Subjects of interest include (but are not limited to):

- EDUCATION
- SOCIOLOGY
- HISTORY
- MEDIA/COMMUNICATION
- RELIGION/THEOLOGY
- WOMEN'S STUDIES

- POLICY STUDIES
- ADVERTISING
- AFRICAN AMERICAN STUDIES
- POLITICAL SCIENCE
- LGBT STUDIES

For additional information about this series or for the submission of manuscripts, please contact Dr. Brock (University of North Carolina at Greensboro) at r_brock@uncg.edu or Dr. Dillard (University of Georgia) at cdillard@uga.com.

To order other books in this series, please contact our Customer Service Department:

(800) 770-LANG (within the U.S.)
(212) 647-7706 (outside the U.S.)
(212) 647-7707 FAX

Or browse online by series at www.peterlang.com.